917.8 FOR 2011

Forbes travel guide. Northwest

ACKNOWLEDEGMENTS

We gratefully acknowledge the help of our representatives for their efficient and perceptive inspections of the lodgings listed. Forbes Travel Guide is also grateful to the talented writers who contributed to this book.

Some of the information contained herein is derived from a variety of third-party sources. Although every effort has been made to verify the information obtained from such sources, the publisher assumes no responsibility for inconsistencies or inaccuracies in the data or liability for any damages of any type arising from errors or omissions.

Neither the editors nor the publisher assume responsibility for the services provided by any business listed in this guide or for any loss, damage or disruption in your travel for any reason.

Front Cover image: ©iStockphoto.com
All maps: Mapping Specialists

ISBN: 9781936010912
Manufactured in the USA
10 9 8 7 6 5 4 3 2 1

CONTENTS

STAR ATTRACTIONS

If you've been a reader of Mobil Travel Guide, you will have heard that this historic brand partnered in 2009 with another storied media name, Forbes, to create a new entity, Forbes Travel Guide. For more than 50 years, Mobil Travel Guide assisted travelers in making smart decisions about where to stay and dine when traveling. With this new partnership, our mission has not changed: We're committed to the same rigorous inspections of hotels, restaurants and spas—the most comprehensive in the industry with more than 500 standards tested at each property we visit—to help you cut through the clutter and make easy and informed decisions on where to spend your time and travel budget. Our team of anonymous inspectors are constantly on the road, sleeping in hotels, eating in restaurants and making spa appointments, evaluating those exacting standards to determine a property's rating.

What kinds of standards are we looking for when we visit a property? We're looking for more than just high-thread count sheets, pristine spa treatment rooms and white linen-topped tables. We look for service that's attentive, individualized and unforgettable. We note how long it takes to be greeted when you sit down at your table, or to be served when you order room service, or whether the hotel staff can confidently help you when you've forgotten that one essential item that will make or break your trip. Unlike any other travel ratings entity, we visit each place we rate, testing hundreds of attributes to compile our ratings, and our ratings cannot be bought or influenced. The Forbes Five Star rating is the most prestigious achievement in hospitality—while we rate more than 5,000 properties in the U.S., Canada, Hong Kong, Macau and Beijing, for 2011, we have awarded Five Star designations to only 54 hotels, 23 restaurants and 20 spas. When you travel with Forbes, you can travel with confidence, knowing that you'll get the very best experience, no matter who you are.

We understand the importance of making the most of your time. That's why the most trusted name in travel is now Forbes Travel Guide.

STAR RATED HOTELS

Whether you're looking for the ultimate in luxury or the best value for your travel budget, we have a hotel recommendation for you. To help you pinpoint properties that meet your needs, Forbes Travel Guide classifies each lodging by type according to the following characteristics:

★★★★★These exceptional properties provide a memorable experience through virtually flawless service and the finest of amenities. Staff are intuitive, engaging and passionate, and eagerly deliver service above and beyond the guests' expectations. The hotel was designed with the guest's comfort in mind, with particular attention paid to craftsmanship and quality of product. A Five-Star property is a destination unto itself.

★★★★These properties provide a distinctive setting, and a guest will find many interesting and inviting elements to enjoy throughout the property. Attention to detail is prominent throughout the property, from design concept to quality of products provided. Staff are accommodating and take pride in catering to the guest's specific needs throughout their stay.

★★★These well-appointed establishments have enhanced amenities that provide travelers with a strong sense of location, whether for style or function. They may have a distinguishing style and ambience in both the public spaces and guest rooms; or they may be more focused on functionality, providing guests with easy access to local events, meetings or tourism highlights.

Recommended: These hotels are considered clean, comfortable and reliable establishments that have expanded amenities, such as full-service restaurants.

For every property, we also provide pricing information. All prices quoted are accurate at the time of publication; however, prices cannot be guaranteed. Because rates can fluctuate, we list a pricing range rather than specific prices.

STAR RATED RESTAURANTS

Every restaurant in this book has been visited by Forbes Travel Guide's team of experts and comes highly recommended as an outstanding dining experience.

★★★★★Forbes Five-Star restaurants deliver a truly unique and distinctive dining experience. A Five-Star restaurant consistently provides exceptional food, superlative service and elegant décor. An emphasis is placed on originality and personalized, attentive and discreet service. Every detail that surrounds the experience is attended to by a warm and gracious dining room team.

★★★★These are exciting restaurants with often well-known chefs that feature creative and complex foods and emphasize various culinary techniques and a focus on seasonality. A highly-trained dining room staff provides refined personal service and attention.

★★★Three Star restaurants offer skillfully prepared food with a focus on a specific style or cuisine. The dining room staff provides warm and professional service in a comfortable atmosphere. The décor is well-coordinated with quality fixtures and decorative items, and promotes a comfortable ambience.

Recommended: These restaurants serve fresh food in a clean setting with efficient service. Value is considered in this category, as is family friendliness.

Because menu prices can fluctuate, we list a pricing range rather than specific prices. The pricing ranges are per diner, and assume that you order an appetizer or dessert, an entrée and one drink.

STAR RATED SPAS

Forbes Travel Guide's spa ratings are based on objective evaluations of more than 450 attributes. About half of these criteria assess basic expectations, such as staff courtesy, the technical proficiency and skill of the employees and whether the facility is clean and maintained properly. Several standards address issues that impact a guest's physical comfort and convenience, as well as the staff's ability to impart a sense of personalized service. Additional criteria measure the spa's ability to create a completely calming ambience.

★★★★★ Stepping foot in a Five Star Spa will result in an exceptional experience with no detail overlooked. These properties wow their guests with extraordinary design and facilities, and uncompromising service. Expert staff cater to your every whim and pamper you with the most advanced treatments and skin care lines available. These spas often offer exclusive treatments and may emphasize local elements.

★★★★ Four Star spas provide a wonderful experience in an inviting and serene environment. A sense of personalized service is evident from the moment you check in and receive your robe and slippers. The guest's comfort is always of utmost concern to the well-trained staff.

★★★ These spas offer well-appointed facilities with a full complement of staff to ensure that guests' needs are met. The spa facil ties include clean and appealing treatment rooms, changing areas and a welcoming reception desk.

TOP HOTELS, RESTAURANTS AND SPAS

HOTELS

★★★★FOUR STAR

The Fairmont Olympic Hotel *(Seattle, Washington)*
Four Seasons Hotel Seattle
(Seattle, Washington)
Four Seasons Hotel Vancouver *(Vancouver, British Columbia)*
Four Seasons Resort Whistler *(Whistler, British Columbia)*
Hastings House Country House Hotel *(Salt Spring Island, British Columbia)*
Shangri-La Hotel, Vancouver *(Vancouver, British Columbia)*
The Sutton Place Hotel Vancouver *(Vancouver, British Columbia)*
Wickaninnish Inn *(Tofino, British Columbia)*

RESTAURANTS

★★★★FOUR STAR

Bishop's *(Vancouver, British Columbia)*
The Georgian *(Seattle, Washington)*
The Herbfarm *(Woodinville, WA)*
La Belle Auberge *(Ladner, British Columbia)*
Lumière *(Vancouver, British Columbia)*
Restaurant Matisse *(Victoria, British Columbia)*
Rover's *(Seattle, Washington)*
West *(Vancouver, British Columbia)*

SPAS

★★★★FOUR STAR

Ancient Cedars Spa *(Tofino, British Columbia)*
CHI Spa at Shangri-La Hotel *(Vancouver, British Columbia)*
The Spa at Four Seasons Whistler *(Whistler, British Columbia)*
Spa at Four Seasons Seattle *(Seattle, Washington)*

YOUR QUESTIONS ANSWERED

WHEN DOES ALASKA HAVE ITS 24 HOURS OF DAYLIGHT AND DARKNESS?

The midnight sun comes to Alaska during the summer, giving the state days filled with more daylight hours. The more north you travel, the longer the days get. On its longest day, June 21, the sun rises in Anchorage at 4:30 p.m. and sets around 11:42 p.m. In Barrow, the northernmost town in the state, the sun keeps blaring for 84 days straight.

On the opposite end of the spectrum, in the winter, the sun hides from Alaska. On the shortest day in December, Anchorage gets six hours of daylight and Barrow adoesn't see the sun for 64 days.

If you are planning to come see the midnight sun, be aware that summer is Alaska's high tourist season, so prices will go up and you'll have to contend with crowds.

WHAT SHOULD I PACK FOR A TRIP TO THE NORTHWEST?

If you are packing for a trip to Alaska, it really depends on which area you visit and what time of the year it is. But a good rule of thumb is to pack lots of layers, even in the summer, when the temperature can dip to 50 F. Of course, in the winter, be sure to add a warm coat, sweaters, long underwear and boots to your luggage. This is the Arctic, after all.

Unlike Alaska, British Columbia has mild winters. But it's advised to tote along a warm jacket and an umbrella to get by there in the cold-weather months. Otherwise, you can pack seasonally appropriate clothes.

Contrary to popular belief, Oregon isn't under a perpetual rain cloud. But it is wise to bring an umbrella with you. The summers are pretty nice, with temperatures topping out in the 80s in most areas, and the winter temperatures hit between the 40s and 20s, so pack some warm gear. Washington, on the other hand, seems to be under a perpetual rain cloud. Its well-known showers pour down between October and early July, though it can rain at any time during the year. So bring along your raincoats, boots and whatever else will keep you dry. The weather is pretty mild year-round in the state, but you should pack a light jacket even in the summer.

Idaho's climate varies depending on the region, but it's a safe bet that you should bring along an umbrella. Boise gets hit with cold winters and very hot summers, so pack accordingly.

WELCOME TO ALASKA

THE MIND-BLOWING BEAUTY OF MILLION YEAR-OLD

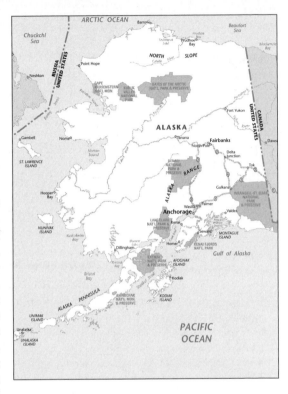

glaciers, a truly unspoiled landscape and plentiful wildlife make Alaska a paradise for nature lovers. Its national forests and parks are America's largest—the state has twice as many caribou as people—and the abundant coastal waters provide some of the best salmon and halibut fishing in the world. Veteran rock and ice climbers routinely assault Mount McKinley, the highest peak in North America at 20,320 feet, and the truly intrepid compete in the annual Iditarod sled dog race.

The great Yukon River cuts the Alaskan interior almost in half, carving tremendous valleys along the way as it makes its 1,265-mile journey from the state's border to the Bering Sea. The mazelike convergence of land and water in the famed Inside Passage of the panhandle was sculpted into its present form by thousands of years of glacial ice scoring its way toward the sea and eventually melting.

Meanwhile, in contrast, there is the relative bustle of Anchorage. Surprisingly cosmopolitan and comfortable, it's home to about half of the state's population and is teeming with first-class restaurants, nightclubs and entertainment.

BEST ATTRACTIONS

ALASKA'S BEST ATTRACTIONS

ANCHORAGE

As the state's largest city, Anchorage teems with things to do. The city has a number of parks, museums, restaurants and theaters, all against a beautiful rustic backdrop.

IDITAROD

The world is fascinated with the "Last Great Race on Earth," which takes mushers and their dog sleds through more than 1,150 miles of extreme and gorgeous terrain.

KENAI

To witness the majestic landscape that Alaska is known for, visit Kenai. The town is full of breathtaking spots, including Katmai National Park & Preserve, which hosts a big bear community and active volcanoes.

SOUTH CENTRAL ALASKA

The plentiful mountains and lakes make the South Central region the state's outdoor playground. Anchor Point is a popular destination for anglers, who have the option of freshwater fishing in the Anchor River for salmon and steelhead trout or saltwater fishing for halibut and salmon on one of the many charter boats based at the local harbor. Eagle River is one of the main gateways to Chugach State Park, which at nearly half a million acres ranks as the third-largest state park in the United States, and contains part of the Iditarod National Historic Trail. Visitors to Eagle River can find outdoor recreational activities to suit their fitness levels: hiking, biking, fishing, canoeing, rafting, camping and rock climbing during the summer, ice climbing, dog mushing, downhill skiing and ice skating during winter. The Kenai area is an undeniably appealing place to visit. Set on the edge of Cook Inlet near the mouth of the Kenai River, the town is surrounded on all sides by untamed wilderness, from the muddy shores and frigid waters of the inlet to the pristine lakes, streams, hills and forests that make up the Kenai National Wildlife Refuge. With panoramic views across Cook Inlet to three of Alaska's most active volcanoes—Mount Redoubt, Mount Spurr and Mount Iliamna—few places can match Kenai's ability to put on a show. Most recently a series of eruptions of Mount Redoubt in 1990, and similar eruptions of Mount Spurr in 1992.

With an average of 325 inches of snow per year, Valdez boasts some of the best snowcat, helicopter and extreme skiing in the world, as well as world-class ice climbing in nearby Keystone Canyon. In recent years, an extensive network of hiking trails has been developed to provide better access to the wild beauty of the area.

These days, Wasilla is best known for its most famous resident, former governor and vice presidential candidate Sarah Palin. It's also home to the Iditarod Trail Sled Dog Race Headquarters, which spotlights the history and evolution of dog sledding through interpretive exhibits and historical artifacts.

In the middle of all of this wilderness is Alaska's biggest city, Anchorage. In the summer, the city comes alive with numerous festivals and exhibits, millions of flowers and seemingly endless outdoor activities, as locals make the most of long daylight hours and mild temperatures. The municipal area is crisscrossed by a network of 120 miles of paved trails, and another 180 miles of wilderness trails popular with mountain bikers, hikers and runners. Within the city limits, Delaney Park, Earthquake Park, Resolution Park and Kincaid Park provide scenic venues for outdoor entertainment and relaxation.

WHAT TO SEE

ANCHOR POINT
ANCHOR RIVER STATE RECREATION AREA
Anchor Point, 907-262-5581; www.dnr.state.ak.us

This area got its name in the 1770s, when Capt. James Cook lost an anchor at the mouth of the river. Today, people venture here to catch glimpses of moose, beaver, mink and bald eagles, along with the beluga whales, harbor seals and sea otters that hang around near the shore of Cook Inlet. You also can see three volcanoes across the inlet: Mount Augustine to the south, and Mount Iliamna and Mount Redoubt to the north.

ANCHOR POINT
907-235-1236

Known for excellent silver and king salmon runs, the Anchor River is also a popular spot to catch steelhead and rainbow trout. Anglers heading out to Cook Inlet for halibut, salmon and rockfish can launch their own boats for a fee at the end of Anchor River Road or can join one of the fishing charters that depart on most days during the summer. Several companies offer charters to anglers, including **Alaska Sport Fishing Tours** (907-235-2556) and **Tall Tales Charters** (907-235-6271).

BEST ATTRACTIONS

WHAT ARE THE BEST PLACES FOR OUTDOOR FUN IN SOUTH CENTRAL ALASKA?

CHECK OUT PORTAGE GLACIER
Although you can't spot the glacier from the shore anymore, tourists still pack this place to see the blue icebergs floating in the water and the exquisite scenery.

VISIT WRANGELL ST. ELIAS NATIONAL PARK AND PRESERVE
The preserve contains North America's largest collection of mountain peaks above 16,000 feet. The centerpiece is Mount St. Elias, the second-highest peak in the U.S.

SPOT A BEAR IN KATMAI NATIONAL PARK & PRESERVE
More than 2,000 bears call Katmai home, and you can safely watch them in action from a platform. You'll also want to check out the park's 14 active volcanoes.

GO HIKING IN VALDEZ
The mountains and rugged landscape in this town make it a great hiking spot. Pick from seven main trails that will take you through waterfalls, a river and forests.

ANCHORAGE
ALASKA AVIATION HERITAGE MUSEUM
4721 Aircraft Drive, Anchorage, 907-248-5325; www.alaskaairmuseum.org
Located on the shores of Lake Hood near Ted Stevens Anchorage International Airport, this private museum aims to preserve and document Alaska's rich aviation history. Interpretive exhibits, vintage photographs, scale models and an extensive collection of aviation memorabilia offer insight into the evolution of flying in Alaska. An onsite hangar houses an extensive collection of preserved and restored aircraft.
Admission: adults $10, seniors and students $8, children 5-12 $6, children 4 and under free. May 15-September 15, daily 9 a.m.-5 p.m.; September 15-May 14, Wednesday-Sunday 9 a.m.-5 p.m.

ALASKA CENTER FOR THE PERFORMING ARTS
621 W. Sixth Ave., Anchorage, 907-263-2900, 877-278-7849; www.alaskapac.org

Opened in 1988, the Alaska Center for the Performing Arts features four state-of-the-art performance spaces and is home to eight resident companies, including the Alaska Dance Theatre, the Anchorage Symphony Orchestra and the Anchorage Opera.

ALASKA NATIVE HERITAGE CENTER
8800 Heritage Center Drive, Anchorage, 907-330-8000, 800-315-6608; www.alaskanative.net

Spotlighting the native cultures of Alaska, the center offers interpretive displays; outdoor demonstrations of traditional hunting, fishing and construction techniques; traditional village exhibits; and live performances of native songs and dances in the 95-seat Welcome House theater.

May-September, daily 9 a.m.-5 p.m.

ALASKA ZOO
4731 O'Malley Road, Anchorage, 907-346-2133; www.alaskazoo.org

With annual attendance at more than 200,000 visitors, the Alaska Zoo is one of the most frequently visited places in the state. It exhibits 38 species of Arctic and subarctic wildlife on 25 acres.

Admission: adults $12, seniors and military personnel $9, children 3-17 $6, children 2 and under free. Daily 10 a.m.-5 p.m.

ANCHORAGE COASTAL WILDLIFE REFUGE AT POTTER MARSH
Seward Highway, 907-267-2556; www.state.ak.us

Known locally as Potters Marsh, this 540-acre refuge at the southern edge of Anchorage is a popular spot for bird-watching. At various times of the year, the marshlands are home to Arctic terns, Canada geese, trumpeter swans, Pacific loons and a variety of other shorebirds. A 1,500-foot wooden boardwalk built out over the marsh enables you to venture far from the parking lot without damaging the wetlands or disturbing the wildlife in the area.

ANCHORAGE MUSEUM AT RASMUSON CENTER
121 W. Seventh Ave., Anchorage, 907-343-6173; www.anchoragemuseum.org

Divided into two distinct parts, the museum's ground floor features six art galleries displaying art of the North, including works by celebrated Alaskan artist Sydney Laurence. The upper floor focuses on Alaskan history and is packed with artifacts, displays and exhibits that depict the lives and cultures of the groups that have shaped Alaska.

Admission: adults $10, seniors, military personnel and students $8, children 3-12 $7, children 2 and under free. September 14-May 8, Tuesday-Saturday 10 a.m.-6 p.m., Sunday noon-6 p.m.; May 1-September 13, daily 9 a.m.-6 p.m.

CHUGACH NATIONAL FOREST
3301 C St., Anchorage, 907-743-9500; www.fs.fed.us

Roughly the same size as Massachusetts and Rhode Island combined, the Chugach (pronounced "CHEW-gatch") is the northernmost national forest, only 500 miles south of the Arctic Circle. One-third of the Chugach is composed of rocks and moving ice. The remainder is a diverse and majestic tapestry of land, water, plants and animals.

CYRANO'S OFF CENTER PLAYHOUSE
413 D St., Anchorage, 907-274-2599; www.cyranos.org

This small, independent downtown theater puts on a slew of plays each year, from classic dramas to contemporary comedies. The atmosphere is decidedly informal, but the productions are first rate.

EARTHQUAKE PARK
Northern Lights Boulevard, Anchorage, 907-276-4118; www.anchorage.net

Located at the west end of Northern Lights Boulevard, this large, forested park was established near the site where a housing development slid into Cook Inlet during the 1964 Good Friday earthquake. The main trail from the parking lot leads to a small exhibit that explains the geological factors that caused the land beneath the subdivision to collapse. The park also serves as an access point to the Tony Knowles Coastal Trail.

EKLUTNA FLATS AND PALMER HAY FLATS
Anchorage, at the head of the Knik Arm in Cook Inlet, 907-267-2182

The Eklutna Flats and Palmer Hay Flats are a tidally influenced wetlands area at the confluence of the Knik and Matanuska rivers. It provides the broadest view of the Matanuska Valley bordered by the Chugach Mountains, a stone's throw to the east. The ancient Talkeetna Mountains rise in the distance.

KEPLER-BRADLEY STATE PARK
550 W. Seventh Ave., Anchorage, 907-269-8400; www.alaskastateparks.org

A fisherman's paradise, this popular state park comprises several trout- and grayling-filled lakes. Kepler-Bradley State Park is within easy driving distance of Anchorage. Trails from the park connect to the Mat/Su Borough Crevasse Moraine Trail System.

PORTAGE GLACIER AND BEGICH, BOGGS VISITOR CENTER
Glacier Ranger District, Girdwood, Portage, 907-783-2326; www.fs.fed.us

Located 50 miles south of Anchorage, Portage Glacier is one of Alaska's most visited tourist attractions. Although the glacier is no longer visible from the shores of Portage Lake, you can still marvel at the massive blue icebergs floating in the water and enjoy the area's spectacular scenery. See the glacier firsthand onboard the M/V Ptarmigan, a sightseeing boat run by Gray Line Tours (907-277-5581 or 800-544-2206; www.graylinealaska.com), located on the shore of the lake just past the visitor center.

WRANGELL ST. ELIAS NATIONAL PARK AND PRESERVE
Copper Center, 907-822-5234; www.nps.gov

This preserve is worth a visit, as it boasts North America's greatest collection of mountain peaks above 16,000 feet, highlighted by 18,008-foot-high Mount St. Elias, the second-highest peak in the United States. It's the nation's largest national park, with more than 13 million acres of rugged wilderness, a landscape of towering mountains, sweeping valleys, massive glaciers and powerful rivers. Wrangell-St. Elias is one of four contiguous parks situated along the U.S.-Canada border, the other three being Glacier Bay National Park and Preserve (Alaska), Kluane National Park Reserve (Yukon Territory) and the Alsek-Tatshenshini Provincial Park (British Columbia). Together, these four parks comprise the world's largest internationally protected area. Wrangell-St. Elias headquarters can be found in Copper Center, a four-hour drive from Anchorage on the Alaska Highway. Two gravel roads provide access into the park. Nabesna Road (42 miles long) offers spectacular scenery, while McCarthy Road (60 miles long) leads to exceptional hiking, fishing and camping. The National Park Service recommends drivers on either of these two roads have a spare tire in tow, as the terrain is rough.

CORDOVA
POINTS NORTH HELI ADVENTURES
Cordova, 877-787-6784; www.alaskaheliski.com

Operating out of the Orca Adventure Lodge, this tour company helicopters brave skiers and snowboarders into the Chugach Mountains, dropping them directly onto the slopes for amazing runs in exceptional powder. Most skiers average 20,000 to 25,000 vertical feet in a day, with five to eight runs.

EAGLE RIVER
EAGLE RIVER NATURE CENTER
32750 Eagle River Road, Eagle River, 907-694-2108; www.ernc.org

The Eagle River Nature Center serves as a gateway to the 500,000-acre Chugach State Park. Indoor and outdoor programs offered by the center teach you about the kinds of flora, fauna and geographic features you might encounter inside the park.

June-August, Sunday-Thursday 10 a.m.-5 p.m., Friday-Saturday 10 a.m.-7 p.m.; October-April, Friday-Sunday 10 a.m.-5 p.m.; May, September, Tuesday-Sunday 10 a.m.-5 p.m.

HOMER
ALASKA ISLANDS AND OCEAN VISITOR CENTER
95 Sterling Highway, Homer, 907-235-6961; www.islandsandocean.org

Opened in December 2003, the Alaska Islands and Ocean Visitor Center is an educational and research facility that offers you an opportunity to learn about the Alaska Maritime National Wildlife Refuge and the Kachemak Bay Research Reserve through interactive exhibits, guided tours and video presentations. One of the primary goals of the center is to enhance people's awareness of the beauty, fragility and diversity of the remote 4.9-million-acre refuge, which stretches from the Arctic Ocean all the way to Alaska's southeast panhandle.

Memorial Day-Labor Day, daily 9 a.m.-6 p.m.

PRATT MUSEUM
3779 Bartlett St., Homer, 907-235-8635; www.prattmuseum.org

The Pratt Museum is home to native and contemporary culture exhibits, natural history artifacts, a gallery of contemporary regional art and a small room filled with live marine plants and wildlife. Outside, the museum grounds include botanical gardens, forest trails teeming with birds and other wildlife and historical structures and artifacts from Homer's pioneer days.

Mid-May-mid-September, daily 10 a.m.-6 p.m.; mid-September-mid-May, Tuesday-Sunday noon-5 p.m.

KENAI
ALAGNAK WILD RIVER
King Salmon, 907-246-3305

The Alagnak Wild River twists and turns across 67 miles of pristine wilderness in the Aleutian Range of southwestern Alaska. The braided river begins at Kukaklek Lake in the Katmai National Preserve and then flows west, widening along the Way, before spilling out into Bristol Bay. In 1980, the Alagnak was included in the National Wild and Scenic Rivers System. White-water rafters are drawn to the river's Class III rapids and ever-changing landscape, ranging from boreal forest to wet sedge tundra. The Alagnak's western stretch, shallow and marked by numerous sandbars, has become a favored destination for fly-fishing. The cool waters of the Alagnak teem with rainbow trout and all five species of Pacific salmon, including the prodigious king salmon, the largest of which can exceed 70 pounds. The Alagnak's designation as a Wild River helps protect the area's abundant wildlife, most notably a large population of brown bears that feeds on the salmon. The Alagnak Wild River is accessible only by boat or seaplane.

CLAM GULCH STATE RECREATION AREA
Kenai Spur Highway, Soldotna, 907-262-5581; www.dnr.state.ak.us

This area is famous for the thousands of razor clams harvested annually from the sandy beaches adjacent to the State Recreation Area. You may dig clams during any low tide, although an Alaska sport fishing license is required. Clam Gulch is on steep bluffs overlooking Cook Inlet, with sweeping views of the Aleutian Mountains and their three tallest peaks: Mount Iliamna, Mount Redoubt and Mount Spurr. The park offers camping and picnic areas.

HISTORIC OLD TOWN KENAI
Kenai Visitors & Cultural Center, 11471 Kenai Spur Highway, Kenai, 907-283-1991; www.visitkenai.com

In an effort to maintain a link with its rich cultural heritage, the city of Kenai has preserved some of its oldest, most historic buildings. Located within sight of the visitor center, the Old Town district consists of everything from grand churches to humble log cabins, each of which helps tell the story of the town's growth and development. Walking maps of the Historic Old Town district are available at the Visitors & Cultural Center on the Kenai Spur Highway.

Mid-May-mid-September, Monday-Friday 9 a.m.-7 p.m., Saturday 10 a.m.-6 p.m., Sunday 11 a.m.-6 p.m.; mid-September-mid-May, Monday-Friday 9 a.m.-7 p.m.

KATMAI NATIONAL PARK & PRESERVE
King Salmon, 907-246-3305; www.nps.gov

Put simply, Katmai is bear country. Katmai National Park and Preserve has one of the world's highest concentrations of brown bears, with more than 2,000 of the giant furry mammals clambering within this remote wilderness along the Alaska Peninsula. The bears are drawn to the area's lakes and rivers, which teem with sockeye salmon. During July and September, it's not uncommon to see dozens of bears gathered at Brooks Falls, feeding on salmon that have migrated up the Naknek River. While the salmon attract bears, the bears in turn attract tourists, thousands of whom make the trip to Katmai via air taxi or boat (no roads lead to the park) to witness North America's largest land predator in its natural habitat. A viewing platform at Brooks Camp provides a safe spot to photograph the brown bears, some of which weigh more than 900 pounds. Katmai is also famous for its 14 active volcanoes in the park. In 1912, the largest volcanic eruption of the 20th century occurred here when the Novarupta Volcano blew its top, launching a plume of smoke and ash 20 miles skyward. The cataclysmic eruption was more powerful than Mount St. Helens's and created a 40-square-mile ash flow within the Valley of Ten Thousand Smokes, so named by botanist Robert Griggs during a 1916 expedition for National Geographic. Today, the area still resembles a lifeless moonscape, possessing a gray landscape devoid of grasses, trees and shrubs. Aside from wildlife viewing, popular activities at Katmai include hiking, sea kayaking and sport fishing.

LAKE CLARK NATIONAL PARK AND PRESERVE
Field Headquarters, 1 Park Place, Port Alsworth, 907-781-2218; www.nps.gov

Lake Clark National Park & Preserve encompasses 4 million acres of pristine wilderness, extending from Cook Inlet, across the craggy peaks of the Chigmit Mountains, farther west to the tundra-covered hills of Interior Alaska. Two active volcanoes can be found in the park: Mount Redoubt and Mount Iliamna. The park's namesake, Lake Clark, stretches for 40 miles. Filled with red salmon, grayling, Dolly Varden and northern pike, Lake Clark offers tremendous fishing opportunities, as do the park's many other lakes and rivers—three of which have been designated National Wild and Scenic Rivers. Fishing season runs from May until October, although a few of the lakes may not fully thaw until June. Hiking is another popular activity, but it requires considerable back-country experience and know-how. The park contains no trails, and even the most fit hikers will be challenged by streams and dense vegetation, particularly near the coast. For those willing to take on the challenge, spectacular rewards await: awe-inspiring scenery, incomparable solitude and frequent wildlife sightings. Dall sheep, moose and black and brown bears live in the park, as do more than 125 species of birds. Beluga whales, harbor seals and sea lions can be seen in Chinitna Bay and Tuxedni Bay. No roads lead to the park, but float-planes regularly shuttle visitors to the waters of Lake Clark from Anchorage, about 150 miles to the northeast.

PALMER
MUSK OX FARM
Glenn Highway, Palmer, 907-745-4151; www.muskoxfarm.org

For more than four decades, this one-of-a-kind nonprofit farm has been raising domesticated musk oxen in the Matanuska Valley. You can tour the grounds and learn about the history of these shaggy holdovers from the last Ice Age. The farm is more than just a tourist attraction, it's an important player in a thriving cottage industry. Each spring, the musk oxen's soft underwool, called qiviut, is combed out and shipped to native communities in Alaska's far north, where it's fashioned into traditional wool garments, which are then sold in stores throughout the state.

Guided tours are given every half hour until 5:30 p.m.

Tours: adults $8, seniors $7, children 5-12 $6, children 4 and under free. Mother's Day-late September, daily 10 a.m.-6 p.m.

SEWARD
ALASKA SEALIFE CENTER
301 Railway Ave., Seward, 907-224-6300, 800-224-2525;
www.alaskasealife.org

Head to the Alaska SeaLife Center to experience Gulf of Alaska marine wildlife, like the Witness 2,000-ton Steller sea lions visible through underwater windows. Puffins frolic and dive in a carefully crafted naturalistic habitat, while harbor seals relax on rocky beaches. Sea stars and a giant Pacific octopus also await you, as well as a collection of intertidal species and deep-sea fish.

Admission: adults $20, students $15, children 4-11 $10, children 3 and under free. Daily 10 a.m.-5 p.m.

EXIT GLACIER
Glacier Road (Herman Leirer Road), Seward, 907-224-7500, www.nps.gov

Originating in the massive Harding Icefield that dominates the landscape on the eastern side of the Kenai Peninsula, Exit Glacier flows for three miles before coming to an end in a scenic river valley just north of Seward. You can walk from the nature center to the foot of the glacier via the Outwash Plain Trail or branch off onto the relatively easy Overlook Loop Trail, which arrives at a small plateau very close to the jagged blue glacier ice. Park service rangers lead one-hour interpretive tours from the nature center to the glacier along these trails twice a day during the summer, at 11 a.m. and 3 p.m.

Nature center: summer, daily 9 a.m.-7:30 p.m.

SOLDOTNA
KENAI NATIONAL WILDLIFE REFUGE
Refuge Visitor Center, 2139 Ski Hill Road, Soldotna, 907-262-7021; www.kenai.fws.gov

Originally created as the 1.7-million-acre Kenai National Moose Range in 1941, this refuge now totals nearly 2 million acres, covering much of the western half of the Kenai Peninsula. Containing every type of Alaskan habitat and supporting an enormous amount of wildlife, including moose, bears, caribou, eagles and lynxes, the refuge is visited by more than half a million travelers each year, many of whom come to try their luck fishing in the nine rivers that run through it. The refuge's visitor center in Soldotna is open year-round and contains exhibits about local wildlife, information about recreational activities available in the area and a range of displays explaining the geological and ecological makeup of the refuge.

Summer, Monday-Friday 8 a.m.-4:30 p.m., Saturday-Sunday 9 a.m.-6 p.m.; Winter, Monday-Friday 8 a.m.-4:30 p.m., Saturday-Sunday 10 a.m.-5 p.m.

VALDEZ
HISTORIC AND SCENIC HIKING TRAILS
Valdez, 907-835-4636; www.valdezalaska.org

With mountains and rugged wilderness surrounding it on all sides, Valdez is graced with some of the best hiking trails in Alaska, some of which follow historic gold prospector routes through the mountains. Of the seven main trails in or near town, the easiest is the Dock Point Trail, a scenic ¾-mile round-trip beginning at the east end of the dock harbor and looping around a narrow peninsula jutting out into Valdez Bay. Hikers looking for more of a challenge can try the historic lower section of the Keystone Canyon Pack Trail, running for 2.6 miles from the Old Richardson Highway Loop to Bridal Veil Falls. Rated easy to moderate, this 1899 trail was abandoned for nearly a century before being hand-cleared and reopened to foot traffic in the late 1990s. This trail provides excellent views of the canyon and the waterfalls, river and forests. Another easy-to-moderate hike nearby is the Goat Trail and Wagon Road, which replaced the northern part of the Keystone Canyon Pack Trail. This 4.8-mile hike takes travelers from Bridal Veil Falls north to mile 18 on the Richardson Highway and offers spectacular views of Snowslide Gulch, Bear Creek and the Lowe River. Other trails in the Valdez area are equally scenic, though not as historic. One runs up Mineral Creek, another along Shoup Bay and a third through Solomon Gulch. The Valdez Convention & Visitors Bureau (200 Fairbanks St.) offers free maps and detailed information about each of the trails in the area.

VALDEZ MUSEUM AND ANNEX

217 Egan Drive, Valdez, 907-835-2764; www.valdezmuseum.org

This museum is full of exhibits that tell the story of Valdez and the Prince William Sound area, starting with the area's origins as a trailhead supply depot during the Klondike Gold Rush of 1897-1898. Other exhibits focus on the 1989 Exxon Valdez oil spill that occurred in Prince William Sound and detail both the massive cleanup effort that was made and the steps that were taken locally and nationally to learn from the accident.

Admission: adults $7, seniors $6, children 14-17 $5, children 13 and under free. Museum: summer, Daily 9 a.m.-5 p.m.; winter, Monday-Saturday 1-5 p.m. Annex: summer, daily 9 a.m.-4 p.m.

WASILLA
IDITAROD TRAIL SLED DOG RACE HEADQUARTERS

Knik Goose Bay Road, Wasilla, 907-376-5155; www.iditarod.com

This rustic log cabin headquarters and visitor center just south of the Parks Highway contains displays and historical artifacts relating to the Iditarod dogsled race. You can view videos of past races, wander through the museum and take dogsled rides during the summer. Unlike many attractions in Alaska, the headquarters stays open all year and is most crowded in the weeks leading up to the race, which officially starts in Wasilla the day after its ceremonial—and much publicized—start in Anchorage. Hours change during the weeks surrounding the Iditarod Trail Sled Dog race, so call for details.

Mid-May - mid-September, daily 8 a.m.-7 p.m.; mid-September-mid-May, Monday-Friday 8 a.m.-5 p.m.

ANCHORAGE
★★★ANCHORAGE MARRIOTT DOWNTOWN

820 W. Seventh Ave., Anchorage, 907-279-8000, 800-228-9290; www.marriott.com

Every guest room at this bright and cheery hotel has oversized picture windows that flood the rooms with natural light while providing excellent views of either Cook Inlet or the Chugach Mountains. Its proximity to the Delaney Park Strip and the Tony Knowles Coastal Trail also make it a great location for guests looking for a bit of outdoor recreation.

398 rooms. Restaurant, bar. Business center. Fitness center. Pool. $251-350

★★★DIMOND CENTER HOTEL

700 E. Dimond Blvd., Anchorage, 907-770-5000, 866-770-5002; www.dimondcenterhotel.com

The Seldovia Native Association owns this contemporary boutique property, which explains the distinctive native art you'll see sprinkled around the hotel. The spacious rooms are equipped with comfortable beds with oversized wooden headboards, Egyptian cotton linens and Aveda bath products. They also come outfitted with 42-inch televisions, microwaves and refrigerators. When you want a workout, you can visit the adjacent Dimond Center Athletic Club, which offers everything from kickboxing to indoor swimming.

109 rooms. Bar. Complimentary breakfast. Business center. Pool. $151-250

★★★HILTON ANCHORAGE

500 W. Third Ave., Anchorage, 907-272-7411, 800-455-8667; www.hilton.com

Located downtown, the towers of this full-service hotel offer sweeping views of the Anchorage area and beyond. On exceptionally clear days, in fact, guests with north-facing rooms can see as far as Mount McKinley, more than 100 miles away. The main draw of the hotel, though, is its comfortable rooms, down duvet-topped beds, and spacious workspaces.

600 rooms. Restaurant. Business center. Fitness center. Pool. Pets accepted. $251-350

★★★THE HOTEL CAPTAIN COOK

939 W. Fifth Ave., Anchorage, 907-276-6000, 800-843-1950; www.captaincook.com

Inside the rooms at this independent hotel, you'll find comforts like down comforters, thick towels, 250-thread-count sheets and blackout curtains, which are a lifesaver during those days of continuous sunshine. The hotel prides itself on service, offering twice-daily housekeeping and nightly turndown services. Other highlights are three full-service restaurants, a selection of boutiques and art galleries, an onsite athletic club and a wealth of original artworks and artifacts on display throughout the public areas.

547 rooms. Restaurant, bar. Fitness center. Pool. $151-250

WHICH HOTEL HAS THE BEST VIEWS?

Alyeska Resort:
Nestled among the gorgeous Turnagain Arm and the majestic Mount Alyeska, the resort is in a prime spot for breathtaking views of hanging glaciers, mountains and the expansive wilderness.

★★★SHERATON ANCHORAGE HOTEL

401 E. Sixth Ave., Anchorage, 907-276-8700, 800-478-8700;
www.sheratonanchoragehotel.com

Located in downtown Anchorage, this hotel is a short walk to the Anchorage Museum of History and Art, the Fifth Avenue Mall and the Egan Convention and Civic Center. Most of the large, comfortable guest rooms have terrific views of the mountain ranges and tidal flats that surround the city. This hotel caters to business travelers, with updated rooms featuring contemporary décor, ample workspace and wireless access.

370 rooms. Restaurant, bar. Complimentary breakfast. Fitness center. Spa. $251-350

GIRDWOOD

★★★ALYESKA RESORT

1000 Arlberg Ave., Girdwood, 907-754-1111, 800-880-3880; www.alyeskaresort.com

Set in the town of Girdwood, about 45 minutes south of Anchorage on the Seward Highway, the resort is surrounded by the Chugach Mountains and the waters of Turnagain Arm. It includes a ski area, a golf course (in Anchorage) and the Alyeska Hotel—a blend of Swiss chateau and modern architecture. The resort offers skiing, snowboarding and heli-skiing in winter; extensive hiking and mountain biking in summer; fine-dining restaurants; state-of-the-art fitness facilities; and all-around super views of hanging glaciers, soaring mountains and miles and miles of pristine wilderness. After a long day outdoors, retreat to your mustard and maroon room and warm up in your bathrobe, or head down to the spa for a hot-stone massage.

307 rooms. Restaurant, bar. Pool. Spa. Golf. $151-250

WHERE TO EAT

ANCHORAGE

★★★CLUB PARIS

417 W. Fifth Ave., Anchorage, 907-277-6332; www.clubparisrestaurant.com

The grand belle of Anchorage's downtown restaurant scene, Club Paris is considered by many to be the best steak house in the city. Opened in 1957, it's part French bistro, part Alaskan saloon. The local landmark has weathered earthquakes, blizzards and urban renewal, and still manages to be enduringly charming and idiosyncratic. Be sure to order the signature four-inch-thick filet mignon.

Seafood, steak. Lunch, dinner. Bar. $36-85

★★★CORSAIR RESTAURANT

944 W. Fifth Ave., Anchorage, 907-278-4502

Featuring ultra-private wraparound booths, discreet soft lighting and a well-trained and knowledgeable staff, Corsair has a gourmet menu that emphasizes French haute cuisine and Alaskan seafood dishes prepared with fresh local ingredients, like the bouillabaisse. Considered one of the top three wine cellars in Alaska, Corsair offers more than 700 vintages in its 10,000-bottle cellar.

French, seafood. Dinner. Closed Sunday. Reservation recommended. Bar. $36-85

HIGHLIGHT

THE LAST GREAT RACE ON EARTH

An event unlike any other, the famed Iditarod Trail Sled Dog Race shakes Alaska out of the winter doldrums, attracting thousands of spectators and volunteers to the state, along with approximately 75 mushers and their respective dog teams. The Iditarod bills itself as the Last Great Race on Earth. That's a bold claim, but it would be difficult to argue that any race demands more of its competitors. Starting in Anchorage and finishing in Nome, the race covers roughly 1,100 miles along the historic Iditarod Trail. The grueling journey tests the conditioning and resolve of the mushers and their dogs as they endure up to 17 days of subzero temperatures and howling winds, traversing an ever-changing terrain of mountain, forest, tundra and coastline.

At its core, Alaska's Iditarod is a celebration of sled dogs and their key role in the state's history and development. Sled dogs demonstrated their importance most prominently during the winter of 1925, when diphtheria afflicted the children of Nome. Medicine could not be delivered to the city, reachable only by plane and boat, as winter storms and a frozen Bering Sea made Nome inaccessible. Sled-dog teams were used to transport a lifesaving serum. Musher Gunnar Kaasen took the reins for the last leg of the trip, pulled by a team of huskies led by a young pup named Balto. The sled-dog team endured fierce winds, blinding snow and temperatures as low as 60 degrees below zero, but made it to Nome and delivered the serum.

In 1973, the first Anchorage-to-Nome Iditarod was held, staged to help preserve the state's mushing heritage, since plane travel had diminished the need for sled dogs. Dick Wilmarth won the inaugural Iditarod, completing the race in just under three weeks—more than twice the pace of today's winning sled teams.

The Iditarod is not the ideal spectator sport, with much of the action unfolding in remote wilderness. Nonetheless, crowds gather at the start and finish lines to cheer on the mushers and their dogs. A great way to be a part of the race is to serve as a volunteer, helping with trail communications, caring for the dogs or transporting supplies. Check out the official Iditarod website (www.iditarod.com) for details about volunteer opportunities.

★★★CROW'S NEST
The Hotel Captain Cook, 939 W. Fifth Ave., Anchorage, 907-343-2217; www.captaincook.com
Featuring one of the best views in Anchorage, this restaurant, located on a top floor of the Captain Cook hotel, is known for its five-course prix fixe menu and an impressive wine list. Hearty menu highlights include grilled filet mignon and foie gras with truffled potatoes, or king crab legs with drawn butter.
American. Dinner. Closed Sunday-Monday. $36-85

★★★MARX BROS. CAFÉ
627 W. Third Ave., Anchorage, 907-278-2133; www.marxcafe.com
A local favorite, this charming wood-clad house was built in 1916. Inside you'll find a cozy ambiance with a fireplace and white-linen-topped tables. The menu features progressive American cooking, with dishes such as pan-roasted salmon with dill cream sauce or tea-smoked duck breast, all paired with an

WHAT IS THE BEST STEAKHOUSE IN ANCHORAGE?

Club Paris:
It may be described as part French bistro and part Alaskan saloon, but Club Paris is hailed as Anchorage's best steak house. It's known for its 14-inch, four-inch-thick juicy filet mignon and other prime cuts.

award-winning wine list.

American. Dinner. Closed Sunday. Reservations recommended. $36-85

★★★SACK'S CAFÉ & RESTAURANT

328 G St., Anchorage, 907-274-4022; www.sackscafe.com

This restaurant has a cheerful, contemporary vibe, with walls coated in a citrus hue and dotted with colorful artwork. It specializes in eclectic New American cuisine. The menu includes everything from pan-seared Alaskan halibut to filet of beef with a blueberry-port glaze.

Contemporary American. Lunch, dinner, Saturday-Sunday brunch. $16-35

GIRDWOOD

★★★SEVEN GLACIERS

Alyeska Resort, 1000 Arlberg Ave., Girdwood, 907-754-2237; www.alyeskaresort.com

Located 2,300 feet above the Girdwood valley floor, the Seven Glaciers restaurant is only accessible by gondola from the Alyeska Resort. From this mountainside perch, it provides views to the north of seven hanging glaciers on a nearby mountain and, to the south, the waters of Turnagain Arm. The restaurant features Alaskan seafood—like halibut, king crab and sockeye salmon—matched with an extensive wine list. For the finish, try the signature Baked Alyeska, a caramel nougat Bavarian with a flourless chocolate cake center and meringue with chocolate shavings and caramelized pecans.

Northwest. Dinner. Closed mid-April-mid-May and October-mid-November. Children's menu. Bar. $36-85

★★★TEPPANYAKI SAKURA

Alyeska Resort, 1000 Arlberg Ave., Girdwood, 907-754-2237; www.alyeskaresort.com

Located inside the Alyeska Resort, Teppanyaki Sakura serves Japanese cuisine with flair and features a U-shaped seating arrangement from which guests can watch the master chef prepare their food. Reservations are limited to only 18 diners per seating and the menu offers four set courses from which to choose, including Wagyu strip loin and black cod with miso. A sushi bar offers additional seating.

Japanese. Dinner. Closed Tuesday-Wednesday. Bar. $36-85

WHERE TO SHOP

ANCHORAGE

ANCHORAGE FIFTH AVENUE MALL

320 W. Fifth Ave., Anchorage, 907-258-5535; www.simon.com

One of the largest malls in the state, it contains 110 shops on the first three levels and a food court on the fourth. Expect to find national chain stores, like Gap, Coach and Nordstrom, as well as uniquely Alaskan shops, like the Iditarod Store and Alaska Wild Berry Products, which sells wild berry jams, chocolates and smoked salmon.

Monday-Friday 10 a.m.-9 p.m., Saturday 10 a.m.-8 p.m., Sunday 11 a.m.-6 p.m.

SAXMAN NATIVE VILLAGE

This village demonstrates the cultural and artistic legacy of the Tlingit of southeast Alaska. It has 28 totem poles and a traditional winter house once used by the tribe.

SHELDON JACKSON MUSEUM

Tucked in Sheldon Jackson College, this museum has the state's best collection of native arts and crafts, including Eskimo masks, Haida headdresses and more.

SHELDON MUSEUM AND CULTURAL CENTER

Exhibits examine the Tlingit people, the area's original inhabitants. Be sure to visit the museum's front yard, where master native craftsmen create totem poles.

TOTEM BIGHT STATE HISTORICAL PARK

The state park carries the largest collection of totem poles in the world. Check out the detailed, authentic structures made of natural materials.

INSIDE PASSAGE

Inside Passage's lush landscape and fjords make it a perfect home for wildlife like bald eagles, sea lions and porpoises. The region is also a base for Tlingit, Haida and Tsimshian tribes, and impressive examples of their rich cultures are seen all over the area. Haines is a town rich in history and natural beauty. Located near the northern end of the Inside Passage, it's surrounded by soaring mountains, deepwater inlets and miles of rugged forests and massive glaciers. Learn more about the area by visiting the Sheldon Museum, home to a fascinating mix of pioneer and Gold Rush memorabilia as well as an extensive collection of Chilkat Tlingit art and artifacts.

Squeezed onto a narrow slip of land between the waters of Gastineau Channel and the base of 3,576-foot-tall Mount Juneau, Juneau, Alaska's capital city, is literally and figuratively overshadowed by the vast wilderness that surrounds it. Located in the middle of the Tongass National Forest two-thirds of the way up the Inside Passage, Juneau is a former Gold Rush town that has managed to strike it rich with tourists. Because no roads connect Juneau to the outside world, all visitors must arrive by air or sea. This is an enormous benefit for the city, as it is most striking when viewed against a backdrop of massive glaciers, dense forests, towering peaks and meandering waterways.

Ketchikan is a town of about 8,500 people, but it hosts nearly 750,000 visitors during the summer. It's the first Alaskan stop for most cruise ships touring the Inside Passage and proudly declares itself to be Alaska's First City. Deep in the heart of the Tongass National Forest, the town is also the closest community to Misty Fjords National Monument, a 2.3-million-acre wilderness of massive glaciers, deep saltwater fjords, pristine forests and abundant wildlife. Closer to town, the protected waters of the Inside Passage attract massive runs of salmon each year (hence Ketchikan's claim to be the Salmon Capital of the World). The most famous section of the old town area is Creek Street, a former red-light district that now houses an appealing blend of restaurants, art galleries and small shops built on pilings over Ketchikan Creek. It's a pedestrian-only zone and a great place to wander around, do a bit of shopping and grab a bite to eat.

The Ketchikan area is also rich in native culture. Totem Bight State Park, eight miles north of town, contains a historic collection of totem poles set along a scenic trail. Saxman Totem Park, two miles south of town, contains totem poles as well as workshops where you can watch native carvers create poles, canoes and other artwork using the same techniques employed by their ancestors. The Southeast Alaska Discovery Center in the middle of downtown has a wide range of exhibits, including a selection of contemporary poles, samples of native basketry and a model of a traditional fish camp.

Petersburg is both geographically and culturally far removed from the rest of the towns that dot the Inside Passage. In a region with centuries-old ties to Russian and native cultures, this remote fishing port at the northern tip of Mitkof Island proudly celebrates its rich Norwegian heritage.

One of the oldest Western settlements in Alaska, Sitka was established at the beginning of the 19th century as a fur trading outpost and fort by the Russian American Company. Modern Sitka retains strong ties to its past as evidenced by the Russian architecture of Saint Michael's Cathedral in the middle of downtown (a replica of the original that burned to the ground in 1966), the restored Russian Bishop's house across from Crescent harbor and Russian Cemetery at the end of Observatory Street. Evidence of the older Tlingit civilization can be found on the east end of town at the Sheldon Jackson Museum, which contains a stunning display of native arts and crafts. Further down the road is Sitka National Historic Park, which features a collection of 15 totem poles set along a meandering forest trail.

WHAT TO SEE

HAINES
SHELDON MUSEUM AND CULTURAL CENTER
First Avenue and Main Street, Haines, 907-766-2366; www.sheldonmuseum.org

Established in 1924, the Sheldon Museum houses a wide variety of historical and artistic artifacts relating to the different cultures that reside in the Chilkat Valley. Through onsite displays and exhibits of rare and elaborate native handicrafts, you can learn about the Tlingit culture that dominated the area before the arrival of European settlers. The museum also focuses on the role Haines played in the Klondike Gold Rush, with displays and memorabilia that tell

BEST ATTRACTIONS

WHAT ARE THE BEST PLACES TO LEARN ABOUT NATIVE CULTURE?

SAXMAN NATIVE VILLAGE
This village demonstrates the cultural and artistic legacy of the Tlingit of southeast Alaska. It has 28 totem poles and a traditional winter house once used by the tribe.

SHELDON JACKSON MUSEUM
Tucked in Sheldon Jackson College, this museum has the state's best collection of native arts and crafts, including Eskimo masks, Haida headdresses and more.

SHELDON MUSEUM AND CULTURAL CENTER
Exhibits examine the Tlingit people, the area's original inhabitants. Be sure to visit the museum's front yard, where master native craftsmen create totem poles.

TOTEM BIGHT STATE HISTORICAL PARK
The state park carries the largest collection of totem poles in the world. Check out the detailed, authentic structures made of natural materials.

the story of the miners who set off on the nearby Dalton Trail leading into the interior and the gold fields of the Klondike. Most summer afternoons, you have the chance to observe master native craftsmen fashioning totem poles in the front yard of the museum.

Admission: adults $5, children 12 and under free. Mid-May-mid-September, Monday-Friday 10 a.m.-5 p.m., Saturday-Sunday 1-4 p.m.; mid-September-mid-May, Monday-Saturday 1-4 p.m.

JUNEAU
ALASKA STATE MUSEUM
395 Whittier St., Juneau, 907-465-2901; www.museums.state.ak.us
Permanent collections and traveling exhibits highlight Alaska's native peoples, its natural history, the Alaska-Yukon gold rushes and the American period of the state's history. A children's room features a one-third scale model of the

stern of the ship Discovery, used by Capt. George Vancouver during his famous explorations of Alaska.

Admission: adults $5 (in winter $3), children 18 and under free. Mid-May-mid-September, daily 8:30 a.m.-5:30 p.m.; mid-September-mid-May, Tuesday-Saturday 10 a.m.-4 p.m.

JUNEAU-DOUGLAS CITY MUSEUM

Fourth Avenue and Main Street, Juneau, 907-586-3572; www.juneau.org

Located across the street from the State Capitol, the Juneau-Douglas City Museum was founded to preserve and display materials relating to the cultural and historical development of the Juneau-Douglas area. The small galleries are packed with artifacts and memorabilia of the groups and events that have influenced the development of the Juneau-Douglas region, from ancient Tlingit tribes to turn-of-the-century mining corporations to modern-day tour companies.

Admission: adults $4, children 12 and under free. Mid-May-mid-September, Monday-Friday 9 a.m.-5 p.m., Saturday-Sunday 10 a.m.-5 p.m.; mid-September-mid-May, Tuesday-Saturday 10 a.m.-4 p.m.

THE LAST CHANCE MINING MUSEUM

1001 Basin Road, Juneau, 907-586-5338

Listed on the National Register of Historic Places and Alaska Gold Rush Properties, this museum is housed in an historic compressor building associated with the former Alaska Juneau Gold Mining Company, which operated in the town from 1912 until 1944. The museum explores the history of the region's mining industry with exhibits of industrial artifacts associated with hard rock gold mining.

Admission: $4. Daily 9:30 a.m.-12:30 p.m., 3:30-6:30 p.m.

MENDENHALL GLACIER

8510 Mendenhall Loop Road, Juneau, 907-789-0097; www.fs.fed.us

Mendenhall Glacier is about 12 miles from downtown Juneau at the northern end of the Mendenhall Valley. The glacier originates in the Juneau Icefield and stretches for 13 miles before terminating at the northern end of Mendenhall Lake, the waters of which conceal roughly half of the glacier's 200-foot-thick toe. Five trails originate in and around the visitor center, providing scenic walks during the summer.

Summer, daily 8 a.m.-6:30 p.m.

MOUNT ROBERTS TRAMWAY

490 S. Franklin St., Juneau, 907-463-3412, 888-461-8726; www.alaska.net

The Mount Roberts Tramway runs from the cruise ship dock in downtown Juneau up the side of Mount Roberts to an elevation of about 1,800 feet, providing passengers with magnificent views of Juneau, Douglas Island and the Gastineau Channel.

May-September, daily 9 a.m.-9 p.m.

WICKERSHAM STATE HISTORIC SITE

213 Seventh St., Juneau, 907-586-9001; www.dnr.state.ak.us

A beautiful Victorian house dating from 1898, this site was home to James Wickersham, one of the most influential men in the development of Alaska during its pioneer days. As a district court judge, Wickersham was responsible for bringing law and order to more than a quarter-million square miles of Alaska's interior at the turn of the century. The list of his other accomplishments is equally amazing. He served as a delegate to Congress, helping to create Mount McKinley National Park, the Alaska Railroad and the territory's first college, later named the University of Alaska. He also won home rule for Alaska in 1912, which gave the territory an elected legislature, was one of the first to introduce a statehood bill for Alaska and was the first Caucasian man to attempt to climb Mount McKinley. His home is now a museum filled with artifacts, photographs and furnishings that tell the story of his trailblazing spirit and devotion to the territory.

Admission: free. Summer, daily 10 a.m.-noon, 1-5 p.m.

KETCHIKAN

SAXMAN NATIVE VILLAGE

South Tongass Highway, Ketchikan, 907-225-4846; www.capefoxtours.com

A short drive south of Ketchikan, the village offers a window to the cultural and artistic heritage of the Tlingit tribe of southeast Alaska. It includes a park filled with 28 totems recovered from surrounding villages and restored by members of the Civilian Conservation Corps during the early part of the 20th century. Also onsite is the Beaver Clan House, a replica of a traditional winter house once used by the Tlingits. At the Saxman Carving Center, observe master totem carvers and their apprentices at work.

SOUTHEAST ALASKA DISCOVERY CENTER

50 Main St., Ketchikan, 907-228-6220; www.fs.fed.us

As one of four Public Lands Information Centers in Alaska, this center's mission is to provide information about the cultures, people, ecosystems and history of Alaska's southeast. Throughout the day, the onsite theater shows Mystical Southeast Alaska, a short multimedia presentation that provides a general introduction to the region. In the center's exhibit halls, life-size ecosystem displays, historic artifacts, and scenic and wildlife photographs give visitors a more detailed view of the region's beauty and diversity.

Admission: adults $5, children 15 and under free. May-September, daily 8 a.m.-5 p.m.; October-April, Tuesday-Saturday 8 a.m.-4 p.m.

TOTEM BIGHT STATE HISTORICAL PARK

9883 N. Tongass Highway, Ketchikan, 907-247-8574; www.dnr.state.ak.us

In 1938, the U.S. Forest Service began salvaging and reconstructing magnificent examples of Tlingit, Haida and Tsimshian symbolic carvings. Decaying totem poles were copied in freshly cut cedar logs using traditional tools and techniques; even the paints used were made of natural materials, like clam shells and salmon eggs. Today, this state park houses the largest collection of totem poles in the world.

PETERSBURG

CLAUSEN MEMORIAL MUSEUM

203 Fram St., Petersburg, 907-772-3598; www.clausenmuseum.net

This small city-run museum in the center of town focuses on the historical development of Petersburg and Mitkof Island, on which the town is located. Exhibits and artifacts relating to Tlingit culture introduce you to the earliest society that lived in the region while fishing gear and nautical memorabilia bring to life the history of the Norwegian fishermen who settled in the region during the latter part of the 19th century. Logging tools and artifacts also are on display, providing insight into another industry that helped fuel Petersburg's economy during the 20th century.

Admission: adults $3, children 12 and under free. May-early September, Monday-Saturday 10 a.m.-5 p.m.; early September-mid-December, Tuesday-Saturday 10 a.m.-2 p.m.

PETROGLYPH BEACH STATE HISTORIC PARK
Wrangell, 907-874-2381; www.wrangell.com

Soak up some sun and see the petroglyphs, or rock carvings by Native Americans, at this beach, which offers some of the best examples that still survive today.

SITKA

OLD SITKA STATE HISTORICAL SITE
Halibut Point Road, Sitka, www.dnr.state.ak.us

Seven miles north of downtown, Old Sitka is where the original 1799 Russian-American Company settlement was located. After the Russian fort was destroyed during fighting with the local Tlingit tribe in 1803, the Russians responded by attacking and capturing the nearby Tlingit settlement of Shee Atika. The Russians then built another settlement on the site, naming it New Archangel. When the United States purchased Alaska from the Russians in 1867, the town's name was changed to Sitka, a European version of the area's Tlingit name. The Old Sitka site contains numerous outdoor displays that tell the history of the native and Russian settlements that once thrived in the area. If you have time to spare, walk the site's network of paths, which includes the Forest and Muskegs Trail, the Estuary Life Trail and the slightly longer Mosquito Cove Loop Trail. Overnight visitors can stay at Starrigavan Campground, a U.S. Forest Service facility on the northern edge of the historic site.

SHELDON JACKSON MUSEUM
104 College Drive, Sitka, 907-747-8981; www.museums.state.ak.us

A small, oddly shaped museum on the Sheldon Jackson College campus near downtown Sitka, it houses what is generally regarded as one of the best collections of native arts and crafts in the state. It is also Alaska's oldest museum, founded in 1887 by the Rev. Sheldon Jackson, who sought to create a museum that would preserve and exhibit the cultural and artistic history of native Alaskan cultures. Highlights of the collection include Eskimo masks, Tlingit and Haida headdresses and a full-sized Aleut baidarka, a specialized form of sea kayak.

Admission: adults $4 ($3 in winter), children 18 and under free. Mid-May-mid-September, daily 9 a.m.-5 p.m.; mid-September-mid-May, Tuesday-Saturday 10 a.m.-4 p.m.

SITKA NATIONAL HISTORICAL PARK
103 Monastery St., Sitka, 907-747-0110; www.nps.gov

Sitka National Historical Park is one of Alaska's smallest but most popular national parks, with nearly 300,000 visitors making the trip every year. Located in a temperate rainforest at the mouth of the Indian River on Baranof Island, the park marks the site of the 1804 Battle of Sitka, a fight that pitted the native Tlingit Indians against the Russians. Another popular attraction is the Russian Bishop's House, constructed in 1843 when the tsar ruled Alaska. The log structure survives as one of four remaining examples of Russian-period architecture in North America. The park also features a remarkable collection of original and replica totem poles from villages throughout southeastern Alaska. The park's visitor center offers talks, exhibits and slide programs. Alaska's oldest federally designated park, Sitka National Historical Park is a short drive from downtown Sitka.

ST. MICHAEL'S CATHEDRAL
240 Lincoln St., Sitka, 907-747-8120; www.sitka.org

A local landmark since its construction in 1848, this beautiful Russian Orthodox cathedral is actually a replica of the original, which burned in 1966. Featuring classic Russian Orthodox architectural elements, like a large onion dome and three-bar crosses, the cathedral houses an exquisite collection of historic icons and religious artifacts dating back to the days when Russian culture dominated the region. Because the cathedral is still in use, visitors are permitted to wander around inside only during posted hours, when religious services are not being conducted.

TONGASS NATIONAL FOREST
204 Siginaka Way, Sitka, 907-747-6671; www.fs.fed.us

Tongass National Forest, the largest national forest in the United States, is the very definition of wilderness. In fact, one-third of the Tongass' 5.7 million acres is managed as wilderness so that Alaska retains its undeveloped character. Expect to see eagles, bears, deer, birds, fish and a variety of other animals in this vast national forest.

SKAGWAY

ARCTIC BROTHERHOOD HALL
Broadway, Skagway, 907-983-2854, 888-762-1898; www.skagway.org

Easily the most recognizable structure in Skagway, if not all of Alaska, this two-story wooden building dating to 1899 features an exterior covered with more than 10,000 pieces of driftwood. Built by the Fraternal Order of the Arctic Brotherhood, the building served as a social, cultural and charitable center for its members during Skagway's heyday as a boomtown. In its current incarnation, it is home to the Skagway Visitor Center and an excellent place to begin a sightseeing tour of the area.

Mid-May-mid-September, Sunday-Friday 8 a.m.-6 p.m., Saturday 9 a.m.-6 p.m.; mid-September-mid-May, call for hours.

KLONDIKE GOLD RUSH NATIONAL HISTORICAL PARK
Second Avenue and Broadway, Skagway, 907-983-2921; www.nps.gov

Most stampeders abandoned Skagway, along with dreams of instant riches, in 1898. The town now has a year-round population of only 800, although the historical park receives around 750,000 annual visits. The 33-mile-long Chilkoot Trail is administered by the park, and it makes for a challenging but rewarding three- to five-day hike. Nestled within the Taiya Inlet and surrounded by snow-capped mountains, the park offers guided tours of the Skagway Historic District. Many visitors arrive in Skagway by boat, as the town is served by the Alaska Marine Highway.

WHITE PASS & YUKON ROUTE OF THE SCENIC RAILWAY OF THE WORLD

White Pass & Yukon Route Depot, Second Avenue and Spring Street, Skagway, 907-983-2217, 800-343-7373; www.whitepassrailroad.com

Built in only 20 months during the Klondike Gold Rush, the White Pass & Yukon Route connecting Skagway with Whitehorse, Yukon Territory remains one of the most spectacular railways in the world. (It's been designated an International Historic Civil Engineering Landmark.) Modern travelers on this rail line can choose from four different trips. The White Pass Summit Excursion is a three-hour, 40-mile round-trip trek that climbs 2,865 feet from Skagway to the summit at White Pass. Covering many of the railway's most scenic sections, this tour is the least expensive from Skagway and the most popular. The Lake Bennett Excursion takes 8.5 hours and travels an additional 20 miles on the line to Canada's Lake Bennett, where the Chilkoot Trail comes to an end. The railway also offers a Chilkoot Trail Hikers Service for those interested in hiking up the 33-mile historic Chilkoot Trail and then hopping aboard the train as it heads back to Skagway. Another option is the combination bus and train service, which transports travelers from Skagway to Whitehorse. Prices and departure times vary, and reservations are required for all excursions.

WHERE TO STAY

JUNEAU
★★★GOLDBELT HOTEL
51 Egan Drive, Juneau, 907-586-6900, 888-478-6909; www.goldbelthotel.com

Located next to the Centennial Convention and Visitors' Center, the Goldbelt Hotel is one of the largest in town and has good waterfront views. A native-owned hotel, it boasts one of the most extensive collections of Tlingit art found anywhere in Alaska. In the lobby and other public spaces you'll find authentic shields, masks, necklaces, jewelry, baskets and bowls. Rooms are large and basic, and the hotel includes a restaurant and free wireless access.

105 rooms. Restaurant, bar. $61-150

RECOMMENDED

JUNEAU
ADLERSHEIM WILDERNESS LODGE
Mile 33 Glacier Highway, Juneau, 907-723-8245, 888-874-6227; www.yankeecove.com

When you want a place off the beaten path, this remote 9-acre bed and breakfast puts you in the middle of the Tongass National Forest on the shores of Yankee Cove. The wilderness retreat has its own dock, where you can set out on a fishing charter or whale-watching tour. Each of the individually decorated suites has its own Alaskan theme. The light-wood-filled rooms all have two-person color therapy soaking tubs to help you unwind after a day hiking in the forest and checking out the area wildlife.

3 rooms. Complimentary breakfast. $251-350

PEARSON'S POND LUXURY INN AND ADVENTURE SPA

4541 Sawa Circle, 907-789-3772, 888-658-6328; www.pearsonspond.com

This hotel calls itself an "adventure spa," but don't expect to get pampered with facials and pedicures. Pearson's believes the best way to renew your spirit and relax is to get moving and to be in nature. You'll definitely be in nature here, since the inn is in a rain forest near the Mendenhall Glacier. There's a slew of activities available: take morning yoga class on the dock, borrow the hotel's kayaks or boats to hit the water, go fishing, or bike or hike along the trails. When you need a break from the action, head to your room, which is outfitted with a kitchenette, fireplace, Jacuzzi and deck overlooking the gorgeous scenery.

5 rooms. Business center. Fitness center. Complimentary breakfast. $251-350

PROSPECTOR HOTEL

375 Whittier St., Juneau, 907-586-3737; www.prospectorhotel.com

Next door to the Juneau Convention Center, this hotel is convenient for those in town on business. The hotel's complimentary Wi-Fi and the rooms' big work desks with ergonomic leather chairs will also come in handy for those who are working during their stay. The rooms also come with cherry-wood furnishings, microwaves and refrigerators. Try to reserve one of the suites or the executive king rooms, which have a nice waterside view of the Gastineau Channel.

62 rooms. Restaurant, bar. Pets accepted. $61-150

KETCHIKAN
GILMORE HOTEL

326 Front St., Ketchikan, 907-225-9423, 800-275-9423; www.gilmorehotel.com

If you're looking for less rustic accommodations, this hotel may be a good fit. It sits across from the state's busiest port, where cruise ships dock. But you can still get waterfront views of Tongass Narrows from some of the rooms. The powder blue, cream and coffee rooms also come with free Wi-Fi; the luxury rooms have featherbeds, satin comforters and flat-screen TVs. This 1927 boutique hotel is

---

WHICH HOTEL HAS THE BEST AMENITIES?

True to its name, **Pearson's Pond Luxury Inn and Adventure Spa** wants you to go out and have an adventure. The hotel helps you out by providing kayaks, boats, fishing gear and bikes—anything that you might need.

listed on the National Register of Historic Places.

38 rooms. Restaurant, bar. Complimentary breakfast. Business center. $61-150

WHERE TO EAT

JUNEAU
★★★THE GOLD ROOM
Westmark Baranof Hotel, 127 N. Franklin St., Juneau, 907-463-6222; www.westmarkhotels.com

A historic restaurant at the Westmark Baranof Hotel, the Gold Room features an Art Deco skylight rediscovered after a fire in the 1980s as well as a huge wall mural by Alaskan artist Sydney Lawrence. The menu is upscale, with dishes such as Parmesan halibut and grilled steak, and the wine list is extensive.

American. Dinner. Children's menu. Bar. $36-85

KETCHIKAN
★★★HEEN KAHIDI
Cape Fox Lodge, 800 Venetia Way, Ketchikan, 907-225-8001; 866-225-8001; www.capefoxlodge.com

Heen Kahidi, which translates as "house by the river," is perched on the side of a bluff overlooking downtown Ketchikan and the waters of the Tongass Narrows. The casual dining area features massive wooden roof beams and a river rock fireplace. The menu is a mish-mash of many different types of cuisine, from burgers and barbecue to empanadas and fettuccine Alfredo.

American, seafood. Breakfast, lunch, dinner. Bar. $16-35

RECOMMENDED

KETCHIKAN
BAR HARBOR RESTAURANT
2813 Tongass Ave., Ketchikan, 907-225-2813; www.barharborrestaurantktn.com

If you want to taste the local specialty, halibut and chips, come to Bar Harbor. The menu also features local catch in dishes, such as tacos with cod or halibut. If you're not in a seafood mood, there are a bunch of meaty dishes on offer. The flavorful prime rib is a good choice. Take your meal outside to get a view of the water and the docked ships.

Seafood. Dinner. Reservations recommended. Outdoor seating. $16-35

SITKA
LUDVIG'S BISTRO
256 Katlian St., Sitka, 907-966-3663; www.ludvigsbistro.com

This tiny dining room tries to channel the Mediterranean with cheery, bright walls and eclectic art, and the tapas menu does the same. Try the tapas featuring local seafood, like the king crab medallions with smoked paprika and lemon zest aioli or the pepper-bacon-wrapped Alaskan scallops with truffle oil. Among the larger dishes, go for the wild Alaskan paella mixta, full of scallops, prawns, king salmon, calamari, rockfish, chicken and chorizo.

Mediterranean. Dinner. $16-35

THE CHANNEL CLUB
2906 Halibut Point Road, Sitka, 907-747-7440; www.sitkachannelclub.com

You'll get a beautiful view of the Sitka Sound if you dine at this restaurant. You'll also get super-fresh seafood, like the seared halibut with lemon beurre blanc and grilled salmon with red pepper coulis. There's also a number of steaks available, like the 12-ounce organic bone-out rib-eye or the 8-ounce filet mignon.

Steakhouse, seafood. Dinner. Children's menu. Bar. $16-35

KODIAK

Located on Chiniak Bay at the northeastern tip of Kodiak Island, the town of Kodiak is home to more than 770 commercial fishing vessels that ply the waters of the Gulf of Alaska and the Bering Sea in search of king crab, salmon, halibut, cod, shrimp and many other varieties of seafood. Although the Alutiiq people have called the island their home for nearly 8,000 years, it wasn't until the arrival of Alexander Baranov in 1792 that a permanent settlement was established next to the sheltered natural harbor he christened St. Paul.

Kodiak still maintains ties to its Russian heritage, most notably in the Holy Resurrection Russian Orthodox Church, with its blue onion-dome spire and Russian cross; the Baranov Museum nearby, which was built by Baranov's men as an otter pelt warehouse; and in numerous street, place and business names throughout the town.

Kodiak today offers far more than just fresh Alaskan seafood, sunshine and spectacular views. An estimated 3,000 Kodiak brown bears live on the island along with large numbers of deer, foxes, mountain goats, bald eagles and shore birds. The waters near shore are home to orcas, humpback whales, sea otters and Steller sea lions.

WHAT TO SEE

ANIAKCHAK NATIONAL MONUMENT AND PRESERVE
King Salmon, 907-246-3305; www.nps.gov

The Aniakchak Caldera, a volcanic crater measuring almost six miles in diameter, is a spectacular sight and a truly awesome example of nature's power. Created over the last 3,400 years by a series of volcanic eruptions—the most recent occurring in May 1931—the caldera has explosion pits, lava flows and cinder cones. The largest cone, Vent Mountain, rises 1,400 feet above the caldera floor. The walls of the caldera vary in height, generally ranging between 2,000 and 4,400 feet. Surprise Lake glistens within the caldera and serves as the source of the Aniakchak River, which offers an unparalleled white-water rafting experience. The river cuts a 1,500-foot opening (known as the Gates) in the caldera wall, and then briskly flows east, winding around the mountains of the Aleutian Range, before spilling out into Aniakchak Bay and the Pacific Ocean. With its remote location along the Alaska Peninsula, the Aniakchak National Monument and Preserve can be accessed only via floatplane.

BARANOV MUSEUM
101 Marine Way, Kodiak, 907-486-5920; www.baranovmuseum.org

Housed in the oldest wooden building in Alaska, this historical museum was built by the Russian-American Company as an otter pelt warehouse during Kodiak's heyday as a Russian fur trading post. Now, it's home to a collection of photographs, exhibits, artworks and artifacts tracing Kodiak's history from the time the Alutiiq Indian culture thrived in the area through the Russian fur trading frenzy and into Alaska's territorial era and early statehood years.

Admission: adults $3, children 3 and under free. Summer, Monday-Saturday 10 a.m.-4 p.m., Sunday noon-4 p.m.; winter, Tuesday-Saturday 10 a.m.-3 p.m.

FORT ABERCROMBIE STATE HISTORIC PARK
Kodiak District Office, 1400 Abercrombie Drive, Kodiak, 907-486-6339; www.dnr.state.ak.us

This scenic oceanside park on 186 acres north of downtown Kodiak was the site of a defensive military installation during World War II and still contains reminders of its wartime function. Today the site plays a completely different role—that of scenic park, crisscrossed by a ribbon of trails passing through meadows, trout-filled lakes and seaside cliffs with excellent whale-watching vantage points. Only 3½ miles from downtown and connected to it by a paved bike trail, the park is a popular spot for outdoor enthusiasts. Hiking and camping are available onsite, as is a visitor center run by the Alaska Department of Natural Resources.

KODIAK ISLAND
907-486-4782, 800-789-4782; www.kodiak.org

Unlike the frozen wilderness that's usually associated with Alaska, Kodiak Island is known as the state's Emerald Isle, thanks its tree-lined fjords. Located off the state's southern coast, it is one of the largest commercial fishing ports in the nation and is famous for its Kodiak brown bears. Outdoor activities include fishing, kayaking, hiking, biking and wildlife viewing.

KODIAK NATIONAL WILDLIFE REFUGE VISITOR CENTER
1390 Buskin River Road, Kodiak, 907-487-2600; www.kodiak.fws.gov

Located beside the Buskin River a half-mile from Kodiak Airport, this visitor center explains the animals, plants and ecosystems that make up the 1.9-million-acre Kodiak National Wildlife Refuge. Encompassing two-thirds of Kodiak Island and a few neighboring islands, the refuge is a haven for red foxes, river otters, weasels, Sitka deer, mountain goats and 250 species of birds, including an estimated 600 pairs of bald eagles. The most famous inhabitants, though, are the approximately 3,000 Kodiak brown bears that roam the island. The largest of the

HIGHLIGHT

WHAT IS THERE TO DO AT DENALI NATIONAL PARK & PRESERVE?

Like Alaska and Mount McKinley, Denali (www.nps.gov/dena) is big—really big. It ranks among the largest national parks, covering more than 6 million acres of pristine wilderness, a broad expanse of land roughly the same size as Massachusetts. Situated within the 600-mile-long Alaska Range, the park's sharp-edged mountains were carved by sprawling glaciers, many of which are still at work—the park contains more than 20 glaciers that are longer than five miles, including one, Kahiltna, that stretches 43 miles. Denali also possesses abundant wildlife, including moose, caribou, Dall sheep and grizzly bears, as well as smaller mammals, such as marmots and snowshoe hares.

Hiking and camping are among the most popular activities at Denali. Although the park has few trails, one worth exploring is the Mount Healy Overlook Trail, a 2½-mile trek that leads to a stellar view of the fast-flowing Nenana River and majestic peaks of the Alaska Range. The Nenana River offers incredible white-water rafting, with stretches of the river categorized as Class IV rapids. Bicycling is another favorite activity, particularly on the 90-mile-long Park Road. Bikes may be transported on the Park Road shuttle bus, allowing for a one-way bike ride to the center of Denali followed by a one-way bus ride back to the visitor center. For those seeking to truly test their mettle, Mount McKinley stands as one of the most difficult climbs in the world. While not a technically difficult climb, bitterly cold temperatures, fierce winds and 16,000 feet of snowline make for a daunting expedition. The park is open year-round, and a surprising number of visitors arrive in the winter to go cross-country skiing or dog sledding.

Native Alaskans have lived at Denali for many centuries. In fact, Mount McKinley (named for President William McKinley) was originally named Denali, which among the indigenous Athabascan people means "Great One." With the stroke of a pen, President Woodrow Wilson established Mount McKinley National Park in 1917. Congress changed the park's name to Denali National Park and Preserve 63 years later.

Denali is accessible by car. The park's headquarters sit on Highway 3, 125 miles south of Fairbanks and 240 miles north of Anchorage. Denali's mountaineering headquarters are in Talkeetna, about 100 miles north of Anchorage. The highly regarded Alaska Railroad runs the Denali Star line between Anchorage and Fairbanks, with stops in Talkeetna and Denali.

brown bears, they average 10 feet tall and weigh as much as 1,600 pounds. The refuge is accessible only by boat or floatplane, so the visitor center also serves as an invaluable resource for travelers planning trips into the area.

Memorial Day-Labor Day, Monday-Friday 8 a.m.-7 p.m., Saturday-Sunday noon-4 p.m.; Labor Day-Memorial Day, Monday-Friday 8 a.m.-4:30 p.m.

WELCOME TO IDAHO

WHEN THE IDAHO TERRITORY WAS CREATED, IT included much of Montana and Wyoming. President Abraham Lincoln had difficulty finding a governor who was willing to come to this wild and rugged land. Some appointees, including Gilman Marston and Alexander H. Conner, never appeared.

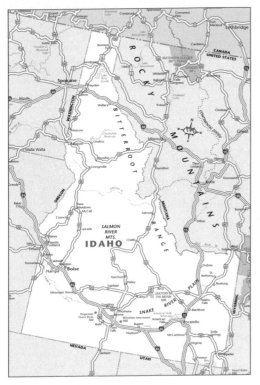

They had good reason to be tentative. The area was formidable and still is, for there is not just one Idaho; there are at least a half-dozen: a land of virgin forests; a high desert covering an area bigger than Rhode Island and Delaware combined; gently sloping farmland, where soft Pacific winds carry the pungency of growing alfalfa; an alpine region of icy, isolated peaks and densely forested valleys hiding more lakes and streams than have been named, counted, or even discovered; an atomic energy testing station only a few miles from the Craters of the Moon, where lava once poured forth and congealed in fantastic formations; and the roadless, nearly uninhabited, 2.3 million-acre Frank Church-River of No Return Wilderness, where grizzly bears, moose and bighorn sheep still run wild.

Stretching south from Canada for nearly 500 miles and varying dramatically in terrain, altitude and climate, Idaho has the deepest canyon in North America, Hell's Canyon, which is 7,913 feet deep. The largest stand of white pine in the world is in the Idaho Panhandle National Forests, and the finest big game areas in the country are the Chamberlain Basin and Selway. Idaho

BEST ATTRACTIONS

IDAHO'S BEST ATTRACTIONS

BOISE
As the state capital and Idaho's largest city, Boise offers a plethora of things to do, from visiting the Basque Museum to getting active in Boise National Forest.

LAVA HOT SPRINGS
This city's natural hot water springs reportedly have healing properties. The all-natural mineral water has no chemicals, no odor and keeps at a toasty 102 to 112 F.

SUN VALLEY
People flock to this resort area for skiing, hiking, ice skating and more. Ernest Hemingway made Sun Valley his home, as do a number of other famous people.

boasts the largest wilderness area in the United States in Frank Church-River of No Return Wilderness, and the largest contiguous irrigated area in the United States was created by the American Falls and several lesser dams. Idaho's largest county, named after the state itself, would hold the entire state of Massachusetts; its second-largest county, Owyhee, would hold New Jersey.

In addition to superlative scenery, fishing and hunting, visitors can find diversions such as buried bandit treasure, lost gold mines, boat trips down the turbulent Salmon River (the "River of No Return") and ghost mining towns. For those who prefer less strenuous activities, Sun Valley and Coeur d'Alene have luxurious accommodations.

NORTHERN IDAHO

Northern Idaho is known for its beauty, with pristine lakes and verdant forests offering much to see and do. Nestled amid lakes and rivers, Coeur d'Alene ("cor-da-LANE") is a tourist and lumbering community, but particularly a gateway to a lush vacation area in the Idaho Panhandle. The city is the headquarters for the three Idaho Panhandle National Forests. The Clearwater River, starting in the Bitterroot Mountains and plunging through the vast Clearwater National Forest, joins the Snake River at Lewiston. The two rivers and the mountains that surround the town give it one of the most picturesque settings in the state. Tucked between Moscow Mountain and the scenic rolling hills of the Palouse, Moscow is a quaint college town. It is home to the University of Idaho, and Washington State University is only a 15-minute drive west, just across the state line in Pullman. Moscow bills itself as the Heart of the Arts, an appropriate moniker given the town's well-attended arts festivals, renowned summer theater program and vibrant live music scene. Tourists come out to Sandpoint to hit the slopes in the winter and they opt for hiking and horseback riding in the spring and summer

WHAT TO SEE

BONNERS FERRY
KOOTENAI NATIONAL WILDLIFE REFUGE
Riverside Road, Bonners Ferry, 208-267-3888; www.fws.gov

This 2,774-acre refuge was created as a resting area for waterfowl during migration. Its wide variety of habitats supports many species of birds and mammals, including bald eagles.

COEUR D'ALENE
LAKE COEUR D'ALENE
www.coeurdalene.org

Partially adjacent to the Idaho Panhandle National Forest, this lake is 26 miles long with a 109-mile shoreline. It is considered one of the most scenic in the country and is popular for boating, fishing and swimming.

MUSEUM OF NORTH IDAHO
115 N.W. Blvd., Coeur d'Alene, 208-664-3448; www.museumni.org

Exhibits at this museum examine steamboating, the timber industry and Native American history. There is also a big game trophy collection.

Admission: adults $3, children $1, families $7. April-October, Tuesday-Saturday 11 a.m.-5 p.m.

SILVERWOOD THEME PARK
27843 N. Highway 95, Athol, 208-683-3400; www.silverwoodthemepark.com

A turn-of-the-century park and village with Victorian buildings, Silverwood includes restaurants, a saloon, a general store, theater featuring old newsreels and classic movies, aircraft museum, air shows and entertainment. Most come for the heart-pumping 65 rides, which include roller coasters and water slides.

HIGHLIGHT

WHAT ARE THE TOP THINGS TO DO IN NORTHERN IDAHO?

GO SWIMMING IN LAKE COEUR D'ALENE

The 26-mile-long lake is considered one of the most scenic in the country. Take in the views and then cool off with a dip.

SEEK THRILLS AT SILVERWOOD THEME PARK

Hit the 65 roller coasters and other rides at this theme park. When you finish your adrenalin rush, visit the turn-of-the-century park within Silverwood.

EXPLORE HELLS CANYON NATIONAL RECREATION AREA

Hells Canyon is the deepest gorge in America. Admire its beauty while partaking in jet boat tours, auto tours, horseback riding and more in the recreation area.

(If you purchase your tickets online ahead of time, you'll get a small discount.)
Admission: adults $41.99, seniors and children 3-7 $21.99. Memorial Day weekend-Labor Day, daily.

GRANGEVILLE

HELLS CANYON NATIONAL RECREATION AREA

541-426-5546; www.fs.fed.us

Created by the Snake River at the Idaho/Oregon border, Hell's Canyon is the deepest gorge in North America, running 1 1/2 miles from He Devil Mountain (elevation 9,393 feet) to the Snake River at Granite Creek (elevation 1,408 feet). The recreation area includes parts of the Nez Perce and Payette National Forests in Idaho and the Wallowa-Whitman National Forest in Oregon. Activities include float trips, jet boat tours, auto tours, backpacking, and horseback riding and boat trips into the canyon from Lewiston, Grangeville and Riggins, and via Pittsburg Landing or the Hells Canyon Dam. Be sure to inquire about road conditions before planning a trip; some roads are rough and open for a limited season.

NEZ PERCE NATIONAL FOREST
104 Airport Road, Grangeville, 208-983-1950; www.fs.fed.us

Nez Perce offers more than 2.2 million acres with excellent fishing, camping, picnicking, cross-country skiing and snowmobiling. The Salmon, Selway, South Fork Clearwater and Snake rivers, all classified as wild and scenic, flow through or are adjacent to the forest. Pack and float trips are available.

LEWISTON

CLEARWATER NATIONAL FOREST
12730 Highway 12, Orofino, 208-476-4541; www.fs.fed.us

Clearwater National Forest stretches almost 2 million acres with trout fishing, hunting, skiing and snowmobiling trails, camping, picnicking and lookout towers.

HELLS GATE STATE PARK
5100 Hells Gate Road, Lewiston, 208-799-5015; www.visitidaho.org

Hells Gate State Park draws visitors with swimming, fishing, boating, hiking, paved bicycle trails, a horseback riding area, picnicking and a playground.
March-November.

NEZ PERCE NATIONAL HISTORICAL PARK
Highway 95 S., Spalding, 208-843-7001; www.nps.gov

The park is composed of 38 separate sites scattered throughout Washington, Oregon, Montana and Idaho. All of the sites relate to the culture and history of the Nez Perce; some are linked to the westward expansion of the U.S. into their homelands.

MOSCOW

APPALOOSA MUSEUM AND HERITAGE CENTER
2720 W. Pullman Road, Moscow, 208-882-5578; www.appaloosamuseum.org

The museum features exhibits of paintings and artifacts relating to the Appaloosa horse, a rugged animal that usually has a white or other solid-colored coat with small spots. Other displays look at early cowboy equipment, saddles and Nez Perce clothing and tools. It also houses the national headquarters of the Appaloosa Horse Club, Inc.
Monday-Friday noon-5 p.m., Saturday 10 a.m.-4 p.m.

SANDPOINT

CEDAR STREET BRIDGE PUBLIC MARKET
334 N. First Ave., Sandpoint, 208-263-1685; www.cedarstreetbridge.com

Inspired by the Ponte Vecchio in Florence, Italy, the Cedar Street Bridge shops provide panoramic views of Lake Pend Oreille and nearby mountains. Among the shops is the North Idaho Artisans, a community of artists who sell things as varied as eco-friendly clothing and chainsaw art.
Daily.

ROUND LAKE STATE PARK
10 miles south on Highway 95, then two miles west, 208-263-3489

Approximately 140 acres of coniferous woods, Round Lake State Park offers swimming, fishing, ice fishing, ice-skating, boating, hiking, cross-country skiing, sledding, tobogganing and snowshoeing.

WALLACE
NORTHERN PACIFIC DEPOT RAILROAD MUSEUM
219 Sixth St., Wallace, 208-752-0111; www.visitidaho.org

Northern Pacific Depot Railroad Museum houses artifacts, photographs and memorabilia that portray the railroad history of the Coeur d'Alene Mining District.

Admission: adults $2, seniors $1.50, children $1. April-October, hours vary.

SIERRA SILVER MINE TOUR
420 Fifth St., Wallace, 208-752-5151; www.silverminetour.org

A 75-minute guided tour through an actual silver mine includes demonstrations of mining methods, techniques and operation of modern-day equipment. Tours depart every 30 minutes.

Admission: adults $12.50, seniors $11, children 4-16 $8.50, children under 4 free. May-mid-October, daily.

WALLACE DISTRICT MINING MUSEUM
509 Bank St., Wallace, 208-556-1592; www.wallaceminingmuseum.org

The museum hosts material on the history of mining, including a 20-minute video, old mining machinery and information on mine tours and old mining towns in the area.

May-September, daily 10 a.m.-5 p.m.; October-April, Monday-Saturday 10 a.m.-5 p.m., Sunday 10 a.m.-3 p.m.

WHERE TO STAY

COEUR D'ALENE
★★★THE COEUR D'ALENE RESORT
115 S. Second St., Coeur d'Alene, 208-765-4000, 800-688-5253; www.cdaresort.com

This lakeside resort has a park-like setting and offers a multitude of outdoor activities, including boat cruises, waterskiing and marina access to downhill skiing, championship golf and nearby shopping. This spot is particularly notable for golfers, both for its premier golf academy and its floating green, accessible by a small boat. A European-style spa offers a full range of services, while five lounges and bars entertain. Sophisticated Northwestern regional cuisine is highlighted at Beverly's restaurant, and Tito Macaroni's serves Italian fare.

336 rooms. Restaurant, bar. Pool. Spa. Pets accepted. Golf. Tennis. $61-150

RECOMMENDED

COEUR D'ALENE
THE ROOSEVELT
105 E. Wallace Ave., Coeur d'Alene, 208-765-5200, 800-290-3358; www.therooseveltinn.com

Built in 1905 and listed on the National Register of Historic Places, the four-story building was converted from a schoolhouse into a cozy bed and breakfast in 1994. The inn, named in honor of Theodore Roosevelt, features 15 antique-furnished rooms with Victorian-inspired floral patterns. A complimentary gourmet breakfast awaits each morning.

15 rooms. Complimentary breakfast. Pets accepted. No children under 6. $61-150

LEWISTON
RED LION HOTEL
621 21st St., Lewiston, 208-799-1000, 800-232-6730;
www.redlionlewiston.com

In the rooms at this Lewiston hotel, you'll find 32-inch flat-screen TVs, mini-fridges, microwaves and free Wi-Fi. But the action happens at the onsite microbrewery, M.J. Barleyhoppers. There you can kick back with a handcrafted ale and play a game of pool. If you're in search of something a bit more upscale, head to the Exchange Lounge, which serves wine, cognac and other spirits.

181 rooms. Restaurant, bar. Business center. Fitness center. Pool. $61-150

SANDPOINT
SELKIRK LODGE
Schweitzer Mountain Resort, 10000 Schweitzer Mountain Resort, Sandpoint, 208-263-9555; www.schweitzer.com

Part of the massive Schweitzer Mountain Resort, which also has condos and cabin accommodations on its property, Selkirk Lodge offers Alpine-style slopeside rooms. Some of the rooms come with microwaves and refrigerators. Of course, the reason to stay here is to be close to Schweitzer's 6,400-foot summit, where you can see Canada and three states on a clear day. In the winter, skiing is the thing to do, and in the summer, people visit to do some hiking and mountain biking. After a day on the mountain, unwind with a glass of vino from the onsite Chimney Rock Grill's award-winning wine list.

82 rooms. Restaurant, bar. Pool. Spa. Ski in/ski out. $151-250

WESTERN PLEASURE RANCH
143 Upper Gold Creed, Sandpoint, 208-263-9066, 888-863-9066; www.westernpleasureranch.com

When you need an escape, come to this family owned dude ranch that sits in Panhandle National Forest. Aside from the big open spaces and beautiful country scenery, the draw is the horses. In cold-weather months, travelers come for horse-drawn sleigh rides and skiing. During warmer months, they come out to do some horseback riding. The main lodge has a recreation room where you can shoot some pool or watch a John Wayne flick as well as a hot tub. The simple rooms are individually decorated but channel the rustic surroundings with lots of wood.

6 rooms. Restaurant. $151-250

WHERE TO EAT

COEUR D'ALENE

★★★BEVERLY'S

The Coeur d'Alene Resort, 115 S. Second St., Coeur d'Alene,
208-765-4000, 800-688-5253;
www.cdaresort.com

This seventh-floor restaurant is the signature dining room at the Coeur d'Alene Resort. Enjoy great lake views, a fine wine cellar and Northwest-inspired cuisine, including the popular firecracker prawns with angel hair pasta or the pan-seared halibut with king crab orzo.

International. Breakfast, lunch, dinner, late-night, brunch. Children's menu. Bar. $36-85

RECOMMENDED

COEUR D'ALENE

CEDARS FLOATING RESTAURANT

The Coeur d'Alene Resort, 115 S. Second St., Coeur d'Alene,
208-664-2922; www.cedarsfloatingrestaurant.com

Dine in Idaho's only floating restaurant. Buoyed by 600,000 pounds of concrete-encased Styrofoam, Cedars floats at the intersection of Lake Coeur d'Alene and the Spokane River. So you're sure to have gorgeous views while noshing on fresh seafood like cedar-plank-smoke roasted Pacific salmon and prime meats like the filet mignon.

Steakhouse, seafood. Dinner. Outdoor seating. Children's menu. $36-85

MOSCOW

NECTAR

105 W. Sixth St., Moscow, 208-882-5914;
www.moscownectar.com

This homey restaurant, with exposed brick and low lighting, specializes in simple upscale comfort food. Ribbons of pappardelle are flavored with truffle butter, Parmesan-Reggiano and a poached egg. Meatloaf gets a boost with a bacon wrapping and a chipotle-barbecue glaze. Aside from serving Pacific Northwest cuisine, Nectar also dubs itself a wine bar. If you have trouble navigating the lengthy global wine list, try one of the flights.

Contemporary American. Dinner. Closed Sunday. Bar. $16-35

WHICH NORTHERN IDAHO RESTAURANT HAS THE BEST VIEW?

What makes **Cedars Floating** stand out from the other eateries is that it's the state's only floating restaurant. Buoyed by 600,000 pounds of concrete-encased Styrofoam, Cedars Floating offers the best views of the water because it's in the water.

RED DOOR

215 S. Main St., Moscow, 208-882-7830; www.red-door-restaurant.com

The Red Door is a favorite among locals, who constantly fill the fire-hued dining room. It's probably because of inventive dishes like tender braised baby goat leg with Thai peanut sauce and fresh peaches over coconut rice, or the pan-seared sockeye salmon with a mirin-pear sauce and morel cashew risotto. Finish it off with some of the peach cobbler, and it might become a favorite of yours.

Contemporary American. Dinner, Saturday-Sunday brunch, late-night. Reservations recommended. Outdoor seating. $36-85

SANDPOINT
DISH HOME COOKING

1319 Highway 2, Sandpoint, 208-265-6100; www.sandpointdish.com

Locals line up to get a seat in the packed, bright dining room, whose walls are painted in chartreuse and deep cerulean, punctuated with funky artwork. Once they snag a seat, they wait for dishes to fill the wood table: free-range chicken off the spit with an achiote spice rub and jalapeño aioli, thick polenta fries tossed with fontina cheese, and a hearty lasagna with layers of roasted garlic, capicola, Italian sausage, mushrooms, ricotta and fontina cheese and roasted garlic marinara.

Contemporary American. Lunch, dinner. $16-35

SOUTHERN IDAHO

The main reason people come to Southern Idaho is Boise. The capital and largest city in Idaho, Boise is also the business, financial, professional and transportation center of the state. You'll find museums, restaurants and a national forest all within city limits. That's not to say there aren't other cities worth visiting in this neck of the woods. At the southern tip of Payette Lake, McCall is a resort area for one of the state's chief recreational areas. Fishing, swimming, boating and waterskiing are available on Payette Lake. McCall is also the headquarters for Payette National Forest. Located at the confluence of the Weiser and Snake rivers, the town of Weiser is a center for tourism for Hells Canyon National Recreation Area

WHAT TO SEE

BOISE
BASQUE MUSEUM AND CULTURAL CENTER

611 Grove St., Boise, 208-343-2671; www.basquemuseum.com

The only museum in North America dedicated solely to Basque heritage, it contains historical displays, paintings by Basque artists, changing exhibits and a restored boarding house used by Basque immigrants in 1900s.

Admission: adults $5, seniors and students $4, children 6-12 $3, children 5 and under free. Tuesday-Friday 10 a.m.-4 p.m., Saturday 11 a.m.-3 p.m.

HIGHLIGHT

WHAT ARE THE BEST THINGS TO DO IN SOUTHERN IDAHO?

SEE UNIQUE ART AT THE BASQUE MUSEUM AND CULTURAL CENTER

Check out this museum, the only one in North America dedicated to Basque heritage. Highlights include paintings by Basque artists and historical displays.

GET ACTIVE IN BOISE NATIONAL FOREST

The possibilities of activities on this forest's more than 2.5 million acres are endless: look out at the scenic byways, go rafting, swim, ski, mountain bike and more.

VISIT THE IDAHO HISTORICAL MUSEUM

Learn more about this vast state and its history at this museum. Don't miss the excellent exhibits on Idaho Native Americans and Oregon Train pioneers.

BOISE NATIONAL FOREST
1249 S. Vinnell Way, Boise, 208-373-4100; www.fs.usda.gov
This 2,646,341-acre forest includes the headwaters of the Boise and Payette rivers, two scenic byways, abandoned mines and ghost towns and access to the Sawtooth Wilderness and the Frank Church-River of No Return Wilderness. You will find trout fishing, swimming, rafting, hunting, skiing, snowmobiling, mountain biking, motorized trail biking, hiking, picnicking and camping available in the forest.

DISCOVERY CENTER OF IDAHO
131 W. Myrtle St., Boise, 208-343-9895; www.scidaho.org
Hands-on exhibits explore various principles of science at the Discovery Center, which features a large bubble maker, catenary arch and magnetic sand. *Admission: adults $6.50, seniors $5.50, children 3-17 $4, children 2 and under free. Labor Day-Memorial Day, Tuesday-Thursday 9 a.m.- 5 p.m., Friday 9 a.m.-7 p.m., Saturday 10 a.m.- 5 p.m., Sunday noon-5 p.m.; Memorial Day-Labor Day, Monday-Thursday 9 a.m.-5 p.m., Friday 9 a.m.-7 p.m., Saturday 10 a.m.-5 p.m., Sunday noon-5 p.m.*

HIGHLIGHT

EXPLORING DOWNTOWN BOISE

Boise is a high-spirited city that manages to meld the vestiges of the cowboy Old West with the sophistication of the urban Pacific Northwest. The downtown core is relatively small, which makes it fun to explore on foot.

Begin at the state capitol building, at Capitol Boulevard and Jefferson Street. This vast structure is constructed of local sandstone and faced on the interior with four kinds of marble and mahogany paneling. On the first floor, wander across the rotunda and gaze upward at the interior of the 200-foot dome, ringed with 43 stars (Idaho was the 43rd state in the Union). The legislative chambers are on the third floor. The Idaho capitol is the only geothermally heated state-house in the country: Water from hot springs five blocks away is pumped into the building's radiators.

From the capitol, proceed down Capitol Boulevard to Main Street. From this corner east on Main Street to about Third Street is a district of fine old homes—many renovated into shops and restaurants—that recalls Boise's early 20th-century opulence. Referred to as Old Boise, this street is home to the Egyptian Theatre (at Main and Capitol), an architecturally exuberant early vaudeville theater and movie palace in full King Tut garb.

One block farther west, at Grove and Eighth streets, is the Grove, Boise's unofficial city center. The grove is a brick-lined plaza with a large fountain, public art and a pedestrian area. Summer concerts are held here, and it's the place to gather for skateboarders, cyclists and lunchtime office workers.

Continue down Grove to Sixth Street to the Basque Museum and Cultural Center (611 Grove St.). Idaho contains one of the largest Basque settlements outside of Europe, and this interesting museum tells the story of their culture and settlement in southwest Idaho. Next door, and part of the museum, is the Cyrus Jacobs-Uberuaga House, built as a boarding house for Basque immigrants in 1864. Continue up Capitol Boulevard to Julia Davis Park, a large park along the Boise River that contains many of the city's important museums and cultural institutions.

Follow the posted sign trails to the Idaho Historical Museum (610 N. Julia Davis Drive), which gives an excellent overview of the state's rich historic heritage. Especially good are the exhibits devoted to Idaho Native American history and to Oregon Trail pioneers. Immediately next door is Pioneer Village, a re-created town with vintage buildings dating from the late 19th century. Also in the park is the Boise Art Museum (670 Julia Davis Drive), with a permanent collection that focuses on American Realism.

At the center of Julia Davis Park is Zoo Boise. In addition to the traditional exotic animal favorites from Africa, the zoo is home to a collection of large Rocky Mountain mammals like moose, mountain lions, elk and bighorn sheep. Zoo Boise has the largest display of birds of prey in the Northwest. Return to the downtown area along Fifth Street.

IDAHO BLACK HISTORY MUSEUM

508 Julia Davis Drive, Boise, 208-443-0017; www.ibhm.org

Changing exhibits highlight the history and culture of African-Americans, with a special emphasis on Idaho African-Americans. The museum features lectures, films, workshops, storytelling and musical performances.

Admission: free. Saturday-Sunday 11 a.m.-4 p.m.

IDAHO HISTORICAL MUSEUM

610 Julia Davis Drive, Boise, 208-334-2120; www.history.idaho.gov

Detailing the history of Idaho and the Pacific Northwest, the museum features exhibits on Native Americans, fur trade, mining, ranching and forestry.

Admission: adults $5, seniors $4, students and children 6-12 $3, children 5 and under free. May-September, Tuesday-Saturday 9 a.m.-5 p.m., Sunday 1-5 p.m.; October-April, Tuesday-Friday 9 a.m.-5 p.m., Saturday 11 a.m.-5 p.m.

WORLD CENTER FOR BIRDS OF PREY

5668 W. Flying Hawk Lane, Boise, 208-362-3716; www.peregrinefund.org

Originally created to prevent the extinction of the peregrine falcon, the scope of the center has been expanded to include national and international conservation of birds of prey and their environments. You can see the breeding chamber of California condors and other raptors at the interpretive center.

Admission: adults $7, seniors $6, children 4-16 $5, children 3 and under free. March-October, daily 9 a.m.-5 p.m.; November-February, Tuesday-Sunday 10 a.m.-4 p.m.

MCCALL

PONDEROSA STATE PARK

Huckleberry Loop, McCall, 208-634-2164; www.visitidaho.org

Approximately 1,280 acres, Ponderosa takes its name from a large stand of ponderosa pines in the park. Other draws include swimming, waterskiing, fishing, boating, hiking, cross-country skiing, picnicking and camping.

NAMPA

CANYON COUNTY HISTORICAL SOCIETY MUSEUM

1200 Front St., Nampa, 208-467-7611; www.canyoncountryhistory.com

Historical artifacts and memorabilia are housed inside a 1903 train depot that was once used as the offices of the Union Pacific Railroad.

Admission: adults $2, seniors and children 6-17 $1, children 5 and under free. Wednesday-Friday 11 a.m.-5 p.m., Saturday 11 a.m.-2 p.m. (open on Saturday at 10 a.m., May-October)

DEER FLAT NATIONAL WILDLIFE REFUGE

13751 Upper Embankment Road, Nampa, 208-467-9278; www.fws.gov

Watch thousands of migratory waterfowl pause at this 10,500-acre refuge while on their journey.

LAKE LOWELL

13751 Upper Embankment Road, Nampa, 208-467-9278; www.fws.gov

Approximately 8,800 acres, Lake Lowell offers boating, sailing, waterskiing and picnicking.

Mid-April-September, daily.

WHICH SOUTHERN IDAHO HOTEL HAS THE BEST DECOR?

The Mid-Century **Modern Hotel** could easily be a set on a show like *Mad Men*, with retro armchairs, lamps and other details, not to mention the cool bar that serves up classic cocktails. But instead of an ad men clientele, you'll find hipsters.

WHERE TO STAY

BOISE
★★★GROVE HOTEL
245 S. Capitol Blvd., Boise, 208-333-8000, 888-961-5000; www.grovehotelboise.com

Located close to the Boise Convention Center, the comfortable rooms at this hotel feature modern furnishings in brown, silver and gray. The hotel is attached to the 5,000-seat Bank of America Centre, which hosts a variety of sporting and entertainment events. Fine dining is available at Emilios, which offers a menu of New American cuisine. Julia Davis Park and the Boise River are a short walk away.

254 rooms. Restaurant, bar. Fitness center. Pool. $61-150

RECOMMENDED

BOISE
HOTEL 43
981 Grove St., Boise, 208-342-4622; www.hotel43.com

Hotel 43's downtown location right across from the Boise Convention Center makes it a good place for business travelers to bunk, but there's plenty to draw in regular travelers as well. The hotel sits only blocks away from the Greenbelt, which links 850 acres of parks, bike paths and more along the Boise River. The modern rooms are also appealing, with oversized dark wooden headboards that almost touch the ceiling, and a sleek gray, red, orange and gold color palette. Business travelers will make good use of the free wireless Internet access, nice-sized desks and complimentary shoeshines, while pleasure travelers will enjoy the flat-screen TVs and the gratis Arts Passports, which will get you entry into the Boise Art Museum. The swanky Chandlers Steakhouse and Martini Bar will be a meeting place for everyone.

112 rooms. Restaurant, bar. Business center. Fitness center. Pool. $61-150

HYATT PLACE BOISE/TOWNE SQUARE
925 N. Milwaukee St., Boise, 208-375-1200; www.hyattplace.com

Hyatt Place was made with the business traveler in mind. Each room comes with free Wi-Fi, a large desk and a special plug panel so you can connect your laptop and other media devices to the 42-inch television. But this is a hotel for everyone; the very spacious rooms all have separate sitting areas with comfy L-shaped sleeper sofas, and they are decked out in modern décor, with neutral shades and hints of autumn colors. Families will appreciate the pool, the free continental breakfast and the nearby Boise Towne Square Mall.

127 rooms. Restaurant, bar. Complimentary breakfast. Fitness center. Pool. $61-150

OXFORD SUITES

1426 S. Entertainment Ave., Boise, 208-322-8000, 888-322-8001;
www.oxfordsuitesboise.com

Oxford bills itself as an all-suite hotel, but if you're looking for a little more elbow room, steer clear of the hotel-room-like studio suites. Other rooms have larger sitting areas and kitchenettes, but all of them have an elegant, contemporary feel with patterned wallpaper, dark wood headboards and décor that's either cream and chocolate or red and gold. And they all come with microwaves and refrigerators. When you want to unwind, visit the nightly wine reception (Monday-Saturday), where you can imbibe and nosh on appetizers. Or head to the pool or the steam room and sauna.

132 rooms. Bar. Complimentary breakfast. Business center. Fitness center. Pool. $61-150

MODERN HOTEL

1314 W. Grove St., Boise, 208-424-8244; www.themodernhotel.com

Formerly a 1960s Travelodge, this hotel got an extreme Mid-Century modern makeover. This hip hotel regularly hosts some of the coolest events in town, whether they be art shows or Mad Men-themed shindigs. It's all about design here; fabric headboards stretch horizontally almost across the wall and retro armchairs and kitchen table sets give it a '50s vibe. But the spa-like bathrooms have a more updated feel with mosaic tiles, Aveda toiletries, sleek Japanese soaking tubs and separate showers. Be sure to hang out in the cozy courtyard near the fire pits and the bar is a must—its classic cocktails would make Don Draper feel right at home.

39 rooms. Bar. Complimentary breakfast. Business center. Pets accepted. $61-150

OWYHEE PLAZA HOTEL

1109 Main St., Boise, 208-343-4611, 800-233-4611;
www.owyheeplaza.com

This historic downtown hotel has been in business since 1910. Although the rooms have been updated since then, they retain a classic look, with cream-colored rooms and dark wood furnishings. And it has some old-school amenities, like shoeshines and an onsite barbershop and salon. The hotel throws bashes in the pool area, so check it out while you're there or go for a swim.

100 rooms. Restaurant, bar. Pool. Pets accepted. $61-150

WHERE TO EAT

BOISE

BISTRO 45

1101 N. Third St., McCall, 208-634-4515;
www.bistro45mccall.com

At this neighborhood favorite, people congregate to chat over glasses of wine or to play a game of bocce ball in the courtyard. But they also come for the

WHAT IS THE
BEST PLACE
FOR BRUNCH IN
SOUTHERN IDAHO?

Head to **Brick 29 Bistro**
for a standout Sunday
buffet from a James
Beard-nominated chef.
You'll be able to gorge
on everything from eggs
Benedict to delectable
housemade bacon. And
it's a steal at $12.99
per person.

delicious casual fare. Vino is a must at this wine bar; there's a lengthy rotating list of bottle and by-the-glass options. The lighter menu lets the wine be the star, so start off with the baked Brie with roasted garlic and from the list of panini, go for the croque monsieur, with Black Forest ham and cheddar. Then go out and play a round of bocce ball.

Contemporary American. Breakfast, lunch, dinner. Bar. $15 and under

CHANDLERS STEAKHOUSE

Hotel 43, 981 Grove St., Boise, 208-383-4300; www.chandlersboise.com

Chandlers is hailed as the best steak house in town because it serves up flavorful cuts like Cowboy Steak, an aged bone-in rib-eye. But the restaurant does a good job of setting an intimate mood, with the wine cases and bar backlit with a soft blue glow and a jazz singer providing the soundtracks on most evenings. There's an extensive wine menu, but don't miss out on one of the smooth 10-minute martinis—the restaurant has become known for them. The cocktail comes in an ice-encrusted tumbler and is poured at your table. After a couple of these potent martinis, you just might forget all about the steak.

Steakhouse. Dinner. Outdoor dining. $36-85

EMILIO'S

Grove Hotel, 245 S. Capitol Blvd., Boise, 208-333-8000, 888-961-5000; www.grovehotelboise.com

In the lobby of the Grove Hotel, Emilio's has an inviting and sophisticated vibe with its display kitchen, leather chairs and white-linen-topped tables. Begin your meal with an appetizer that's a fun take on upscale cuisine, the lobster tail corndogs, which come wrapped in proscuitto and battered with cornmeal. For the entrée, don't miss the kurobuta pork braised in plum barbecue sauce. It's a complex, elegant dish. A four-course prix fixe menu for $30 is also offered.

Contemporary American. Breakfast, lunch, dinner. Bar. $16-35

RED FEATHER BISTRO

246 N. Eighth St., Boise, 208-429-6340; www.justeatlocal.com

This downtown bistro's exposed stone and brick, metal spiral staircase and backlit wine wall give this place a sleek feel. But the food will make you feel all homey. Dishes like mac and three local cheeses—Ballard Family Farm white cheddar, pepper cheddar and Danish pearl—and buttermilk fried chicken and cornmeal waffles are straight-up comfort food that mom makes, but better. Order the pan-seared Wild Fraser River salmon with sesame-maple glaze for something a little less homey but equally delicious.

Contemporary American. Lunch (Monday-Friday), dinner, Saturday-Sunday brunch, late-night. Outdoor seating. Bar. $16-35

NAMPA
BRICK 29 BISTRO
320 11th Ave., Nampa, 208-468-0029; www.brick29.com

Foodies flock to Brick 29 to sample James Beard-nominated chef Dustan Bristol's inventive upscale comfort food with locally sourced ingredients. Among the appetizers, try the Idaho Jo-Jos, large fries with blue cheese fondue. It's harder to choose a main course: Pockets of housemade ravioli are stuffed with snow crab and goat cheese; rosemary chicken gets an extra kick of flavor with a brandy-apple cider pan sauce; lamb shank is doused in a red wine borde-laise and is accompanied with smoked mushroom risotto. You can't go wrong here—everything tastes exquisite in the airy light-wood-filled dining room.

Contemporary American. Lunch (Monday-Friday), dinner. Bar. $16-35

EASTERN IDAHO

Forests and other natural beauty cover this region of Idaho. Cloud-capped mountains, rocky gorges and the Salmon River make Challis one of the most picturesque in the Salmon River "Grand Canyon" area. It's also the headquarters for Challis National Forest. Shoshone is surrounded by ranches and farms, and the area retains an aura of the untamed old West. Popular recreational activities include boating, fishing and big-game hunting. Hot water pouring out of the mountains and bubbling up in springs, believed to be the most highly mineralized water in the world, makes Lava Hot Springs a busy year-round resort. Fishing, swimming, camping and golf are available in the surrounding area. Once the site of a reservation, Pocatello was named for the Native American leader who granted the railroad rights of way and building privileges. Now the headquarters of the Caribou National Forest are located here.

WHAT TO SEE

BURLEY
CITY OF ROCKS NATIONAL RESERVE
3035 Elba-Almo Road, Almo, 208-824-5519; www.nps.gov

A pioneer stopping place, this 25-square-mile area of granite spires and sculptured rock formations resembles a city carved from stone; granite walls are inscribed with messages and names of westward-bound settlers, and remnants of the California Trail are still visible. Well-known for technical rock climbing, it also offers hiking and picnicking.

CHALLIS
SALMON-CHALLIS NATIONAL FOREST
1206 S. Challis St., Salmon, 208-756-5100; www.fs.fed.us

More than 2.5 million acres of forestland surrounds Challis on all sides, crossed by highway 93 and 75. Attractions include hot springs; ghost towns; nature viewing via trails; a portion of the Frank Church-River of No Return Wilderness; trout fishing; camping; picnicking; and hunting.

MIDDLE FORK OF THE SALMON WILD AND SCENIC RIVER
Highway 93, South Challis St., 208-879-4101; www.fs.fed.us

Middle Fork is one of the premier white-water rafting rivers in the U.S.; permits are required to float this river.

IDAHO FALLS
CARIBOU-TARGHEE NATIONAL FOREST
1405 Hollipark Drive, Idaho Falls, 208-524-7500; www.fs.fed.us

On this forest's approximately 1.8 million acres are two wilderness areas: Jedediah Smith (West slope of the Tetons, adjacent to Grand Teton National Park) and Winegar Hole (grizzly bear habitat, bordering Yellowstone National Park). Attractions include fishing, big-game hunting, camping, picnicking and winter sports at the Grand Targhee Resort ski area. Float trips are available on the Snake River, and the Palisades Reservoir offers boating, sailing, waterskiing and canoeing.

LAVA HOT SPRINGS
LAVA HOT SPRINGS
430 E. Main Lava Hot Springs, 208-776-5221; www.lavahotsprings.com

Outdoor mineral pools, fed by 30 different springs, range from 104 to 112 F. The springs also include an Olympic-size swimming pool with a diving tower.
Daily. Hours, rates vary by attraction.

POCATELLO
IDAHO MUSEUM OF NATURAL HISTORY
Fifth Avenue and Dillon Street, Pocatello, 208-282-3168; imnh.isu.edu

Exhibits on Idaho fossils, especially large mammals of the ice age, are the highlight at this museum, which also shows Native American basketry and beadwork.
Monday-Saturday.

REXBURG
TETON FLOOD MUSEUM
51 N. Center, Rexburg, 208-359-3063; www.rexcc.com

Artifacts, photographs, and films document the 1976 flood caused by the collapse of the Teton Dam, which left 11 people dead and caused $1 billion in damage.
Admission: adults $2, children 12-18 $1, children 11 and under $.50. May-September, Monday 10 a.m.-7 p.m., Tuesday-Saturday 10 a.m.-5 p.m.; October-April, Monday 11 a.m.-7 p.m., Tuesday-Friday 11 a.m.-5 p.m.

HIGHLIGHT

WHAT'S THE BEST WAY TO EXPLORE THE SUN VALLEY AREA?

Begin a tour of the resort towns of Ketchum and Sun Valley at the Ketchum-Sun Valley Heritage and Ski Museum, in Ketchum's Forest Service Park at First Street and Washington Avenue. The museum tells the story of the indigenous Tukudeka tribe, the early mining settlement and the building of Sun River Resort. There is also information about past and present residents, such as Ernest Hemingway, Olympic athletes and the Hollywood glitterati who come to ski. Walk north along Washington Avenue, passing coffee shops and gift boutiques, to the Sun Valley Center for the Arts and Humanities (191 Fifth St. E.), the hub of the valley's art world. The center presents exhibits, lectures and films and is a great place to find out what's going on in Ketchum.

Walk one block east to Main Street. For a city of its size, downtown Ketchum has an enormous number of art galleries, restaurants and high-end boutiques. It would be easy to spend a day wandering the small town center, looking at art, trying on sheepskin coats and stopping for lattes. While you wander, be sure to stop at the Chapter One Bookstore (160 Main St.), which offers a good selection of regional titles. Charles Stuhlberg Furniture (571 East Ave. N.) is filled with the faux-rustic New West furniture and accessories popular with the area's upscale residents. For art galleries, go to Sun Valley Road and Walnut Avenue. The Walnut Avenue Mall (620 Sun Valley Road) is a boutique development with four independent galleries. Directly across the street is the Colonnade Mill (601 Sun Valley Road) with four more top-notch galleries.

Continue east on Sun Valley Road, picking up the walking and biking trail north of the road. Follow the trail one mile east through forest to the Sun Valley Resort, a massive complex with an imposing central lodge, condominium developments, home tracts and golf courses. The lodge was built in 1936 by Averill Harriman, chairman of the Union Pacific Railroad, and was modeled after European ski resorts in Switzerland and Austria. Harriman hired an Austrian count to tour the western United States in search of a suitable locale; the count chose the little mining town of Ketchum for the resort.

Wander the interior of the vast lodge, looking at the photos of the celebrities who have skied here. In its heyday, Sun Valley hosted the likes of Lucille Ball, the Kennedys, Gary Cooper and dozens of other stars of film and politics. Just west of the lodge, easily glimpsed through the windows that look out onto the Bald Mountain ski area, is an outdoor skating rink. Kept frozen even in summer, the rink is usually a favorite with novice ice skaters. On Saturday evenings, professional ice skaters take to the ice to perform.

For a longer hike, return to Sun Valley Road and the walking trail and continue east up Trail Creek, past golf courses and meadows. In a mile, the valley narrows. Here, in a grove of cottonwoods overlooking the river is the Hemingway Memorial, a simple stone bust that commemorates the author, who died in Ketchum in 1961. Etched in the stone are the words Hemingway wrote upon the death of a friend: "Best of all he loved the fall. The leaves yellow on the cottonwoods. Leaves floating on the trout streams. And above the hills the high blue windless skies … now he will be a part of them forever."

YELLOWSTONE BEAR WORLD
6010 S. 4300 W., Rexburg, 208-359-9688; www.yellowstonebearworld.com

This drive-through preserve near Yellowstone National Park features bears, wolves and other wildlife. "Cub Yard" shows bear cubs at play and "Duck Deck" is a waterfowl observation/feeding deck.

Admission: adults $16.95, seniors $14.95, children 3-10 $9.95, children 2 and under free. Early May-October, daily 9 a.m.-5 p.m.

SHOSHONE
SHOSHONE INDIAN ICE CAVES
1561 N. Highway 75, Shoshone, 208-886-2058; www.visitidaho.org

The caves function as a natural refrigerator, with temperatures ranging from 18 to 33 F. They are three blocks long, 30 feet wide and 40 feet high, and local legend has it that long ago a princess was buried under the ice. To this day, visitors report hearing strange voices and footsteps that seem to come from nowhere. On the grounds are a statue of Shoshone Chief Washakie and a museum of Native American artifacts, as well as minerals and gems.

Admission: adults $8, seniors $7, children 4-12 $5, children 3 and under free. Tours: May-September, daily 8 a.m.-7:15 p.m.

WHERE TO STAY

★★★SUN VALLEY LODGE
1 Sun Valley Road, 208-622-2001, 800-786-8259; www.sunvalley.com

Everyone from Ernest Hemingway to Clark Gable has come to Sun Valley to enjoy the area's rustic luxury, and the Sun Valley Lodge has been this resort town place to stay since 1936. The guest rooms and suites are decorated in French-country style with oak furnishings and cozy fabrics. The real draw is Sun Valley's skiing and fishing. The Duchin Lounge's hot buttered rum hits the spot after a day on the slopes; Gretchen's pleases with casual fare; and the Lounge Dining Room is a standout with its upscale American menu.

148 rooms. Restaurant, bar. Pool. Golf. Tennis. $151-250

WHERE TO EAT

★★★GRETCHEN'S
Sun Valley Lodge, 1 Sun Valley Road, Sun Valley, 208-622-2800; www.sunvalley.com

After a day on the slopes, stop at this beautifully decorated restaurant located in the Sun Valley Lodge. Featuring a cozy, country-French atmosphere, Gretchen's serves a variety of specialty salads, pastas, seafood and poultry.

Continental. Breakfast, lunch, dinner. Reservations recommended. Outdoor seating. Children's menu. Bar. $16-35

WELCOME TO OREGON

THIS IS THE END OF THE FAMOUS OREGON TRAIL FROM which came scores of pioneers in covered wagons. The state abounds in the romance of the country's westward expansion. Meriwether Lewis and William

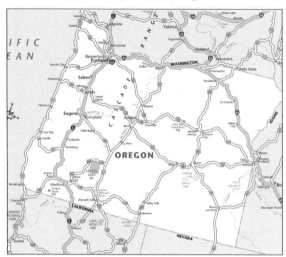

Clark, sent by President Thomas Jefferson to explore the vast area bought in the Louisiana Purchase, ended their explorations here. This was also the scene of John Jacob Astor's fortune-making fur trade and that of Hudson's Bay Company, which hoped to keep the area for England.

English Capt. James Cook was the first European to see the coast in 1778, but it remained for Lewis and Clark to discover what a prize Oregon was. When they returned to St. Louis in 1806, they spread the word. In 1811, Astor's Pacific Fur Company built its post at Astoria, only to be frightened into selling it to the British North West Company during the War of 1812.

Other fur traders, missionaries, salmon fishermen and travelers followed them, but the Oregon country was hard to reach. The first true settlers did not arrive until 1839, four years before a great wagon train blazed the Oregon Trail.

Cattle and sheep were driven up from California, and land was cleared for farms. Oregon was settled by pioneers looking for good land that could support them. Local Native Americans resented the early settlers and fought them until 1880. The Oregon Territory, established in 1848, received a flood of immigrants. More arrived after President James Buchanan proclaimed statehood 11 years later.

The rich forests that flourished in the moist climate west of the Cascade Mountains produced much lumber. Timber is still important: One quarter of Oregon is national forest land. Sustained yield practices by lumber companies ensure a continuing supply.

BEST ATTRACTIONS

OREGON'S BEST ATTRACTIONS

BEND

The Willamette Valley is for wine lovers, but Bend is for beer drinkers. The city has a number of breweries and great restaurants. Not to mention, it's a paradise for outdoors types with Deschutes National Forest and the Mount Bachelor Ski Area.

THE COAST

The state's rugged coastline is a feast for the eyes, with dunes, forests, cliffs and beaches all dotting the landscape. Check out the charming coastal towns as you wind your way through the Coast.

PORTLAND

You'll find endless things to do in the City of Roses, especially outdoors in the many parks. But there are also chic neighborhoods like the Pearl District that offer cool boutiques, hip art galleries and amazing restaurants.

WILLAMETTE VALLEY

Take a tour through Oregon's equivalent to the Napa Valley. The state's own wine country is filled with independent vineyards that churn out amazing vintages and excellent food with which to pair it.

One of the most beautiful drives in Oregon extends from Portland to The Dalles, the end of the Oregon Trail, along the Columbia River. Here is the Columbia Gorge, designated a National Scenic Area, where waterfalls, streams and mountains abound. The area offers many recreational activities such as camping, skiing, snowmobiling, windsurfing and hiking.

Those who love the outdoors or the American West love Oregon. Each year, millions of tourists enjoy the state's magnificent coastline, blue lakes, mountains and forests.

THE COAST

When people want to see scenic Oregon, they come to the coast. Along the 363 miles of coastline, you'll see rugged cliffs, dense forests, dunes, sandy beaches and lots of great little coastal communities. A picturesque beach, legendary rocks and a harbor at the mouth of the Coquille River attract many travelers to Bandon. Beachcombers, whale-watchers and fishermen find Brookings a haven for their activities. Cannon Beach offers great swimming, surfing and surf fishing. Among the large rocks offshore is the 235-foot Haystack Rock, the third-largest monolith in the world. Migrating gray whales often can be spotted heading south from mid-December to early February and returning in early to mid spring. The charming port town of Coos Bay borders a bay that shares its name. The bay itself is the largest natural harbor between San Francisco and Seattle. With some of the highest sand dunes in the world, Florence is within reach of 17 lakes for fishing, swimming and boating. River and ocean fishing, crabbing and clamming are also popular here. You'll find endless things to do in these coastal communities.

WHAT TO SEE

ASTORIA
ASTORIA COLUMN
Follow scenic drive signs to Coxcomb Hill, 503-325-7275; www.astoriacolumn.org

A 125-foot concrete tower commemorates the first settlement with a gift shop, an information booth and an observation deck at the top.

Memorial Day-Labor Day, daily.

COLUMBIA RIVER MARITIME MUSEUM
1792 Marine Drive, Astoria, 503-325-2323; www.crmm.org

The museum features rare maritime artifacts and memorabilia of the Columbia River, its tributaries and the Northwest coast. You can browse exhibits on the fishing industry, discovery and exploration, steamships, shipwrecks, the Coast Guard, the Navy, navigation and steamboats.

Admission: adults $10, seniors $8, children 6-17 $5, children 5 and under free. Daily 9:30 a.m.-5 p.m.

BEST ATTRACTIONS

WHERE ARE THE BEST BEACHES IN OREGON?

ECOLA STATE PARK
This 1,303-acre park offers prime beach real estate that's among the best of the coast. Lewis and Clark ended their famous expedition at this spot.

OSWALD WEST STATE PARK
Surfing and fishing are popular at this coastal park, which also boasts cliffs, dunes and even a rain forest.

SAMUEL H. BOARDMAN STATE SCENIC CORRIDOR
Along the 11 gorgeous miles of coastline at this corridor, you'll find secluded cove beaches as well as rugged cliffs and seaside prairies.

FLAVEL HOUSE
441 Eighth St., Astoria, 503-325-2203; www.cumtux.org

The Flavel House was built by Capt. George Flavel, a pilot and shipping man. The restored Victorian home contains antique furnishings and fine art, along with a collection of 19th- and 20th-century toys.

Admission: adults $5, seniors and students $4, children 6-17 $2, children 5 and under free. May- September, daily 10 a.m.-5 p.m.; October-April, daily 11 a.m.-4 p.m.

FORT CLATSOP NATIONAL MEMORIAL
92343 Fort Clatsop Road, Astoria, 503-861-2471; www.nps.gov

This site marks the Western extremity of the territory explored by Meriwether Lewis and William Clark in their 1804-1806 expedition. The fort is a reconstruction of their winter quarters. The original was built here because of the excellent elk-hunting grounds, easy access to ocean salt, protection from the westerly coastal storms and the availability of fresh water. The visitor center has museum exhibits and provides audiovisual programs. The canoe landing has replicas of dugout canoes of that period. Ranger talks and living history demonstrations are presented mid-June to Labor Day.

April-September, daily.

FORT STEVENS STATE PARK
Astoria, five miles west on Highway 101, then five miles north on Ridge Road, 503-861-1671, 800-551-6949; www.oregonstateparks.org

A 3,763-acre park, Fort Stevens State Park is adjacent to an old Civil War fort and includes the wreck of the Peter Iredale on the ocean shore. Fort Stevens is the only military post in the lower 48 states to be fired upon by foreign forces since 1812. There is a visitor center and self-guided tour at the Old Fort Stevens Military Complex along with ocean beach and lake swimming, fishing, clamming, boating, bicycling and picnicking at Coffenbury Lake.
Daily.

BANDON
BANDON HISTORICAL SOCIETY MUSEUM
270 Filmore Ave., Bandon, 541-347-2164; www.bandonhistoricalmuseum.org
History buffs will find exhibits on the maritime activities of early Bandon and the Coquille River, coastal shipwrecks, Coast Guard operations and an extensive collection of Native American artifacts and old photos.
Admission: adults $2, children free. Monday-Saturday 10 a.m.-4 p.m.

BULLARDS BEACH STATE PARK
52470 Highway 101, Bandon, 541-347-3501; www.oregonstateparks.org
This 1,266-acre park stretches across four miles of ocean beach. Bullards Beach State Park brings in visitors for fishing, boating and picnicking.
May-October, daily.

FACE ROCK STATE PARK
Bandon, four miles south on Highway 101, then one mile west on Bradley Lake Road, 800-551-6949; www.oregonstateparks.org
A 879-acre park in a coastal dune area, Face Rock offers beach access, fishing and picnicking.

WEST COAST GAME PARK
Highway 101, Bandon, seven miles south on Highway 101, 541-347-3106; www.gameparksafari.com
A 21-acre park with more than 450 exotic animals and birds, allows you to meet and walk with free-roaming wildlife. Animal keepers demonstrate the personalities of many large predators residing at the park.
March-November, daily; December-February, weekends and holidays.

BROOKINGS
AZALEA PARK
Highway 101 and North Bank Chetco River Road, Brookings, 541-469-1100; www.brookings.or.us
The name of the 36-acre city park comes from the five varieties of large native azaleas found there, some blooming twice a year. In addition to the blooms, there's an observation point, hiking and picnicking.

HARRIS BEACH STATE PARK
1655 Highway 101 N. Brookings, 541-469-2021, 800-551-6949; www.oregonstateparks.org
Visit this 171-acre park for scenic rock cliffs along the ocean. Or come for the ocean beach, fishing, hiking trails, sights from the observation point, picnicking and improved tent and trailer campsites.

SAMUEL H. BOARDMAN STATE SCENIC CORRIDOR
4655 Highway 101 N. Brookings, 541-469-2021, 800-551-6949;
www.oregonstateparks.org

A 1,473-acre park with observation points along 11 miles of spectacular coastline, the scenic corridor also features fishing, clamming, hiking and picnicking.

CANNON BEACH
ECOLA STATE PARK
Ecola Road, Cannon Beach, two miles north off Highway 101, 503-436-2844,
800-551-6949; www.oregonstateparks.org

Lewis and Clark ended their expedition in what is now a 1,303-acre park with six miles of ocean frontage. Aside from traversing the same land as the famous explorers, you can spot sea lion and bird rookeries on rocks and offshore islands and do whale-watching at observation points.

OSWALD WEST STATE PARK
9500 Sandpiper Lane, Nehalem, 10 miles south on Highway 101, 800-551-6949;
www.oregonstateparks.org

A 2,474-acre park with outstanding coastal headland, Oswald West features towering cliffs, low dunes and a rain forest with massive spruce and cedar trees. The road winds 700 feet above sea level and 1,000 feet below the peak of Neahkahnie Mountain. Visitors come for surfing, fishing and hiking trails.
October 1-April 30, tent site $10, extra vehicle $5; May 1-September 30, tent site $14, extra vehicle $5.

COOS BAY
CAPE ARAGO
Cape Arago Highway, Coos Bay, 15 miles southwest off Highway 101, 541-888-8867,
800-551-6949; www.oregonstateparks.org

This 134-acre promontory juts into the ocean and features two beaches, fishing, hiking and an observation point for whale and seal watching.

CHARLESTON MARINA COMPLEX
63534 Kingfisher Drive, Charleston, nine miles southwest, 541-888-2548;
www.charlestonmarina.com

Boating enthusiasts can come to Charleston Marina to charter boats or to use the launching and moorage facilities, car and boat trailer parking, dry boat storage and travel park. The complex includes a motel, marine fuel dock, tackle shops and restaurants.
Monday-Friday.

SHORE ACRES STATE PARK
89814 Cape Arago Highway, Coos Bay, 541-888-2472, 800-551-6949;
www.oregonstateparks.org

The former grand estate of a Coos Bay lumberman is now a destination for its unusual botanical and Japanese gardens and spectacular ocean views. The park offers an ocean beach, hiking and picnicking.
Daily.

FLORENCE
C&M STABLES
90241 Highway 101 N., Florence, 541-997-7540; www.oregonhorsebackriding.com

Experience the scenery of Oregon coast on horseback. Rides cover the beach and dune trails. If you're looking for something a bit more romantic, saddle up for one of the sunset rides.

Daily 10 a.m.-5 p.m.

CARL G. WASHBURNE MEMORIAL
93111 Highway 101, Florence, 14 miles north on Highway 101, 541-547-3416, 800-551-6949; www.oregonstateparks.org

This verdant 1,089-acre park is a good area for studying plant life. Features include a two-mile beach, swimming, fishing and clamming. Don't be surprised to see elk in the campgrounds and nearby meadows.

HECETA HEAD LIGHTHOUSE
12 miles north on Highway 101, Yachats, 541-547-3416; www.hecetalighthouse.com

Built in 1894, Heceta Head Lighthouse is a picturesque beacon set on rugged cliff.

Admission: free. Parking: $5. Lighthouse Tours: March-October 11 a.m.-5 p.m.

JESSIE M. HONEYMAN MEMORIAL STATE PARK
Three miles south on Highway 101, Florence, 541-997-3641, 800-551-6949; www.oregonstateparks.org

Honeyman Memorial State Park stretches across 522 coastal acres with wooded lakes and sand dunes, an abundance of rhododendrons and an excellent beach. Go there for swimming, waterskiing, fishing, a boat dock and ramps, hiking and picnicking.

SAND DUNES FRONTIER
3 ½ miles south on Highway 101, Florence, 541-997-3544; www.sanddunesfrontier.com

Take an excursion aboard a 20-passenger dune buggy, or get adventurous and drive one yourself. Sand Dunes Frontier also offers miniature golf, a flower garden, a gift shop and a snack bar.

Daily, weather permitting.

SEA LION CAVES
91560 Highway 101 N., Florence, 541-547-3111; www.sealioncaves.com

Descend 208 feet under basaltic headland into a 1,500-foot-long cavern that is home to wild sea lions. These lovable mammals are generally seen on rocky ledges outside the cave in spring and summer and inside the cave in fall and winter. Self-guided tours are available.

Daily from 9 a.m.

SIUSLAW PIONEER MUSEUM
278 Maple St., Florence, 541-997-7884; www.florencechamber.com

Exhibits at Siuslaw Pioneer Museum preserve the history of the area with impressive display of artifacts and items from early settlers and Native Americans.

Tuesday-Sunday noon-4 p.m.; closed January.

GOLD BEACH
CAPE SEBASTIAN STATE SCENIC CORRIDOR
Seven miles south on Highway 101, 800-551-6949; www.oregonstateparks.org

Part of approximately 1,143 acres of open and forested land, Cape Sebastian is a precipitous headland, rising more than 700 feet above the tide with a view of many miles of coastline. A short roadside through the forest area is filled with wild azaleas, rhododendrons and blue ceanothus in season.

JERRY'S ROGUE RIVER JET BOAT TRIPS
Gold Beach, south end of Rogue River Bridge at port of Gold Beach Boat Basin, 541 247-4571, 800-451-3645; www.roguejets.com

Take a six-hour, 64-mile round-trip ride into a wilderness area with a two-hour lunch or dinner stop at Agness. There are also eight-hour (104-mile) and six-hour (80-mile) round-trip whitewater excursions.
May-October, daily.

MAIL BOAT WHITEWATER TRIPS
94294 Rouge River Road, Gold Beach, Mail Boat Dock, 541-247-7033, 800-458-3511; www.mailboats.com

Options at Mail Boat include a 104-mile (round trip) jet boat ride into the wilderness and whitewater of the upper Rogue River; an 80-mile round-trip excursion to the middle of Rogue River; and a 64-mile round-trip jet boat ride with a two-hour lunch stop at Agness. Reservations are recommended.
May-October, daily.

LINCOLN CITY
ALDER GLASS
611 Immonen Road, Lincoln City; www.alderhouse.com

Set in a grove of alder trees, this is the oldest glass-blowing studio in Oregon. See the artisans at work and pick up a lovely glass souvenir for yourself.
Mid-March-November, daily.

CHINOOK WINDS CASINO & CONVENTION CENTER
1777 N.W. 44th St., Lincoln City, 541-996-5825, 888-244-6665; www.chinookwindscasino.com

About 80 miles south of the Washington border on the scenic Oregon coast, Chinook Winds is the largest convention facility between Seattle and San Francisco. With more than 1,200 machines and tables, the modern casino has all the requisite slots, blackjack, keno, poker, roulette, craps, even bingo—with a betting limit of $500. The cavernous showroom sees regular performances by classic rock bands, country artists and comedians, many of them household names. There are also three restaurants (an upscale dining room, a buffet and a deli), a lounge, childcare services and an arcade for the kids. Best of all, when you need a break from the tables, the casino's beachfront location provides a serene escape.

NEWPORT
BEVERLY BEACH STATE PARK
198 N.E. 123rd St., Newport, 541-265-9278, 800-551-6949; www.oregonstateparks.org

Get access to the beach at this 130-acre park. There are also attractions such as fishing, hiking and picnicking.

DEVILS PUNCH BOWL STATE NATURAL AREA

Eight miles north off Highway 101, 800-551-6949; www.oregonstateparks.org

An 8-acre park noted for its bowl-shaped rock formation that fills at high tide, Devils Punch Bowl features ocean-carved caves, marine gardens, a beach, trails and an observation point.

HATFIELD MARINE SCIENCE CENTER OF OREGON STATE UNIVERSITY

2030 S.E. Marine Science Drive, Newport, 541-867-0100; www.hmsc.oregonstate.edu

Hatfield Marine Science Center conducts research on oceanography, fisheries, water quality, and marine biology. You'll want to head there to hike its nature trail and visit the aquarium museum.

ONA BEACH STATE PARK

Eight miles south on Highway 101, 800-551-6949; www.oregonstateparks.org

Go to this 237-acre day-use park for Ona Beach, where you can do some swimming, fishing (boat ramp) and picnicking.

OREGON COAST AQUARIUM

2820 S.E. Ferry Slip Road, Newport, 541-867-3474; www.aquarium.org

The aquarium houses 15,000 animals representing 500 species in 32 habitats. The Swampland exhibit looks at the wetlands and the inhabitants that have been endangered by tragedies like Hurricane Katrina and disasters like the BP oil spill. For a dose of cuteness, visit the seals and the sea otters.

Admission: adults $14.95, seniors $13.45, children 13-17 $12.75, children 3-12 $9.95, children 2 and under free. Early September-late May, daily 10 a.m.-5 p.m.; Memorial Day-Labor Day, daily 9 a.m.-6 p.m.

RIPLEY'S BELIEVE IT OR NOT

250 S.W. Bay Blvd., Newport, 541-265-2206; www.marinersquare.com

See a sideshow without even going to the circus. Ripley's Newport museum of the bizarre features replicas of a backward fountain, King Tut's tomb, the Titanic and the Fiji mermaid.

Admission: adults $10.95, children $5.95, children 4 and under free. October-May, daily 10 a.m.-5 p.m.; June, September, daily 10 a.m.-6 p.m.; July-August, daily 9 a.m.-8 p.m.

SOUTH BEACH STATE PARK

5580 S. Coast Highway, South Beach, 541-867-4715, 800-551-6949; www.oregonstateparks.org

Spread across more than 400 acres, South Beach State Park features a sandy beach, dunes, fishing, hiking and picnicking.

UNDERSEA GARDENS

250 S.W. Bay Blvd., Newport, 541-265-2206; www.marinersquare.com

Descend beneath the sea for an underwater show. Watch native sea life, including a giant octopus, through viewing windows, while guides narrate as scuba divers perform.

Admission: adults $10.95, children $5.95, children 4 and under free. October-May, daily 10 a.m.-5 p.m.; June, September, daily 10 a.m.-6 p.m.; July-August, daily 9 a.m.-8 p.m.

YAQUINA HEAD

750 N.W. Lighthouse Drive, Newport, 541-574-3100; www.blm.gov

The lighthouse here is a popular spot for whale-watching and its fully accessible tidal pool viewing.

Daily.

REEDSPORT
UMPQUA LIGHTHOUSE STATE PARK

460 Lighthouse Road, Reedsport, 541-271-3611; www.oregonstateparks.org

This 450-acre park touches the mouth of the Umpqua River, borders the Umpqua Lighthouse Reservation and skirts the ocean shore for more than two miles. Sand dunes rise 500 feet, making them the highest in U.S. The park has a lovely seasonal display of rhododendrons and also features swimming, fishing, hiking and a whale-watching area.

TILLAMOOK
TILLAMOOK COUNTY CREAMERY ASSOCIATION

4175 Highway 101 N., Tillamook, 503-815-1300; www.tillamookcheese.com

Make a snack stop-off at this popular creamery that's been making cheese since 1894. Fill up on slices of the medium cheddar, which was named the big cheese in the 2010 World Cheese Championships. For heartier fare, visit the café for breakfast or lunch. But be sure to end your visit with one of the 38 ice cream varieties made onsite. Get a fresh-baked waffle cone filled with flavors like Grandma's Cake Batter, Oregon Black Cherry or German chocolate cake.

Visitor center: Labor Day-mid-June, daily 8 a.m.-6 p.m.; mid-June-Labor Day, daily 8 a.m.-8 p.m.

CAPE LOOKOUT STATE PARK

13000 Whiskey Creek Road, 12 miles southwest off Highway 101, Tillamook, 503-842-4891, 800-551-6949; www.oregonstateparks.org

A 1,974-acre park with virgin spruce forest and an observation point, Cape Lookout is one of most primitive ocean shore areas in the state.

WHERE TO STAY

BANDON
★★★LODGE AT BANDON DUNES

57744 Round Lake Drive, Bandon, 541-347-4380, 888-345-6008; www.bandondunesgolf.com

The Lodge at Bandon Dunes sits alongside the windswept coast of the Pacific Ocean. While the scenery is a draw, it's primarily a place for duffers, since the property is home to two of the Northwest's premier 18-hole courses. All guest rooms feature views of the ocean and the golf courses or the dunes and forest, and some have fireplaces and private balconies. Just off the lobby, Gallery Restaurant serves three meals a day, specializing in fresh seafood.

153 rooms. Restaurant, bar. Fitness center. Golf. $151-250

GOLD BEACH
★★★TU TU' TUN LODGE

96550 N. Bank Rogue, Gold Beach, 541-247-6664, 800-864-6357; www.tututun.com

From its flower-filled gardens to its scenic location on the banks of the Rogue

River, the Tu Tu' Tun Lodge offers a peaceful respite. The rustic guest rooms feature wood-burning fireplaces, deep-soaking tubs, overstuffed furnishings and soft bed linens. Inventive Pacific Northwest cuisine is available in the onsite restaurant.

18 rooms. Restaurant, bar. Pool. $151-250

LINCOLN CITY

★★★SALISHAN LODGE & GOLF RESORT

7760 Highway 101, Gleneden Beach, 541-764-2371, 800-452-2300; www.salishan.com

Carved out of a scenic stretch of Oregon coastline, this traditional Pacific Northwest lodge is perhaps best loved for its magnificent views of the region's rugged landscape. Private beach access and an 18-hole, Scottish-style golf course rank among the property's favorite amenities, which also include an indoor tennis center, fitness center and two indoor pools.

205 rooms. Restaurant, bar. Fitness center. Pool. Spa. Pets accepted. Beach. Golf. Tennis. $61-150

RECOMMENDED

ASTORIA

CANNERY PIER HOTEL

10 Basin St., Astoria, 888-325-4996; www.cannerypierhotel.com

Sitting along a dock along the Columbia River, this industrial-looking hotel could easily be mistaken for a commercial cannery. After all, the hotel used to be a fish-packing site. The Cannery Pier embraces its cannery roots with tasteful décor, including exposed steel beams, wooden trusses and walls adorned with historical cannery labels and photographs. The cozy rooms come with hardwood floors, gas fireplaces and microwaves. The best amenity is that all rooms have nice views of the river that you can enjoy on a private balcony, from a window bench inside or even from your bathroom window. If you want to go into town, hop on one of the hotel's 1950s replica bikes or, if you prefer a more chic ride, get chauffeured in an antique car, both of which are free.

46 rooms. Complimentary breakfast. Fitness center. Spa. Pets accepted. $251-350

HOTEL ELLIOTT

357 12th St., Astoria, 877-378-1924; www.hotelelliott.com

The old-school lit-up marquee at the entrance to Hotel Elliott tips you off that this is a property

---

WHICH HOTELS HAVE THE BEST VIEWS?

Cannery Pier Hotel: This hotel sits on a dock, which means that every room has great vistas of the Columbia River, which you can enjoy from your deck or your bathtub.

Hallmark Resort: Gaze out of your hotel room window at Hallmark and you'll see the water, Tillamook Lighthouse and gargantuan Haystack Rock.

Salishan Lodge & Golf Resort: The Salishan Lodge is planted in the midst of the thick verdant forests on the rustic Oregon coastline. Admire the rugged, peaceful landscape from your room.

Surfsand Resort: As its name implies, Surfsand is a beachfront resort. Located along the Pacific Ocean, it's only steps from your room to Haystack Rock.

with a past, but the 1914 hotel is firmly planted in the present with perks like heated tile floors in the bathrooms, sweet-smelling cedar-lined closets, DVD players and free Internet access. The rooms do maintain a classic feel with mahogany-, gold- and eggplant-colored bedspreads and curtains and cozy wood fireplaces. Make it a point to visit the five-story hotel's rooftop terrace, where you can sit back in big wooden chairs and admire the view of the river and the nearby Victorian houses.

32 rooms. Bar. $61-150

CANNON BEACH
HALLMARK RESORT
1400 S. Hemlock St., Cannon Beach, 503-436-1566, 888-448-4449; www.hallmarkinns.com

You'll get a great view of the water, the Tillamook Lighthouse and the 235-foot Haystack Rock, the world's third-largest monolith, at this oceanfront resort. Most rooms have a two-person Jacuzzis and fireplaces. If you are bringing the family, you can opt for kitchen suites or on-the-water beach houses. When you need a break from the ocean, you can take a dip in one of the two salt-water pools or relax in the onsite spa.

142 rooms. Business center. Fitness center. Pool. Spa. Pets accepted. $61-150

SURFSAND RESORT
148 W. Gower, Cannon Beach, 503-436-2274, 800-547-6100; www.surfsand.com

Surfsand centers all its activity around the beach, with seasonal Sunday weenie roasts and bonfires, complimentary sand toys, beachside cabana service and a s'mores add-on that gets you all the fixings for the gooey treats. But when the sun goes down, you'll find plenty in your room to keep you busy: LCD televisions in the rooms and bathrooms, DVD players and free DVD libraries, and fireplaces so that you can warm up after swimming in the ocean.

82 rooms. Restaurant, bar. Fitness center. Pool. Pets accepted. $151-250

LINCOLN CITY
THE O'DYSIUS HOTEL
120 N.W. Inlet Court, Lincoln City, 541-994-4121, 800-869-8069; www.odysius.com

This hotel appeals to water lovers, with the Pacific Ocean to the immediate west, the D-River (the world's shortest river) bordering to the south and Devils Lake a short walk to the east. Each cozy room has a fireplace and a whirlpool tub. In the morning, a free continental breakfast of fruit and pastries is delivered to your room so that you can grab a quick bite before hitting the beach.

30 rooms. Complimentary breakfast. No children allowed. $151-250

WHERE TO EAT

LINCOLN CITY
★★★BAY HOUSE
5911 S.W. Highway 101, Lincoln City, 541-996-3222; www.bayhouserestaurant.com

Located at the south end of the city, the restaurant offers spectacular views of Siletz Bay. The menu features upscale American fare, including dishes such as pan-seared halibut in toasted tangerine sauce and grilled salmon with vegetable cous cous.

American. Dinner, brunch. Bar. $16-35

RECOMMENDED

ASTORIA
SILVER SALMON GRILLE
1105 Commercial St., Astoria, 503-338-6640;
www.silversalmongrille.com

This restaurant makes the most of its Oregon Coast location and serves fresh local fish. Try the toasted-pecan-crusted salmon with Gulf shrimp and Brie-champagne cream or the halibut fish and chips. Indecisive types should go for the Silver Salmon Seafood Trio, with petite silver salmon, pan-fried oysters and coconut beer prawns. In case you don't feel like seafood, order the thick filet mignon.

American, seafood. Lunch, dinner. $16-35

CANNON BEACH
DOOGER'S
1371 S. Hemlock, Cannon Beach, 503-436-2225;
www.cannon-beach.net

When you crave a steaming bowl of clam chowder, grab a bowl at Dooger's. The restaurant is known for its chowder; if you really enjoy it, pick up one of the restaurant's do-it-yourself chowder kits for you to take home with canned clams, potatoes and spices. For hardier fare, Dooger's also offers seafood entrees, such as the Admiral's Platter, which teems with crab legs, razor clams, salmon, scallops, prawns, halibut and calamari.

Seafood, steak. Breakfast, lunch, dinner. Children's menu. Bar. $36-85

WAYFARER RESTAURANT AND LOUNGE
1190 Pacific Drive, Cannon Beach, 503-436-1108;
www.wayfarer-restaurant.com

Dine at this Northwestern Pacific oceanfront restaurant and you'll have a nice view of the Haystack Rock. Start off with avocado fingers, beer-battered avocado slices with blue cheese dipping sauce, or the Dungeness crab cakes with shrimp mousse. For the entrée, stick to the seafood portion of the menu, like herb-breaded and butter-seared razor clams with chili jelly or pan-seared salmon topped with Dungeness crab and béarnaise sauce.

Seafood. Breakfast, lunch, dinner. $16-35

WHICH RESTAURANTS HAVE THE BEST SEAFOOD?

Bay House
The Bay House ranks among the best restaurants on the coast. Its menu is filled with succulent seafood like pan-seared halibut in toasted tangerine sauce.

Dooger's
People come to Dooger's for one main reason: to slurp down a bowl of its trademark clam chowder.

Wayfarer Restaurant and Lounge
The menu at the Wayfarer is studded with seafood selections, everything from rockfish to Dungeness crab to razor clams.

COOS BAY
PORTSIDE
63383 Kingfisher Road, Charleston, 541-888-5544; www.portsidebythebay.com

Admire the views of Coos Bay from this seafood restaurant while you dine on regional specialties, such as the deep-fried Dungeness crab legs or the salmon Charleston, bacon-wrapped salmon medallions, shrimp and crab doused in hollandaise sauce. For a light dessert to cap a heavy meal, have the lime and lemon ice, which gets some oomph from a shot of grenadine and orgeat syrup.
Seafood. Lunch, dinner. Reservations recommended. Outdoor seating. Children's menu. Bar. $16-35

PORTLAND

Green in both color and consciousness, Portland is a city that's spectacular to look at, live in, visit and experience. With approximately 42 inches of annual average rainfall, the city stays visually green year-round, but it also leads the way in eco-practices like recycling efforts, sustainable building and a great public transportation system that includes buses, a light rail and a downtown streetcar service. Getting around by bicycle is part of the collective consciousness here, and the city makes it easy with well-marked bike lanes on many roads, plus a 40-mile bike loop around the city.

The largest city in the state, Portland is divided by the Willamette River and its northern tip straddles both the Willamette and the Columbia rivers. Here, there's something for everyone: a nationally recognized culinary community, a vibrant arts scene, nature and outdoor opportunities around every neighborhood—after all, the Columbia River Gorge, Mount Hood and Mount Saint Helens are nearby—plus a close proximity to mountains and beaches. You can easily hike into one of the many areas featuring breathtaking waterfalls and relaxing hot springs in the morning, then enjoy a gourmet dinner and attend the opera, a concert or the ballet that night.

Swimming, boating, fishing and camping opportunities are ample, but if staying city central is more your thing, there's plenty of quirky boutiques, funky neighborhoods and the largest bookstore you may ever visit to keep you occupied. Another perk: Portland has a rockin' music scene. Bands such as Pink Martini, the Dandy Warhols and the Decemberists started here, and you can find live music at a number of historic venues every night of the week. Business visitors swarm the city's convention centers, including the Oregon Convention Center, the Memorial Coliseum complex and the Metropolitan Exposition Center. You'll also see lots of college students traipsing around town, since Lewis & Clark College, Portland State University, the University of Portland and Reed College are all located here.

Of course, one of the reasons to visit is the verdant surroundings. Aside from the many parks sprinkled throughout Portland, the City of Roses boasts the spectacular international Rose Test Garden and annual Rose Festival (May/June). Overall, Portland's casual vibe and perfect blend of culture and nature appeal to many.

WHAT TO SEE

BENSON STATE RECREATION AREA
30 miles east on I-84, 800-551-6949; www.oregonstateparks.org

Thirty miles east of Portland, near Multnomah Falls, the Benson State Recreation Area has a lake that's perfect for fishing, swimming and boating (non-motorized boats only). The first weekend of June, try your luck angling for rainbow trout on Free Fishing Day with your own pole, or one the park provides. Picnicking is popular here, and a reservable group shelter is available. The park even has a disc golf course.

Daily. $5 or $30 annual day-use pass.

COUNCIL CREST PARK
S.W. Council Crest Drive, Portland, 503-823-7529; www.portlandonline.com

Council Crest Park is not just the city's highest park; it's Portland's highest point, topping off at 1,073 feet above sea level. That may not sound very high, but it's enough to afford wonderful views of the Tualatin Valley, the Willamette River, Mount St. Helens and the truly high and mighty Mount Hood. Don't miss the bronze mother-and-child fountain near the entrance. Originally installed in another area of the park in 1956, the statue was stolen in the '80s and found almost 10 years later in a northeast Portland backyard during a narcotics raid.

Daily.

CROWN POINT STATE SCENIC CORRIDOR
40700 Historic Columbia River Highway, Corbett, 503-695-2261, 800-551-6949;
www.oregonstateparks.org

This 307-acre park possesses a 725-foot-high vantage point alongside the Columbia River Gorge, allowing for spectacular views of the gorge's rock walls, which rise 2,000 feet above the water. The historic Vista House, an octagonal sandstone structure with a domed ceiling, was designed by Edgar Lazarus in 1916 as a rest-stop observatory and viewpoint for travelers along the Columbia Gorge Highway. The recently restored house is free to enter and features a museum, gift shop and interpretive display of Gorge historical and geological items.

Admission: free. March 14-October 31, daily; closed rest of the year.

CRYSTAL SPRINGS RHODODENDRON GARDEN
Southeast 28th Avenue and Woodstock Boulevard, Portland, 503-771-8386; www.portlandonline.com

The pathways at Crystal Springs wind through a 9 ½-acre woodland setting, passing some 2,500 rhododendrons, azaleas and companion plants. A spring-fed lake attracts many species of birds and waterfowl. Green thumbs and nature walkers alike can enjoy meandering the many paths throughout the garden. The first Saturday in April, get a look at hundreds of early-blooming rhodo-dendrons, or visit on Mother's Day, when an even larger array is on display. The garden is also available for weddings and special events.

Admission: Labor Day-February, free; March-Labor Day, $3. Garden hours: April-September, daily 6 a.m.-10 p.m.; October-March, daily 6 a.m.-6 p.m.

DABNEY STATE RECREATION AREA

19 miles east off Interstate 84, at Stark Street Bridge on Highway 30, 800-551-6949; www.oregonstateparks.org

East of Portland, this 135-acre park is a popular summertime destination thanks to its idyllic swimming hole and picnic area. The park even offers electric cooking stations to fry up those hamburgers and tofu dogs. Many visitors catch their own meal by fishing for salmon and steelhead in the Sandy River. Other amenities include a group shelter, walking trails, a beach, a boat ramp and a disc-golf course.

Admission: $5 daily day-use fee, $3 daily day-use fee for reservable picnic sites and disc golf.

FOREST PARK

N.W. 29th Avenue and Upshur Street to Newberry Road, Portland, 503-823-7529; www.portlandonline.com

This big strip of greenery encompasses more than 5,100 wooded acres, making it the largest wilderness park within city limits in the United States. Take advantage of its 74 miles of hiking, bicycling and equestrian trails. Try Wildwood Trail, which begins at the Vietnam Veterans Living Memorial in Hoyt Arboretum and extends 27 miles, ending deep in the park beyond Germantown Road. Some 100 bird species and 60 mammal species inhabit the park.

Daily 5 a.m.-10 p.m.

THE GROTTO

Sandy Boulevard (Highway 30) at N.E. 85th Avenue, Portland, 503-254-7371; www.thegrotto.org

The National Sanctuary of Our Sorrowful Mother—commonly called the Grotto—is a 62-acre Catholic shrine and botanical garden. Created in 1924, the Grotto cuts into the side of a 110-foot cliff and is surrounded by a variety of beautiful plants and flowers. An elevator takes you to the Natural Gallery in the woods, where you'll find more than 100 statues. The landscaped upper level has a meditation chapel overlooking the Columbia River with Mount St. Helens visible in the distance.

Daily 9 a.m.-8:30 p.m.

GUY W. TALBOT STATE PARK

Columbia River Highway, Troutdale, 800-551-6949; www.oregonstateparks.org

These 371 lush acres served as the estate of Guy Webster Talbot and his family until the property was donated to the state in 1929. The park is a wonderful picnicking destination, as it is rarely crowded and features lovely surroundings, including 250-foot-high Latourell Falls, the second-highest falls along the Columbia River Gorge. A reservable picnic shelter is available.

Daily.

HOWELL TERRITORIAL PARK AND THE BYBEE HOUSE

13901 N.W. Howell Park Road, Portland, 503-797-1850; www.oregonmetro.gov

The Howell Territorial Park, occupying 93 pastoral acres on Sauvie Island, is home to the Bybee House, an impressive example of Greek Revival architecture. Originally a private residence, the Bybee House was purchased in 1961 by Multnomah County and soon after restored to appear as it would have at the time of its construction in 1858.

Admission: free. Daily sunrise-sunset.

HIGHLIGHT

WHAT ARE THE BEST PLACES FOR OUTDOOR FUN IN PORTLAND?

GO FOR A BIKE RIDE IN FOREST PARK
Biking is big in Portland, and here you can pedal along 74 miles of trails in the largest city wilderness park in the country.

GAZE AT MULTNOMAH FALLS
There are a number of beautiful cascading waters along the Columbia River Gorge. But Multnomah, the U.S.'s second-highest year-round waterfall, is particularly striking.

WALK AROUND THE PEARL DISTRICT
This hot neighborhood is a great place to peruse trendy boutiques and galleries. The artsy enclave is home to the Art Institute and the Portland Institute for Contemporary Art.

STROLL THROUGH THE PORTLAND JAPANESE GARDEN
The 5.5-acre oasis is hailed as the most authentic Japanese gardens outside of Japan. Come see the beautifully designed Sand and Stone and the Strolling Pond gardens.

SHOP AT THE PORTLAND SATURDAY MARKET
Head to this weekly open-air market, one of the largest and oldest of its kind in the United States. Vendors hawk everything from hand-woven scarves to barbecue.

HOYT ARBORETUM
4000 S.W. Fairview Blvd., Portland, 503-865-8733; www.hoytarboretum.org
Spanning 187 acres, Hoyt Arboretum boasts more than 900 species of trees and shrubs, including one of the largest collections of conifers in the United States. The arboretum sits upon a ridge overlooking the Oregon Zoo. One-, two- or four-mile self-guided walks are available; maps available at the visitor center.
Tours: $3. Daily 6 a.m.-10 p.m. Guided tours (90 minutes): July-August, Saturday 9 and 11 a.m.

LEWIS AND CLARK STATE RECREATION SITE

16 miles east on I-84, 800-551-6949; www.oregonstateparks.org

Situated near the confluence of the Columbia and Sandy rivers, this park offers picnic tables, a beach and a boat ramp. Anglers and swimmers are a common sight in the cool waters of the Sandy River. Hiking is popular here, particularly along a trail that leads to Broughton's Bluff. The park's namesakes camped in and explored the area in November 1805.

Daily.

MOUNT TABOR PARK

S.E. 60th Avenue and Salmon Street, Portland, 503-823-2223; www.portlandonline.com

Get active at this 195-acre park, which has a basketball court, a volleyball court, a horseshoe pit, a playground, a picnic shelter and tennis courts, as well as an off-leash area for dogs. One thing that isn't active in the park is an extinct volcano, making Portland one of only two U.S. cities to have one.

Daily 5 a.m.-midnight.

MULTNOMAH FALLS

I-84 to Multnomah Falls turnoff, Bridal Veil, 503-695-2372; www.fs.fed.us

Multnomah Falls is chief among the many waterfalls along the phenomenally scenic Columbia River Gorge highway. Gushing 620 feet from Larch Mountain, it is the second-highest year-round waterfall in the United States. It draws nearly 2 million tourists each year.

OAKS AMUSEMENT PARK

7805 S.E. Oaks Park Way, Portland, 503-233-5777; www.oakspark.com

Opened in 1905, Oaks Park is one of the oldest continuously operating amusement parks in the nation and is a local favorite for its small-scale, old-school style of family entertainment. Classic rides still exist here, including Tilt-a-Whirl, bumper cars, go-carts, a Ferris wheel and a 1912-built carousel. Adrenalin junkies can get their fix on thrill rides such as the Looping Thunder Roller Coaster, which throws you on stomach-churning 360-degree loops, and the Disk'O, a rocking, spinning machine with unique motorcycle-style seats arranged in an outward-facing circle. Acorn Acres houses more tame kid rides. Don't leave without taking a ride down the old-fashioned but still fun Big Pink Slide. A skating rink and historic dance pavilion are also part of the park's spread.

Admission: free. Ride bracelets: $11.75-$14.75; individual ride tickets: $2.25 each or seven for $13. Rides: late March-early October. Skating rink: year-round. Hours vary.

OREGON HISTORICAL SOCIETY

1200 S.W. Park Ave., Portland, 503-222-1741; www.ohs.org

Get your history fix at the Oregon Historical Society, which features a broad range of exhibits and collections within its museum and research library. The history of Oregon and the Pacific Northwest is documented through photographs, audio recordings, artifacts and books. Exhibitions include "License to Drive," a fun collection of Oregon license plates from past to present, and "The Benson Automobile," the first car completely built in the state by garage inventors. Make sure you take time to visit the "Battleship Oregon" exhibit. The ship, known as "The Bulldog of the Navy," was an important force in the Spanish-American War and helped modernize the U.S. Navy during that period.

Admission: adults $11, seniors and students $9, children 6-18 $5, children 5 and under free. Tuesday-Saturday 10 a.m.-5 p.m., Sunday noon-5 p.m.

OREGON MUSEUM OF SCIENCE AND INDUSTRY

1945 S.E. Water Ave., Portland, 503-797-6674, 800-955-6674; www.omsi.edu

The museum has six exhibit halls and labs featuring fun exhibits on astronomy, electronics, Earth science, biology and dinosaurs. Check out "Identity: An Exhibition of You," a physical, psychological and social identity exhibit where you can age your face and morph your photo into a different gender or ethnicity. The museum is also home to a planetarium and OMNIMAX theater, as well as the U.S.S. Blueback, the Navy's last non-nuclear, fast-attack submarine. OMSI After Dark ($10 admission) is a series of monthly adult-only evenings that include a DJ, cash bar, live demos and activities, planetarium and OMNIMAX shows, as well as a special dinner menu at the OMSI Café made from local, sustainable ingredients (check website for specific dates; they change monthly).

Admission: adults $12, seniors and children 3-13 $9. Planetarium, OMNIMAX, laser light shows and select other attractions additional; check website for specific pricing. Labor Day-Memorial Day, Tuesday-Sunday 9:30 a.m.-5:30 p.m.; October-May, daily, 9:30 a.m.-7 p.m.

OREGON ZOO

4001 S.W. Canyon Road, Portland, 503-226-1561; www.oregonzoo.org

Opened as the Washington Park Zoo in 1887, the Oregon Zoo houses large and small creatures, ranging from elephants and giraffes to millipedes and scorpions. It specializes in breeding and protecting rare and endangered species and has about 1,029 living specimens, 54 of which are considered either endangered or threatened. Notable animals to visit include the gray wolf, Malayan sun bear and black rhinoceros, a rhino species that's considered the most endangered in the world due to poaching. Also check out the Island Pigs of Asia area, with rare Visayan warty pigs and babirusa pigs. The newest addition is the Red Ape Reserve, featuring orangutans and white-cheeked gibbons. The zoo is a five-minute ride from downtown Portland on the MAX light rail. A separate zoo railway links to the popular Washington Park.

September 16-May 14, daily 9 a.m.-4 p.m.; May 15-September 15, daily 8 a.m.-6 p.m. Admission: adults $10.50, seniors $9, children 3-11 $7.50.

PITTOCK MANSION

3229 N.W. Pittock Drive, Portland, 503-823-3623; www.pittockmansion.com

This restored French château-style mansion, dating to 1914, was built by early Portland pioneers Henry (who took over The Oregonian newspaper in 1860 and turned it into a daily) and Georgianna Pittock as their family home, and was later turned in to a museum of the family's heritage and a tribute to Pacific Northwest craftsmanship. The grounds include 46 forested and landscaped acres. Indoors, the home features impressive nods to English, French and Turkish designs. The museum store is housed in what was once the family's garage and features specialty wares such as hand-blown glass, porcelain collectibles, textiles and jewelry from local artists and vendors. Spectacular views of rivers, the city and snowcapped mountains, including Mount St. Helens and Mount Hood, are a bonus. Seasonal events and exhibitions such as Summer Evenings at Pittock Mansion and Immerse Yourself in Architecture are offered throughout the year.

Admission: adults $8, seniors $7, children ages 6-18 $5, children 5 and under free. Hours vary by season; check website for details. Closed January.

PORTLAND ART MUSEUM

1219 S.W. Park Ave., Portland, 503-226-2811; www.pam.org

Founded in 1892, the Portland Art Museum holds a permanent collection of more than 42,000 pieces of art, including European paintings and sculptures from the Renaissance to the present; 19th- and 20th-century American works; a noted collection of Northwest Coast Native American art; Asian, pre-Columbian, West African, classical Greek and Roman art; British silver; and creative photography. Notable works include drawings by Picasso, Matisse and Cézanne, as well as paintings by famed landscape painter George Inness and post-war photography by Minor White.

Admission: adults $12, seniors and students $9, children free. Free fourth Friday of every month 5-8 p.m. Tuesday, Wednesday and Sunday 10 a.m.-5 p.m., Thursday-Friday 10 a.m.-8 p.m., Sunday noon-5 p.m.

PORTLAND CHILDREN'S MUSEUM

4015 S.W. Canyon Road, Portland, 503-223-6500; www.portlandcm.org

Located in Washington Park across from the Oregon Zoo, this museum offers plenty of hands-on play spaces, including the Clay Studio, where kiddies can sculpt till their little hands get tired, and Grasshopper Grocery, a pint-sized market with miniature carts and aisles of mock food. A new feature is Kid's Build: Project 2010, which allows children ages 5 and up the chance to build, stack, sort and experiment with recycled and traditional building materials. For younger visitors, the Baby's Garden offers a lily-pad water bed, fish aquarium and tree with a slide.

Monday-Thursday, Saturday 9 a.m.-5 p.m., Friday 9 a.m.-8 p.m., Sunday 11 a.m.-5 p.m.

PORTLAND JAPANESE GARDEN

611 S.W. Kingston Ave., Portland, 503-223-1321; www.japanesegarden.com

This 5.5-acre enclave of tranquility is considered one of the most authentic Japanese gardens outside of Japan. Opened in 1967, the masterfully designed garden possesses five formal styles: Natural Garden, Sand and Stone Garden, Tea Garden, Strolling Pond Garden and Flat Garden. Check out the gift store for an eclectic array of arts and crafts merchandise, most from Japan.

Admission: adults $9.50, seniors and students $7.75, children 6-17 $6.75, children 5 and under free. April-September, Monday noon-7 p.m., Tuesday-Sunday 10 a.m.-7 p.m.; October-March, Monday noon-4 p.m., Tuesday-Sunday 10 a.m.-4 p.m.

PORTLAND SATURDAY MARKET

Waterfront Park, S.W. Ankeny and Naito Parkway, Portland, 503-222-6072; www.portlandsaturdaymarket.com

This is one of the largest, oldest open-air community markets in the United

States. It features more than 250 vendor booths with arts and crafts made by Pacific Northwest artisans and a wide variety of foods. Here, you'll find treasures like Gypsy Camp upholstery-fabric handbags, Touch the Sky hand-woven scarves, Oregon Jewelry and Ornaments' pendants and more depicting nature scenes, plus a dizzying array of games, toys, metal sculptures and more. Refuel after shopping with ethnic food from one of the many food stalls; Beirut Café serves up heart-shaped falafel, and My Brother's BBQ cooks up a Creole-style barbecue sandwich. Indulge your sweet tooth with a scoop of homemade ice cream from Great NW Ice Cream, famous for crazy concoctions like beer ice cream made with Black Butte Porter brew. Street entertainers, face painters and the like enliven the atmosphere. Live music keeps the place humming, with bands taking the stage midday.

Early March-late December, Saturday 10 a.m.-5 p.m., Sunday 11 a.m.-4:30 p.m.

ROOSTER ROCK STATE PARK
East on I-84, 503-695-2261, 800-551-6949; www.oregonstateparks.org

A short drive east of Portland, Rooster Rock offers three miles of sandy beaches along the Columbia River. The park is a popular destination for windsurfing, disc golf, boating, fishing, swimming, hiking and picnicking. Don't panic if you run into some naked people: One of Oregon's two designated nude beaches is at the park's eastern edge.

Admission: daily use $5; reservable picnic shelters $3.

STERNWHEELER COLUMBIA GORGE
110 S.E. Caruthers St., Portland, cruises leave from Marine Park in Cascade Locks, 503-224-3900, 800-224-3901; www.portlandspirit.com

Climb aboard the *Columbia Gorge*, an authentic triple-deck paddle wheeler, and enjoy great views as you journey along the Columbia River. A variety of excursions are offered, including champagne brunch cruises, dinner cruises and special holiday Cinnamon Bear cruises featuring characters, storytelling, magic and music.

WASHINGTON PARK
400 S.W. Kingston, Portland, 503-823-7529; www.washingtonparkpdx.org

Head to Washington Park to frolic on 129 scenic acres on a hill overlooking the city. On a clear day, the views are simply spectacular, with Mount Hood towering majestically in the east and Mount St. Helens visible on the northern horizon. The Shakespeare Garden, Lewis and Clark Memorial Holocaust Memorial and Sacajawea Statue can be found in the park, as well as the International Rose Test Garden, Japanese Garden and Portland Children's Museum. Washington Park facilities include softball and soccer fields, lighted tennis courts, covered picnic areas, a playground and hiking trails.

Daily 5 a.m.-10 p.m.

WORLD FORESTRY CENTER
4033 S.W. Canyon Road, Portland, 503-228-1367; www.worldforestry.org

This is a museum for nature lovers. The World Forestry Center, located in Washington Park near the Oregon Zoo, is composed of the Forest Discovery Center, a 20,000-square-foot museum celebrating the importance and diversity

SPECIAL EVENTS

CHAMBER MUSIC NORTHWEST

522 S.W. Fifth Ave., Portland, 503-294-6400; www.cmnw.org

The nationally acclaimed chamber music festival offers 25 concerts featuring a mix of 50 to 60 national and international artists, such as Sylvia McNair and Sheridan Seyfried, each summer. A catered picnic precedes each concert. Children under seven are only permitted at Family Concerts.

Mid-June-late July.

PORTLAND MARATHON

Portland, 503-226-1111; www.portlandmarathon.org

The world-class running event (the traditional 26.2-mile marathon with an entry fee of $135) features 10,000 runners and competition from the U.S. and abroad and is a qualifying race to gain entry to the prestigious Boston Marathon. In 1983, the course became one of the first to be officially measured and certified by the Association of International Marathons. Starting in downtown Portland, the course combines flat terrain and some hills and winds through the waterfront district, historic Old Town, residential neighborhoods and over the picturesque St. John's and Broadway Bridges. Six miles of the course border the eastern bluff of the Willamette River, making for beautifully varied terrain throughout the marathon.

Early October.

PORTLAND ROSE FESTIVAL

5603 S.W. Hood Ave., Portland, 503-227-2681; www.rosefestival.org

If you're visiting the city in late spring or early summer, the Rose Festival is not to be missed; in fact, it received the title of Best Festival in the World in 2007 from the International Festivals & Events Association. The idea for the fest bloomed after the success of the 1905 World's Fair in Portland; organizers thought the city needed a yearly world-class event. The city's popular rose culture prompted officials to make the event a celebration of the rose, a symbol of beauty, toughness and durability, characteristics shared by the pioneering Oregonians of the day. Held annually since 1907, the fest honors Pacific Northwest heritage and is named after the flower that's synonymous with the city. The Grand Floral Parade is impressive, touted as one of the country's top all-floral parades with more than 20,000 blooms adorning the floats. And if flowers aren't your thing, there's plenty more to experience, including championship auto racing, hot-air balloons, an air show, a carnival and fleet week with Navy ships.

Late May to mid-June.

ST. PATRICK'S IRISH FESTIVAL

Kells, 112 S.W. Second Ave., Portland, 503-227-4057; www.kellsirish.com

When people want to be transported to the Emerald Isle, they come to Kells to hear live Irish music every night of the week and to puff away in the cigar room. Around St. Patrick's Day, this pub becomes party central during one of the largest Irish festivals in the Pacific Northwest. You'll see pipers, dancers and, of course, traditional food like Irish lamb stew, shepherd's pie and soda bread during the five-day fest.

Mid-March.

MUSICFEST NW

Multiple venues around Portland; www.musicfestnw.com.

Get ready to wave your hands in the air like you just don't care. Indie, hip-hop and punk music fans descend on venues around town for what's quickly become the third-largest indoor music festival in the country, featuring local, regional and national acts from the unknown to the well- known—past bands include The Decemberists and Smashing Pumpkins. Created and hosted by Portland's alt-weekly newspaper Willamette Week, this festival is the place to discover new music and new friends. Tickets cost $65 and for an all-show pass it's $90. VIP tickets are also offered for $175.

Mid-September.

OREGON BALLET THEATRE

818 S.E. Sixth Ave., www.obt.org

There's just something magical about watching a ballet, and the Oregon Ballet Theatre captivates audiences with breathtaking shows such as The Sleeping Beauty, and of course, at holiday time, The Nutcracker. New for spring 2011 is Song & Dance, a show that juxtaposes Nicolo Fonte's sultry couples in Left Unsaid against a hip-hop showcase called Speak by Trey McIntyre, then ends with a lively collage of tributes to Hollywood musicals and Broadway numbers.

OREGON SYMPHONY

Arlene Schnitzer Concert Hall, 1037 S.W. Broadway, orsymphony.org

Boasting 76 full-time musicians, the Oregon Symphony continues to produce stellar classical, youth and pops concerts for eager listeners at the downtown Schnitzer venue (which seats more than 2,700), as well as community concerts in Portland parks. Upcoming notable performances in 2011 include a special

continued on page 80

SPECIAL EVENTS *continued*

Johnny Mathis Valentine's Day concert and Hilary Hahn, one of the country's best young classical musicians, playing Tchaikovsky. For Halloween, Alfred Hitchcock's *Psycho* will play on the big screen with the symphony providing the creepy live soundtrack.

PORTLAND PIRATE FESTIVAL

Cathedral Park, North Edison Street and Pittsburg Avenue under the St. John's Bridge, north Portland
Ahoy, mateys! Don your best pirate garb and bring the kids out for some swash-buckling fun. The little ones will stay entertained with a variety of rides, puppet shows, hands-on crafts and airbrush tattoos, while the older set rocks out to a mix of music from bands such as the Dreadnoughts and the Pirates Charles. Watch sword-clashing historical re-enactments and take in the sights of performance artists, including jugglers and fire-breathers.
Mid-September.

OREGON BREWER'S FESTIVAL

Waterfront Park, downtown Portland, www.oregonbrewfest.com
Beer connoisseurs come together for this annual summer celebration, which offers up more than 80 different craft beers from breweries around the country. Local brewers like Widmer Brothers, MacTarnahan's and Rogue Ales present their best suds alongside visitors including Alaskan Beer, California's Blue Frog Grog & Grill and Hawaii's Kona Brewing Company and many more. Past festivals presented unique concoctions like Bitch Creek ESB, an extra special brown; Captain Shaddock IPA, a grapefruit India Pale Ale; and Destination, a Honey Red Ale. Food vendors and live music make the event an all-out party.
Last weekend in July.

of tree life, plus two sustainably managed working tree farms and the World Forest Institute, the center's information services division that provides data to manufacturers, consultants, researchers and others in the forestry field. The museum's most popular exhibit is a 70-foot-tall talking tree, a replica Douglas fir that teaches tree biology in five different languages: English, French, Japanese, Spanish and German.
Daily 10 a.m.-5 p.m. Admission: adults $8, seniors $7, children $5.

WHERE TO STAY

★★★AVALON HOTEL & SPA
0455 S.W. Hamilton Court, Portland, 503-802-5800; www.avalonhotelandspa.com
The relatively new Avalon Hotel & Spa is in the recently revitalized south

waterfront area of Portland and offers an unusual perk: It sits on the bank of a protected wildlife area, and many rooms have a river view, which you can enjoy from the balcony. Traditional furnishings, earth and medium wood tones create a homey feel to the guest rooms. The Spa Chakra is also noteworthy, with 11 treatment rooms, a full-service salon and an ample menu of pampering treatments—wind down a busy day with the Supreme Maintenance package, which includes an energizing facial, an exfoliating body treatment and a mani/pedi. The Aquariva Italian Kitchen and Wine Bar shares the river view, and a complimentary continental breakfast is served daily on each floor of the hotel.

99 rooms. Restaurant, bar. Complimentary breakfast. Fitness center. Spa. $151-250

★★★EMBASSY SUITES PORTLAND DOWNTOWN

319 S.W. Pine St., Portland, 503-279-9000, 800-362-2779; www.embassyportland.com

This downtown Portland hotel has a historic location, housed in a building that originally opened in 1912. The restored lobby's gold-leafed columns, marble stairways and crystal chandeliers may hint at the building's age, but the guest rooms have been updated with flat-screen TVs and high-thread count linens. Traditional-style furnishings, like printed upholstered sofas, wingback chairs and dark-wood poster beds, create a comfy feeling. When you need some entertainment, head to the game cellar for video games, a pool table, air hockey and large-screen TV for movie viewing. Forget about a cold morning meal here; daily breakfasts are cooked to order and even better, they are free.

276 rooms. Restaurant, bar. Fitness center. Pool. $151-250

★★★GOVERNOR HOTEL

614 S.W. 11th Ave., Portland, 503-224-3400, 800-554-3456; www.govhotel.com

This historic building has housed a hotel for more than 100 years, and a fresh remodel perfectly combines the original feel of its Arts & Crafts architectural style with modern amenities, including flat-screen TVs, a soothing beige and cream color scheme and contemporary furniture. Some rooms include working fireplaces. Jake's Grill, the onsite restaurant, is popular with locals for its seasonal, fresh seafood and grilled steaks.

100 rooms. Restaurant, bar. Fitness center. Pool. $151-250

★★★THE HEATHMAN HOTEL

1001 S.W. Broadway, Portland, 503-241-4100, 800-551-0011;www.heathmanhotel.com

If it's a classy, cultural feel you want, the Heathman Hotel delivers. The wood-paneled Tea Court serves high tea daily, the library features author-signed books from thrill-master Stephen King and the razor-tongued chef and TV host Anthony Bourdain. Andy Warhol's endangered species artwork, a series of 10 vibrantly colored screenprints the artist made to portray endangered animals from around the world, hangs on each floor. Located close to Portland attractions such as the Arlene Schnitzer Concert Hall, Portland Art Museum and Oregon Historical Society Museum, the Heathman is a popular spot for weekenders. Rooms include treats such as Peet's French press coffee, L'Occitane soaps, twice-daily maid service and a choice of mattresses—Tempur-Pedic, pillow-top or feather-top.

150 rooms. Restaurant, bar. Business center. Pets accepted. $151-250

★★★HILTON PORTLAND & EXECUTIVE TOWER
921 S.W. Sixth Ave., Portland, 503-226-1611, 800-445-8667;
www.portland.hilton.com

The Hilton Portland & Executive Tower boasts all
of the things you'd expect from a Hilton, and it's the
largest Green-Seal Certified hotel on the West Coast.
Set in Portland's entertainment and cultural district,
this hotel has comfortable rooms featuring feather
beds and flat-screen TVs. Executive Tower rooms are
spacious, and king suites in the tower include a leather
recliner and 20-story-high views. The fitness center is
stocked with Precor cardio equipment (each with its
own TV) and includes a waveless lap pool. The hotel's
is just one block to the MAX light rail, so exploring
Portland sans car is a snap.

*782 rooms. Restaurant, bar. Business center. Fitness center. Pool.
Pets accepted. $151-250*

★★★HOTEL DELUXE
729 S.W. 15th Ave., Portland, 503-219-2094;
www.hoteldeluxeportland.com

Movie buffs will want to check into this downtown
hotel. The décor salutes Hollywood's golden era
with elegant Art Deco-inspired designs and displays
of nearly 400 photos from Tinseltown films, such as
Marilyn Monroe's *Some Like It Hot*, in the lobby and
throughout the hotel's hallways. Rooms are decorated
in vibrant citrus colors and with 1920s to 1940s
Hollywood-style accents, including one-of-a-kind
crystal lamps and elegant padded headboards compli-
mented by mahogany furniture. Be sure to make a date
for dinner and a movie: Enjoy cocktail hour in the
intimate Driftwood Room bar, fill up with a hearty
meal at Gracie's restaurant, then see recent flicks by
local filmmakers in the onsite screening room. During
the summer, movies are shown weekly on the rooftop
with beverage and snack service. For a special romantic
occasion, reserve the Marlene Dietrich suite, which has
an 8-foot round bed.

*130 rooms. Restaurant, bar. Business center. Fitness center. Pets
accepted. $151-250*

★★★HOTEL LUCIA
400 S.W. Broadway, Portland, 503-225-1717, 877-225-1717;
www.hotellucia.com

Calling all hipsters: Minimalist modern style in a cozy,
cool setting is what you'll find at the Hotel Lucia. Black-
and-white photos from former President Ford photog-
rapher (and Oregon native) David Hume Kennerly add
interest throughout the hotel. Typhoon! restaurant offers

both Thai and American fare, and the hip Bo Restobar serves up Asian-fusion meals and top-notch cocktails. Additional perks include a pillow menu, a spiritual menu so you can order your preferred religious text, and 24-hour room service.

127 rooms. Restaurant, bar. $151-250

★★★HOTEL MONACO PORTLAND

506 S.W. Washington St., Portland, 503-222-0001, 888-207-2201; www.monaco-portland.com

When you check into the Hotel Monaco, Timmy will likely greet you with a wagging tail. The friendly yellow Labrador is the resident director of pet relations at this dog-friendly hotel, and guests can regularly be seen hanging out with their own canines in the lobby. The theme of this hotel is patron of the arts, and guests are given canvases, paint and brushes to create their own masterpiece at the wine receptions held every evening in the lobby. The updated rooms feature classic striped walls and an energizing periwinkle, persimmon and espresso color theme. Unwind and let the spa come to you with in-room treatments such as a Calm Mind massage and an aromatherapy facial provided by the adjacent Dosha Spa, a Portland favorite.

221 rooms. Restaurant, bar. Spa. Pets accepted. $151-250

★★★HOTEL VINTAGE PLAZA

422 S.W. Broadway, Portland, 503-228-1212, 800-263-2305; www.vintageplaza.com

This elegant Kimpton hotel's name is appropriate—the hotel is housed in a historic building that was constructed in 1894 as the Imperial Hotel, and it's listed on the National Register of Historic Places. The hotel is also aptly named because of its dedication to wine: The rooms are nicknamed for local wineries, and every Wednesday, representatives from one of Oregon's 136 wineries give a class and tasting. A recent renovation includes stylish room décor in cream, olive and chocolate tones, and the beds feature eye-catching persimmon-colored leather headboards. Try to snag a Starlight room (there are nine) to enjoy conservatory windows that let you see the stars right from your bed. Pets receive the royal treatment here, with a personalized welcome board, bed, massage and doggie day care.

117 rooms. Restaurant, bar. Pets accepted. $151-250

★★★MARRIOTT PORTLAND CITY CENTER

520 S.W. Broadway, Portland, 503-226-6300, 888-236-2427; www.marriott.com

The Marriott Portland Downtown is conveniently located within the city's business and financial district. Guest rooms are decorated in warm beige, brown and cream tones and accented by elegant wood furniture; the pillow-top mattresses are sure to lull you into a restful sleep. Some rooms overlook a city park. Concierge-level rooms on upper floors offer skyline views and a weekday buffet breakfast, plus complimentary hors d'oeuvres Sunday through Thursday evenings.

503 rooms. Restaurant, bar. Pool. Pets accepted. $151-250

★★★MARRIOTT PORTLAND DOWNTOWN WATERFRONT

1401 S.W. Naito Parkway, Portland, 503-226-7600, 888-236-2427; www.marriott.com

If a view of the river is on your hotel wish list, the Marriott Portland Downtown Waterfront has it. Rooms have either a skyline or river view, and the renovated rooms feature down comforters and duvets. Swim year-round in the indoor pool, which is surrounded by windows and gives a view of the greenery outside. Dining options include Allie's American Grille (breakfast only) and Champions Restaurant and Sports Bar (lunch and dinner), where you can sample local microbrews. If those don't tempt your taste buds, head to the nearby Portland Riverplace Marina for additional dining—and shopping—options.

503 rooms. Restaurant, bar. Fitness center. Pool. Pets accepted. $151-250

★★★PARAMOUNT HOTEL

808 S.W. Taylor St., Portland, 503-223-9900; www.portlandparamount.com

This 15-story boutique hotel is in downtown Portland within walking distance of Pioneer Square and the Center for the Performing Arts. It's also directly across the street from Portland's newly opened Director Park, an oasis in the middle of downtown. The oversized rooms feature upscale furnishings like a velvet-covered reading chair and ottoman and fireplaces in some. Suites have double-sided fireplaces dividing the living and sleeping areas. For a romantic stay, book a Balcony Guest Room, featuring French doors that open to a Romeo & Juliet balcony. Dragonfish Asian Café offers eclectic pan-Asian cuisine.

154 rooms. Restaurant, bar. Pets accepted. $151-250

★★★RIVER PLACE HOTEL

1510 S.W. Harbor Way, Portland, 503-228-3233, 800-227-1333; www.riverplacehotel.com

Enjoy on-the-water accommodations at the aptly named River Place Hotel. The Craftsman-inspired lobby is a nod to the Pacific Northwest, and rooms are furnished in soothing creams and coffee tones. Pamper yourself with a stay in one of the Fireplace Suites, which have city and water views and a crackling blaze to keep you warm. Dine at the upscale Three Degrees Waterfront Bar & Grill (no jeans allowed) and enjoy half-price selections during daily happy hour from 4 to 7 p.m. If you'd rather be out in the water, rent a kayak from the hotel and hit the river.

84 rooms. Restaurant, bar. Pets accepted. $151-250

★★★SHERATON PORTLAND AIRPORT HOTEL

8235 N.E. Airport Way, Portland, 503-281-2500, 800-325-3525; www.starwoodhotels.com

You won't miss your flight if you stay at this newly renovated, business-focused travel hotel, which sits right on airport grounds. The signature SweetSleeper bed, elegant furnishings and evening turndown service create a luxurious setting, while free wireless Internet helps you stay connected. The heated indoor pool, whirlpool and sauna will melt your stresses away and make you forget the rumbling planes nearby. The Columbia Grill & Bar serves comforting American fare nearly around the clock (5 a.m-1 a.m.) and offers a huge variety of local microbrews. So take a load off and grab a beer here before running off to your flight.

218 rooms. Restaurant, bar. Fitness center. Pool. Pets accepted. $151-250

RECOMMENDED

ACE HOTEL

1022 S.W. Stark St., Portland, 503-228-2277; www.acehotel.com

A stay at this unique hotel won't break the bank. Instead, it will deliver stylish and quirky rooms, a helping of local flavor and a taste of luxury. Opened in 2007, the Ace aimed to fill a void in the hotel industry, providing comfort and style at a reasonable price for a discerning, creative crowd—think young screenwriters and guitarists. To create a space where this selective set would want to spend its time, the Ace team carefully restored a 1912 hotel between downtown and the Pearl District, retaining the historical character while updating the place to create a design it describes as "warm minimalism." Next, the staff hired a fleet of local artists to leave its mark in the guest rooms, making each one unique and endeavoring to achieve an elegantly disheveled look in all of them. Custom-printed Pendleton wool blankets adorn the organic rubber latex beds. Through the lobby, local brewer Stumptown aromatically roasts divine coffee, and Clyde Common, an adjoining restaurant serving local fare, draws crowds late into the night.

79 rooms. Restaurant, bar. $61-150

ALOFT PORTLAND AIRPORT AT CASCADE STATION

9920 N.E. Cascades Parkway, Portland, 503-200-5678, 877-462-5638; www.aloftportlandairport.com

A downsized version of the chic W hotels chain, Aloft retains all of the hip, modern cachet of its older sibling and will be a hit with frequent travelers who like being a stone's throw from the airport and outside of the downtown hubbub. The guest rooms are urban contemporary with built-in bookcase headboards, nine-foot ceilings and expansive windows. The handy connectivity center recharges all your gadgets and even lets you plug into the 42-inch LCD TV for viewing your photos on the big screen. Re:fuel is the 24-hour self-serve gourmet eatery; get a cocktail and a light meal at w xyz bar, open until midnight.

136 rooms. Bar. Fitness center. Pool. $151-250

HERON HAUS

2545 N.W. Westover Road, Portland, 503-274-1846; www.heronhaus.com

This restored 1904 Tudor-style bed and breakfast really turns on the charm: It has an enclosed sunroom, a library and a small apple and pear orchard. Although it's in a historic area, the Heron Haus isn't an isolated rustic getaway; it's 10 minutes from the city center and even closer to the trendy N.W. 23rd Nob Hill shopping district, featuring boutiques and favorite shops such as Urban Outfitters, Pottery Barn and more. Each of the quaint guest rooms retains the architectural interest of the period, like built-in bookshelves and bay windows, and is furnished in simple, cottage-style décor complete with plaid blankets and fireplaces. It's important to note that all guest rooms are on the second and third floors, and there is no elevator.

6 rooms. Complimentary breakfast. $151-250

THE NINES, PORTLAND

525 S.W. Morrison St., Portland, 877-229-9995; www.starwoodhotels.com

This relatively new luxury hotel lives up to its name, inspired by the phrase "dressing to the nines" and because it occupies the top nine floors of the historic Meier & Frank building. The eighth-floor lobby is a huge, open-air space that offers several sitting areas for intimate conversations, as well as the

Urban Farmer organic restaurant, where fresh is the only way. The library includes a pool table and Gus Van Sant painting donated by the man/artist/director himself, and whimsical art such as nude mannequins make a lasting impression. The rooms are impressive designer spaces with a refreshing palette of turquoise, white and beige, and they come decked out with sexy velvet sofas. Even sexier: Some rooms include marble infinity tubs.

331 rooms. Restaurant, bar. Business center. Fitness center. Pets accepted. $151-250

PORTLAND'S WHITE HOUSE BED AND BREAKFAST

1914 N.E. 22nd Ave., Portland, 503-287-7131, 800-272-7131; www.portlandswhitehouse.com

Tucked away in the historic Irvington neighborhood, this White House lookalike (built in 1911 as a summer home by a wealthy lumber baron) will impress you as much as the gorgeous homes in the area. Each of the rooms, five in the main house and three in the carriage house, has private baths and antique furnishings. Vegetarians and vegans will be pleasantly surprised by the fresh, local, seasonal and sustainable complimentary breakfast (specialty: crème brûlée French toast); carnivores can enjoy hormone-free meats served as side dishes. Shopping, dining, fitness facilities and local attractions are all nearby.

8 rooms. Complimentary breakfast. $151-250

WHERE TO EAT

★★★HEATHMAN

Heathman Hotel, 1001 S.W. Broadway, Portland, 503-241-4100, 800-551-0011; www.heathmanrestaurantandbar.com

Chef Philippe Boulot offers classic French cooking in a tri-level dining room at this restaurant inside the Heathman Hotel. The menu features dishes made from whatever's fresh and local, including Anderson Ranch Willamette Valley lamb with baby squash, potato confit and herbed lamb jus.

American, French. Breakfast, lunch, dinner, late-night. Reservations recommended. Outdoor seating. Children's menu. Bar. $36-85

★★★HIGGINS RESTAURANT AND BAR

1239 S.W. Broadway, Portland, 503-222-9070; www.higgins.ypguides.net

This tri-level French bistro is housed in a historic building complete with a vintage pressed-tin ceiling. The menu focuses on fresh local, organic ingredients, such as the Pacific Oysters on the half-shell with carrot-habanero granité.

American. Lunch, dinner, late-night. Reservations recommended. Children's menu. Bar. $16-35

★★★JAKE'S GRILL

611 S.W. 10th Ave., Portland, 503-220-1850, 888-344-6861; www.mccormickandschmicks.com

A favorite in downtown Portland, this dark-wood paneled steakhouse has fresh seafood fare and great happy hour deals: a $1.95 bar menu that includes a half-pound cheeseburger and steamed mussels. Specialties include USDA prime top sirloin bordelaise and grilled Columbia River king salmon. Drinks like white wine sangria and Bada Bing (limoncello, rum, lemon juice and a splash of cranberry) are made with premium ingredients, fresh juices and special attention.

American. Breakfast, lunch, dinner, late-night, Saturday-Sunday brunch. Reservations recommended. Outdoor seating. Children's menu. Bar. $16-35

★★★PALEY'S PLACE

1204 N.W. 21st Ave., Portland, 503-243-2403;
www.paleysplace.net

Set in a homey Victorian house, Paley's Place uses fresh, local ingredients to craft its Pacific Northwest regional cuisine, such as American Kobe beef steak tartare. It presents imaginative and beautifully presented entrées, like heirloom bean and spring vegetable cassoulet and rabbit ravioli with housemade bacon, local mushrooms and spring garlic. A cheese menu includes cow, goat and sheep's milk choices. Homemade chocolates arrive with the bill, in keeping with the warm service.

French, Italian. Dinner. Reservations recommended. Outdoor seating. Bar. $16-35

★★★PAZZO RISTORANTE

627 S.W. Washington St., Portland, 503-228-1515;
www.pazzo.com

This authentic northern Italian restaurant is a favorite among the locals, thanks to its intimate, friendly atmosphere with arched brick walls, dark wood and cozy booths. Sample handmade pastas like tortelli, stuffed with whole-milk ricotta, and hearty dishes such as Maiale, a grilled pork chop with local beans, shallots and a Gravenstein apple vinaigrette.

Italian. Breakfast, lunch, dinner, brunch. Reservations recommended. Outdoor seating. Children's menu. Bar. $16-35

★★★PLAINFIELDS

852 S.W. 21st Ave., Portland, 503-223-2995;
www.plainfields.com

Located downtown in a historic Victorian house, Plainfields serves East Indian cuisine, including vegan and vegetarian entrées that will have even meat eaters salivating. Try Sahi Subji Korma, a combination of root vegetables, peas and housemade cheese braised in cardamom nut sauce. Call for more information on the chef's rotating "whimsy menu," seven-course dinners with wine pairings. One past whimsy dinner featured buffalo tartare, cream of morel soup with crisp onion, fava bean cassoulet and Boccone Dolce dessert, meringue layered with Oregon strawberries and whipped cream. An extensive wine list is available.

Indian. Dinner. Reservations recommended. Outdoor seating. $16-35

WHICH PORTLAND RESTAURANTS ARE LOCAL FAVORITES?

Jake's Grill:
Residents flock to this steak house for its delectable meat and seafood, as well as potent cocktails like the Bada Bing, made with limoncello, rum, lemon juice and cranberry.

Pazzo Ristorante:
The intimate booths, dark wood and brick walls at this Italian restaurant lend it a warm, cozy vibe. It draws in the locals, who come in to linger over steaming plates of housemade pasta.

★★★RINGSIDE DOWNTOWN

2165 W. Burnside St., Portland, 503-223-1513;
www.ringsidesteakhouse.com

Opened in the 1940s, RingSide is a classic steakhouse on top of Nob Hill, just a few minutes from the city center. The no-frills menu sticks to classic dishes using USDA prime beef such as tenderloin with brandy cream sauce and mushrooms, and slow-roasted prime rib. Fresh seafood and vintage wines are also par for the course at RingSide. If your appetite isn't big enough for an entrée, try the bar menu's tasty offerings, such as steak bites, chili-lime crab cakes and prawn satay with sweet chili sauce.

Seafood, steak. Dinner, late-night. Reservations recommended. Bar. $36-85

★★★WILDWOOD RESTAURANT AND BAR

1221 N.W. 21st Ave., Portland, 503-248-9663;
www.wildwoodrestaurant.com

This acclaimed Oregon restaurant serves fresh seafood and seasonal Northwest ingredients in elegant combinations. A wood-burning oven turns out crisp pizzas like the lobster, mushroom and roasted garlic pie and adds warmth to the dining room. You may want to try to dine here during Winery Dinner Wednesdays, when you get a three-course prix fixe dinner with wine pairings for $55.

American. Lunch, dinner. Reservations recommended. Outdoor seating. Bar. $16-35

RECOMMENDED

HUBER'S CAFÉ

411 S.W. Third Ave., Portland, 503-228-5686; www.hubers.com

Boasting the title of Portland's oldest restaurant, Huber's was established in 1879 and continues to serve up tasty American dishes and seafood. What keeps people coming back? Huber's specialty, the traditional turkey dinner (available year-round) with sage dressing, mashed potatoes and cranberry sauce. The origin of the meal dates back to the early years, when patrons received a free turkey sandwich and coleslaw with their drink order. Try the signature drink, Spanish Coffee, made tableside.

American, seafood. Breakfast, lunch, dinner, late-night. Reservations recommended. Outdoor seating. Children's menu. Bar. $16-35

WHERE TO SHOP

ALBERTA ARTS DISTRICT

N.E. Alberta Street between N.E. 15th and N.E. 30th streets, Portland

This revitalized artsy area has a funky retro feel and retains the quaint apartment-over-storefront design of days long gone. Here you'll find artsy places like Collage Art Supplies (*1639 N.E. Alberta St., 503-249-2190; www. collagepdx.com*) and Six Days Art Co-Op (*2724 N.E. Alberta St., 503-280-6329; www.sixdaysarts.com*)—touted as "unusual art by unusual artists"—alongside boutiques like Tumbleweed (*1812 N.E. Alberta St., 503-335-3100; www. tumbleweedboutique.com*) and Frock (*1439 N.E. Alberta St., 503-595-0379; www.frockboutique.com*), where you can pick up anything from vintage slips and hand-poured candles to independent designer duds and handmade jewelry.

Alberta Street is also host to Portland's lively Last Thursdays street fairs on the last Thursday of the month and the annual Art Hop *(www.artonalberta.org/ arthop)* held in May.

BLACK WAGON

3964 N. Mississippi Ave., Portland, 503-916-0000; 866-916-0004; www.blackwagon.com

Calling all hip parents. Black Wagon caters to moms and dads who want their kids to look as cool as they do. Outfit your little one in an "I Trike (picture of a tricycle) Portland" onesie and she'll fit right into the city's bike culture. Or pick up some Matthew Porter monkey wall prints, such as a fedora-wearing, Tommy gun-toting primate in "Gangster" and a rocker monkey in "Drummer," to spice up a bland nursery.

Monday-Friday 11 a.m.-7 p.m., Saturday 10 a.m.-7 p.m., Sunday 10 a.m.-5 p.m.

BRIDGEPORT VILLAGE MALL

Lower Boones Ferry Road and S.W. 72nd Ave., Tigard, www.bridgeport-village.com

Take advantage of Oregon's no-sales-tax policy and go on a tax-free shopping binge at this upscale outdoor mall located 15 minutes from downtown Portland. Browse stores like Saks Fifth Avenue Off Fifth, Anthropologie and Crate & Barrel or get pampered at Coldwater Creek, The Spa. Take a rest in the Italian-inspired gazebo and let the kids wear themselves out at the play area in the center court. Need help carrying all those packages? On weekends, stop by guest services for a courtesy shuttle ride back to your car. There's free self-parking or valet for $4.

Monday-Saturday 10 a.m.-9 p.m., Sunday 11 a.m.-6 p.m. (Some stores and movie theater hours may vary.)

FARMHOUSE ANTIQUES

8028 S.E. 13th Ave., Portland, 503-232-6757

This shop sits in the Sellwood neighborhood, an antique collector's paradise with several stores and an antiques mall nearby. The store gets high marks for interesting finds, good presentation, plus a friendly staff. Hot sellers are vintage hats (especially pillbox and wool varieties), but you can also find generous collections of Depression-era glass, Royal Doulton china, and cast-iron and sterling-silver items.

Summer, daily 11 a.m.-5 p.m.; other days and hours vary. Call for information.

HERBIVORE

1211 S.E. Stark St., Portland, 503-281-8368; www.herbivoreclothing.com

Animal lovers will just adore the cruelty-free designs at this vegan-promoting shop. T-shirts are emblazoned with cool slogans like "Eat like you give a damn." You'll also find vegan cookbooks and accessories such as jewelry, wallets, belts and bags.

Monday-Saturday 10 a.m.-6 p.m., Sunday 10 a.m.-5 p.m.

NOB HILL DISTRICT

N.W. 21st and 23rd streets, Portland

Sometimes called N.W. "Trendy-first" and "Trendy-third" for its N.W. 21st and N.W. 23rd streets locale, this is the place to find upscale boutiques, salons, bars

HIGHLIGHT

PORTLAND'S PASSION FOR MICROBREWS

San Francisco has wine and Seattle has coffee, but in unpretentious and easygoing Portland, the beverage of choice is beer. If you appreciate fresh, handcrafted beer, you're certain to enjoy your stay here. Portland has been dubbed America's Microbrew Capital, an appropriate moniker given the city's numerous thriving microbreweries. Beer drinkers flock daily to brewpubs such as the Laurelwood Public House (1728 N.E. 40th Ave.) and BridgePort Brewpub (1313 N.W. Marshall St.), where they enjoy a variety of ales crafted in the Old World tradition, often using locally grown barley and hops.

Portland's beer history dates to 1852, when German brewer Henry Saxer moved to the Oregon Territory, opening Liberty Brewery near First and Davis streets. Saxer's brewery experienced immediate success, and other breweries opened soon after to tap into locals' seemingly insatiable thirst for beer.

In the mid-1980s, Portland's brew tastes focused on European-style microbrews, a trend driven by a law passed by the Oregon state legislature that enabled brewers to sell beer directly to the public. Suddenly, microbreweries and brewpubs were popping up all over the state. Nobody took better advantage of the new law than Mike and Brian McMenamin, who in 1984 opened the Hillsdale Brewery and Public House (www.mcmenamins.com), the state's first brewpub since Prohibition.

The McMenamins admit that their first brew, Hillsdale Ale, needed improvement, but after experimenting with different recipes, they were able to concoct colorfully named beers (Hammerhead, Terminator) that quickly became popular. The McMenamin brothers parlayed these early successes into a brewing empire, opening more than 50 breweries and brewpubs in the Northwest, as well as seven theater pubs and six hotels.

A fun way to experience the city's many microbrews is to book a trip on the Portland Brew Bus (www.brewbus.com). The five-hour Brew Bus tour takes you to three or four local brewers, where you'll sample 15 to 25 beers and record your impressions of each on a complimentary scorecard. The bus often stops at Widmer Brothers Gasthaus Restaurant & Pub (955 N. Russell St.), founded by siblings Kurt and Rob in 1984. Widmer Brothers Brewing Company has emerged as one of the most successful brewers in the Northwest, thanks largely to the popularity of its Hefeweizen, a strongly aromatic beer that goes unfiltered from the lagering tank to the bottle.

Another way to soak in beer in Portland is to attend the Oregon Brewers Festival. Since 1987, OBF (www.oregonbrewfest.com) has been attracting tens of thousands of beer drinkers to Tom McCall Waterfront Park in downtown Portland.

and restaurants among classic Victorian homes and 1920s brick apartment buildings. Notable places to nosh include Papa Haydn, an American-style fine dining restaurant; its next-door sister establishment Jo Bar & Rotisserie, specializing in wood-fired entrées; 23Hoyt, an upscale tavern serving pub grub; and Moonstruck Chocolates, a local chocolatier. Parking is scarce, so taking the Portland Streetcar from downtown is highly recommended.

NOUN: A PERSON'S PLACE FOR THINGS

3300 S.E. Belmont St., Portland, 503-235-0078; www.shopnoun.com

Here you'll find an eclectic mix of new, vintage and local items such as stationery, hand-made jewelry, art and home décor, all hand-picked by owner Stephanie Sheldon. One of the most interesting finds is "Science" glass—beakers, test tubes, glass vials and measuring cups that you can repurpose into vases, pen holders or whatever you can think up. Moufelt Jewelry will catch your eye; the colorful earrings and necklaces are strung on wire with felt ruffles, flowers or dots. Take a break from shopping and indulge in a cupcake from Saint Cupcake, a shop that shares space with Noun. The red velvet with vanilla cream cheese frosting and the toasted coconut cream cupcakes will give you a sugar rush to help you finish your shopping.

Tuesday-Saturday 10 a.m.-7 p.m., Sunday 10 a.m.-5 p.m.

PEARL DISTRICT

Bordered by West Burnside Street, the Willamette River, Broadway and the 405 Freeway, Portland; www.explorethepearl.com

Formerly a dingy warehouse district near downtown west of Burnside Street, "The Pearl" is now an internationally recognized leader in urban renewal. It has been magnificently renovated into an area of modern condos, lofts, trendy boutiques, salons and a plethora of art galleries. The Art Institute of Portland makes its home here, as well as The Portland Institute for Contemporary Art and the Willamette Gallery, to name a few. Make it a point to visit Oblation Papers & Press, a shop that produces beautiful handmade paper, stationery and letterpress items. The pedestrian-friendly neighborhood is on the Portland Streetcar line. The annual arts festival, Art in the Pearl, takes place here on Labor Day weekend.

PIONEER PLACE MALL

700 S.W. Fifth Ave., Portland; www.pioneerplace.com

Take refuge from a rainy day downtown at Pioneer Place, a multilevel shopping mall spanning four city blocks. You'll find shops of all sorts, such as Aldo, Juicy Couture, Coach, Betsey Johnson and Fossil, along with standbys like Gap, H&M, Ann Taylor and J.Crew. In addition to food court meal options, you can also choose from Macaroni Grill and Express Japan Sushi Bar. Treat yourself to some of Portland's finest chocolates at Moonstruck Chocolate Café, which serves a rich hot chocolate that hits the spot on a dreary day. Parking garages adjacent to the mall cost $1.50 per hour up to four hours; the daily max on weekdays is $12 and the daily max on weekends is $5.

Monday-Saturday 10 a.m.-8 p.m., Sunday 11 a.m.-6 p.m.

POWELL'S CITY OF BOOKS

1005 W. Burnside St., Portland, 503-228-4651, 800-291-9676; www.powells.com

A must-stop for bibliophiles, Powell's City of Books stocks more than 1 million new and used titles within a sprawling 68,000-square-foot facility that occupies an entire city block in downtown Portland. First-time visitors should pick up a complimentary store map to help them navigate through a maze of nine color-coded rooms, perusing an inventory that's divided into 122 major subject areas and approximately 3,500 subsections. If you're a collector looking for, say, a signed first edition of The Hobbit, be sure to check out the Rare Book Room, which houses autographed first editions and other collectible volumes.

Daily 9 a.m.-11 p.m.

WASHINGTON SQUARE MALL

Highway 217 at Greenburg, Hall and Scholls Ferry exits, Tigard, www.shopwashingtonsquare.com

A quick 20 minutes from downtown Portland, this massive indoor mall caters to your every shopping whim, from Nordstrom, Pottery Barn and Sears to specialty stores such as Teavana, where you can sample tea brews from around the world and purchase a variety of beautiful Japanese teapots. Pick up some local wares at Made in Oregon or dine at sit-down restaurants including The Cheesecake Factory, seafood eatery Newport Bay and Red Robin.

Monday-Saturday 10 a.m.-9 p.m., Sunday 10 a.m.-7 p.m.

ZA ZEN

3415 S.E. Belmont St., Portland, 503-238-8991; www.zazenshop.com

Located just across the road and down a block from Noun, Za Zen offers affordable and eye-catching women's and men's clothing, jewelry and accessories. You'll rarely see a price tag that reads more than $40, and most items are in the $20-to-$30 range, including cute floral print dresses and super-soft cotton tops from Za Zen's private label, as well as leggings, crocheted sweaters and casual dresses from the brands Mix and Vodka. For a cool accessory, pick up a necklace with Scrabble-tile charms. The sales rack outside is a great place for bargain hunting.

Monday-Friday noon-6 p.m., Saturday noon-5 p.m., Sunday 11 a.m.-6 p.m.

ZELDA'S SHOE BAR

633 N.W. 21st Ave., Portland, 503-226-0363; www.zeldaspdx.com

Indulge your shoe fetish here. This upscale shoe boutique dazzles with its variety of designer footwear, apparel and accessories. You'll find brands like Claudia Ciuti, Frye, Jolie, Swedish Hasbeens and many more. And you can even book a private party for after hours; the $450 package includes eight to 10 guests, champagne, light appetizers and a $200 gift certificate for the guest of honor.

Monday-Saturday 10 a.m.-6 p.m., Sunday noon-5 p.m.

WILLAMETTE VALLEY

People come to the Willamette Valley for one major reason: to sample the area's famous wines. McMinnville is in the center of the wine-producing area. Many of its wineries offer tours, tastings and even have restaurants and wine bars on the premises. Dundee is another wine country location that's filled with wineries as well as restaurants that cater to the wine-loving foodie.

But the Willamette Valley isn't all about getting tipsy from the great wine. Located in the heart of the region and built on the banks of the Willamette River, Corvallis is a center for education, culture and commerce. Siuslaw National Forest headquarters is here. Salem, the state capital and third-largest city in Oregon, also resides in the area. It's a busy place where the state politicians and businessmen do wheeling and dealing. Granted, many times business is conducted over glasses of Willamette Valley wine.

WHAT TO SEE

CORVALLIS
AVERY PARK
1310 S.W. Avery Park Drive, Corvallis, 541-766-6918; www.ci.corvallis.or.us

A 75-acre park on the Marys River, Avery Park is great for outdoor activities. There are bicycle, cross-country and jogging trails, picnicking, a playground and a ball field. You'll also find rose, rhododendron and community gardens, along with a 1922 Mikado locomotive.
Daily.

SIUSLAW NATIONAL FOREST
4077 S.W. Research Way, Corvallis, 541-750-7000; www.fs.fed.us

Siuslaw includes 50 miles of ocean frontage with more than 30 campgrounds, public beaches, sand dunes and overlooks. A visitor center and nature trails are in the Cape Perpetua Scenic Area. Marys Peak, the highest peak in the Coast Range, has a road to picnic grounds and a campground near the summit. Camping and dune buggies are allowed in designated areas. The forest contains 630,000 acres, including the Oregon Dunes National Recreation Area.

TYEE WINE CELLARS
26335 Greenberry Road, Corvallis, 541-753-8754; www.tyeewine.com

Located on a 460-acre Century farm, Tyee Wine Cellars offers tastings, tours, interpretive hikes and picnicking. Try to taste the pinot noir, pinot gris, chardonnay and gewürztraminer; the vineyard specializes in those wines.
July-August, Friday-Monday; April-June, October-December, weekends and by appointment.

DAYTON
DOMAINE DROUHIN OREGON
6750 Breyman Orchards Road, Dayton, 503-864-2700; www.domainedrouhin.com

In a barely-40-year-old wine region, the Drouhin family's 128 years of experience and Burgundian winemaking roots certainly give them the edge in authenticity. Third-generation winemaker Robert Drouhin established

Domaine Drouhin in 1987 in the Dundee Hills. His daughter, Véronique, who holds a degree in enology, later assumed responsibility for the family's new-world label. Her first vintage was the highly celebrated 1991 release, and her subsequent pinot noirs have continued to garner regular raves from the press and connoisseurs.

Wednesday-Sunday 11 a.m.-4 p.m.

DOMAINE SERENE

6555 N.E. Hilltop Lane, Dayton, 503-864-4600; www.domaineserene.com

This wine born in Yamhill County's Red Hills has beaten top vintages from Burgundy, California and Oregon in blind tastings. Perhaps Domaine Serene owes its worldwide critical acclaim to its founders' vigilance. The focus here is on achieving the best wines using environmentally friendly farming practices—always done with human hands—and low crop yields. The resulting pinot noirs and chardonnays have consistently proved to be concentrated award-winners.

Wednesday-Monday 11 a.m.-4 p.m. Tours available by appointment.

DUNDEE

ARGYLE WINERY

691 Highway 99W, Dundee, 503-538-8520, 888-427-4953;www.argylewinery.com

Located front and center on the main drag in Dundee, Argyle Winery has an elegant tasting room tucked inside a Victorian house that was once the town's city hall. Here, you can taste Argyle's respected pinot noirs and sparkling wines around the long bar or lounge on the wraparound front porch. Rumor has it you may also encounter a ghost, whose presence inspired the name of Argyle's Spirithouse Pinot Noir. Ask the tasting room staff for the full story over your flight of wines.

Daily 11 a.m.–5 p.m.

THE FOUR GRACES VINEYARDS

9605 N.E. Fox Farm Road, Dundee, 800-245-2950; www.thefourgraces.com

As one of the newer kids on the block, this intimate winery, which started in 2003, is doing something right. The stop, right between Newberg and Dundee, will feel more like a respite in Grandma's kitchen than another tasting room along the wine trail. The hospitality is quaintly old-fashioned, too. In fact, the caterers—yes, there's food included with your flights—dog-sat for us while we sipped, letting us focus on the light, crisp flavors of some of Oregon's best pinot gris. If you like whites, don't miss these. The pinot noirs are worth more than a couple of swirls as well, and the quaint ambience here challenges the pretense of winemaking tradition.

Daily 10 a.m.–5 p.m.

SOKOL BLOSSER

5000 N.E. Sokol Blosser Lane, Dundee, 503-864-2282, 800-582-6668; www.sokolblosser.com

Part of the small club of early pinot pioneers in Oregon, Bill Blosser and Susan Sokol Blosser planted their first vines in 1971. Underscoring earth-friendly practices in recent years, Sokol Blosser has been leading the way toward more sustainable winemaking in the Willamette Valley. In 2002, the winery built a cellar certified as Leadership in Energy and Environmental Design by the U.S.

Green Building Council, and began using organic farming practices on its 80 acres. Three years later, it received the USDA's stamp of approval as a certified organic winery. The latest move toward sustainability was cemented with the handing over of the winery reins in 2008 to Bill and Susan's children, Alex and Alison Sokol Blosser. Pick up a few bottles of the acclaimed Evolution, a delicious white blend that's just right for picnic lunches.

Daily 10 a.m.-4 p.m. Tours: Friday-Sunday 11:30 a.m. and 2:30 p.m.

EUGENE

ARMITAGE COUNTY PARK
90064 Coburg Road, six miles north off I-5 on Coburg Road, Eugene, 541-682-2000; www.lanecounty.org

A 57-acre park on a partially wooded area on the south bank of the McKenzie River, Armitage features fishing, boating, hiking and picnicking.

HENDRICKS PARK RHODODENDRON GARDEN
Summit and Skyline drives, Eugene, 541-682-5324

More than 6,000 aromatic plants bloom in this 20-acre, internationally known garden. You'll sniff rare species and hybrid rhododendrons from the local area and around the world. The park includes walking paths, hiking trails and a picnic area. The peak bloom happens mid-April to mid-May.
Daily.

HULT CENTER FOR THE PERFORMING ARTS
1 Eugene Center, Eugene, Seventh Avenue and Willamette Street, 541-682-5000; www.hultcenter.org

The performing arts center offers more than 300 events each year ranging from Broadway shows and concerts to ballet performances.

JORDAN SCHNITZER MUSEUM OF ART
1223 University of Oregon, 1430 Johnson Lane, Eugene, 541-346-3027; uoma.uoregon.edu

Peruse diverse collections at this museum, which bridges Eastern and Western art. Be sure to check out its large selection of Asian art representing the cultures of China, Japan, Korea and Cambodia as well as American and British works of Asian influence. The museum also features Persian miniatures and ceramics, photography and works by contemporary artists and craftsmen from the Pacific Northwest, including those of Morris Graves.
Admission: adults $5, seniors $3, children free. Tuesday, Thursday-Sunday 11 a.m.-5 p.m., Wednesday 11 a.m.-8 p.m.

OWEN MUNICIPAL ROSE GARDEN
North end of Jefferson Street along the Willamette River, Eugene, 541-682-4800; www.eugene-or.gov

Treat your nose at this aromatic 5-acre park with more than 300 new and rare varieties of roses, as well as wild species. It is a recognized test garden for experimental roses. The best blooms sprout up late June to early July.
Daily.

SCIENCE FACTORY CHILDREN'S MUSEUM & PLANETARIUM

2300 Leo Harris Parkway, Eugene, 541-682-7888; www.sciencefactory.org

The Science Factory encourages hands-on learning and features planetarium shows and exhibits illustrating physical, biological and earth sciences and related technologies. Stop by the Lizard Terrarium to see various reptiles from all over the world.

Admission: adults and children 3 and up $7, seniors $6, children 2 and under free. Wednesday-Sunday 10 a.m.-4 p.m.

SOUTH BREITENBUSH GORGE NATIONAL RECREATION TRAIL

Eugene, access is two miles on Road 4685 at Roaring Creek, 541-225-6300; www.fs.fed.us

Meandering through giant trees in an old-growth grove, this popular trail follows the South Breitenbush River. A small Forest Service-operated campground is near the trailhead.

SPENCER BUTTE PARK

Ridgeline and Willamette streets, Eugene, 541-682-4800; www.eugene-or.gov

The park has 305 acres of wilderness, with Spencer Butte Summit, at 2,052 feet, dominating the scene.

WILLAMETTE NATIONAL FOREST

East via Highways 20, 126 or 58, 541-225-6300; www.fs.fed.us

Covering 1.5 million acres, Wilamette National Forest is home to more than 300 species of wildlife and the Cascade Mountain Range summit. Come here for the fishing, hunting, hiking, skiing, snowmobiling and camping.

WILLAMETTE PASS SKI AREA

Cascade Summit, south via Interstate 5, east on Highway 58, 541-345-7669; www.willamettepass.com

The ski area features double and triple chairlifts, a ski patrol and school, ski and snowboard rentals, a lodge, a lounge and a restaurant. The longest run is 2.1 miles, and the peak vertical drop is 1,583 feet. Night skiing is allowed in late December to late February on Fridays and Saturdays.

Late-November-mid-April.

MCMINNVILLE

EVERGREEN AVIATION & SPACE MUSEUM

500 N.E. Capt. Michael King Smith Way, McMinnville, 503-434-4180; www.sprucegoose.com

The centerpiece of this museum is Howard Hughes's famous "Spruce Goose" aircraft.

Admission: adults $20, seniors $19, children $18. Daily 9 a.m.-5 p.m.

THE EYRIE VINEYARDS

935 N.E. 10th Ave., McMinnville, 503-472-6315, 888-440-4970;www.eyrievineyards.com

If we're going to talk about wine in the Willamette Valley, we should start with Eyrie (pronounced "EYE-ree"). Founders David and Diana Lett are the Oregon wine industry's first family. Nicknamed "Papa Pinot," David Lett—a young, enthusiastic recent grad at the time—and his family moved to the Willamette Valley in 1966 to test his theory that Burgundian varietals could thrive in the Oregon climate. His success speaks for itself. Lett was the first to plant pinot noir, chardonnay and other grapes in the Willamette Valley and the first to plant pinot gris this side of the Atlantic. He partnered with the other early groundbreakers in Oregon wine—Adelsheim, Erath, Ponzi and Sokol Blosser—sharing clippings and joining forces to persevere in spite of the lack of recognition they received throughout the '70s. The Eyrie tasting room and winery in McMinnville are separate from the vineyards, but worth a stop to taste the original pinot that set the bar for the rest of the valley.

Wednesday-Sunday noon–5 p.m.

GALLERY THEATER

210 N. Ford St., McMinnville, 503-472-2227; www.gallerytheater.org

The theater features musical, comedy and drama productions by the Gallery Players of Oregon.

Friday-Sunday.

NEWBERG

ADELSHEIM VINEYARD

16800 N.E. Calkins Lane, Newberg, 503-538-3652; www.adelsheim.com

Two of Oregon's pinot pioneers, David and Ginny Adelsheim began planting their original 15-acre Willamette Valley vineyard in 1972. Almost 40 years later, the estate includes nine vineyards and 168 acres, and produces nearly 50,000 cases of wine annually. Entrenched in the Willamette Valley pinot tradition, Adelsheim was one of the wineries where Véronique Drouhin studied up on Oregon winemaking as an intern for the 1986 vintage, before beginning her family's stateside business in earnest. Today, Adelsheim's grounds in the rolling Chehalem Mountains include a charming tasting room and patio.

Wednesday-Sunday 11 a.m.-4 p.m.

BRICK HOUSE VINEYARDS

18200 Lewis Rogers Lane, Newberg, 503-538-5136; www.brickhousewines.com

Twenty years ago, Brick House owner Doug Tunnell, a former CBS News international correspondent, decided to return to his Oregon home and launch a vineyard. The result was a venture that produces fine varietals traditionally from Burgundy: pinot noir, chardonnay and gamay noir. As one of only a handful of certified organic wineries in the Willamette Valley, Brick House wines are grown using traditional methods, without fertilizers or pest control sprays. Even the trellis posts must fit within USDA guidelines. Yet Brick House manages to bottle pinots that will proudly stand up to any other chemically enhanced glass around.

Memorial Day-Thanksgiving, daily. By appointment only the rest of the year.

PENNER-ASH WINE CELLARS

15771 N.E. Ribbon Ridge Road, Newberg, 503-554-5545; www.pennerash.com

This young Willamette Valley winery has come a long way in less than a decade. Winemaker Lynn Penner-Ash left her post at the helm of Rex Hill (not far down the Valley from her new digs) in 2002. Since then, the label has grown from its first 125 cases of pinot produced in 1998 to the more than 8,000 cases of pinot noir and syrah churned out of its new state-of-the-art facility. The multi-level,

WHAT ARE THE BEST VINEYARD HOTELS?

Black Walnut Inn
Oenophiles should stay at the Black Walnut Inn, which has its own vineyard. Its Yamhill Valley location allows easy access to many of the local wineries.

Youngberg Hill Vineyards Inn
This inn is surrounded by 22 acres of pinot noir and pinot gris grapes. The 20-year-old organic vineyard also gives you the chance to taste its wines.

gravity-flow winery (practically an industry standard now) was designed to allow nature to do a lot of the physical labor for the employees, as well as to eliminate the damage that comes from pumping wine from one processing stage to another—further refining Penner-Ash's already clearly demonstrated command of pinot.
Thursday-Sunday 11 a.m.-5 p.m. Tours available by appointment.

SALEM

BUSH BARN ART CENTER
600 Mission St. S.E., Salem, 503-581-2228; www.salemart.org
You won't find any animals in this remodeled barn. It houses two exhibit galleries and offers monthly shows and a sales gallery featuring Northwest artists.
Tuesday-Friday 10 a.m.-5 p.m., Saturday-Sunday noon-5 p.m.

HISTORIC DEEPWOOD ESTATE
1116 Mission St. S.E., Salem, 503-363-1825; www.historicdeepwoodestate.org
It's all about authentic details at this Queen Anne-style house and carriage house designed by W. C. Knighton. The Deepwood Estate features stained-glass windows, golden oak woodwork, a solarium, Lord and Schryver gardens with a wrought-iron gazebo from 1905, boxwood gardens, a perennial garden with English teahouse and a nature trail.
Admission: adults $4, seniors and students $3, children 6-12 $2, children 5 and under free. Tours: May 15-September 15, Sunday-Friday noon-4 p.m.; September 16-May 14, Wednesday-Thursday, Saturday 11 a.m.-3 p.m.

HONEYWOOD WINERY
1350 Hines St. S.E., Salem, 503-362-4111, 800-726-4101; www.honeywoodwinery.com
Oregon's oldest producing winery offers tours, a tasting room and a gift shop. Its best-sellers include a sweet red and the Dom Pierre almond sparkling wine.
Monday-Friday 9 a.m.-5 p.m., Saturday 10 a.m.-5 p.m., Sunday 1-5 p.m.

STATE CAPITOL
900 Court St. N.E., Salem, 503-986-1388; www.leg.state.or.us
Built with marble for a modern Greek design, the Capitol is topped with a fluted tower and a bronze, gold-leafed statue symbolic of the pioneers who carved Oregon out of the wilderness.
Tours: June-August, daily; September-May, by appointment.

CAPITOL MALL

900 State St., Salem, 503-986-1388; www.leg.state.or.us

Flanked by four state buildings in Modern Greek style, the Capitol Mall includes the Public Service, Transportation, Labor and Industries buildings and the State Library.

WHERE TO STAY

EUGENE

★★★HILTON EUGENE AND CONFERENCE CENTER

66 E. Sixth Ave., Eugene, 541-342-2000, 800-445-8667; www.hiltoneugene.com

Located in downtown Eugene, the Hilton is adjacent to the Hult Center for the Performing Arts, which offers Broadway shows, concerts and other performances. The hotel's Big River Grille serves Pacific Northwest cuisine and the lobby bar offers local microbrews. If you want to get a workout, head to the gym, rent one of the bicycles and tour downtown, or swim some laps in the indoor swimming pool.

269 rooms. Restaurant, bar. Business center. Fitness center. Pool. Pets accepted. $61-150

★★★VALLEY RIVER INN

1000 Valley River Way, Eugene, 541-743-1000, 800-543-8266; www.valleyriverinn.com

Adjacent to Valley River Center, Eugene's largest shopping mall, the Valley River Inn offers an attractive riverside setting on the north bank of the Willamette River. Rooms feature down duvets, plush bathrobes and free Wi-Fi. Many of the rooms also feature river views.

257 rooms. Restaurant, bar. Business center. Fitness center. Pool. Pets accepted. $151-250

RECOMMENDED

CORVALLIS

HARRISON HOUSE BED & BREAKFAST

2310 N.W. Harrison Blvd., Corvallis, 541-752-6248, 800-233-6248; www.corvallis-lodging.com

Located within walking distance of Oregon State University, this bed and breakfast inside a Dutch-Colonial home is convenient to area kayaking, rafting and hiking opportunities.

5 rooms. Restaurant. Complimentary breakfast. $61-150

DUNDEE

BLACK WALNUT INN

9600 N.E. Worden Hill Road, Dundee, 866-429-4114; www.blackwalnut-inn.com

Set amid vineyards and orchards, the elegant Black Walnut Inn resembles a Tuscan villa set among the hills of Italy. This luxurious bed and breakfast will make you feel at home in the Willamette Valley, delivering super-soft, plush beds and a complimentary gourmet breakfast. Each room in the all-suite property comes with either a patio and garden area or a balcony so you can take in the views of the vineyards, Mount Hood, Mount Jefferson and the Willamette Valley.

9 rooms. Complimentary breakfast. $251-350

INN AT RED HILLS

1410 N. Highway 99W, Dundee, 503-538-7666; www.innatredhills.com

Each of the rooms at the inn is uniquely decorated, though all come drenched in caramel, white and other neutral hues with dark-wood furniture. But this being wine country, the main attractions at this hotel are its food and drinks. The wine bar, Press, focuses on local bottles and a small-plates menu of local cheeses, spreads and charcuterie. For fine dining, try the onsite Farm to Fork, which sources all of its ingredients from within 200 miles of the hotel. All the fresh fare, like Dungeness crab pot pie, is designed to complement wine. The restaurant will make up picnic baskets for you to tote along during your wine-tasting or bike-riding adventures.

20 rooms. Restaurant, bar. $151-250

MCMINNVILLE

STEIGER HAUS BED AND BREAKFAST

360 S.E. Wilson St., McMinnville, 503-472-0821; www.steigerhaus.com

Make the most of this bed and breakfast's lovely wooded surroundings. Take a stroll through the garden to see the rhododendrons, wildflowers and other Northwest flora. Or relax on the ivy-covered deck and terraces. In fact, ask to have your complimentary breakfast, with fresh berries, peaches and hazelnuts, alfresco.

5 rooms. Complimentary breakfast. No children under 10. $61-150

YOUNGBERG HILL VINEYARDS INN

10660 S.W. Youngberg Hill Road, McMinnville, 503-472-2727, 888-657-8668; www.youngberghill.com

Set on a hillside above the Willamette Valley, this inn overlooks Youngberg Hills' award-winning pinot noir vineyards. Covered decks wrap the inn's perimeter, affording views of the valley below and nearby mountain peaks. You can taste the grapes that make the region famous at the inn's daily 4 p.m. complimentary wine tasting.

8 rooms. Complimentary breakfast. No children under 6. $151-250

SALEM

THE GRAND HOTEL IN SALEM

201 Liberty St. S.E., 503-540-7800, 877-540-7800; www.phoenixgrandhotel.com

Formerly known as the Phoenix Grand, the Grand Hotel in Salem is a good base for business travelers, since it's adjacent to the Salem Conference Center and has a 24-hour business center and free Wi-Fi. The rooms, which have a classic look with deep red and gold décor, also have spacious desks for when you have to do some after-hours work for that presentation.

193 rooms. Restaurant, bar. Complimentary breakfast. Business center. Fitness center. Pool. Spa. $151-250

WHERE TO EAT

EUGENE

★★★SWEETWATERS

Valley River Inn, 1000 Valley River Way, Eugene, 541-743-1000, 800-543-8266; www.valleyriverinn.com

With views of the Willamette River, this casual restaurant serves Northwest cuisine and Mediterranean-inspired dishes. Fresh seafood, game meats, exotic fruits and local ingredients make up the majority of the menu. Try the chile-crusted sautéed Pacific black cod or the pan-seared elk medallions with smoked blue cheese grits.

American. Breakfast, lunch, dinner, Sunday brunch. Reservation recommended. Outdoor seating. Children's menu. Bar. $16-35

RECOMMENDED

DUNDEE

DUNDEE BISTRO & WINE BAR
100-A S.W. Seventh St., Dundee, 503-554-1650; www.dundeebistro.com

Owned by the Ponzi family, wine pioneers in the area, this establishment is one of the Willamette Valley's first forays into the restaurant world. The menu is crafted with all wine-friendly dishes, like pork loin with goat cheese risotto that pairs nicely with the Ponzi Pinot. The pizzas—like the portobello with béchamel, sweet onions, potatoes and provolone—are a can't-fail choice here. Of course, the restaurant takes its wine seriously, with the staff attending mandatory weekly wine training sessions, so don't pass up a selection from the lengthy list.

American. Lunch, dinner. Outdoor seating. $16-35

FARM TO FORK
Inn at Red Hills, 1410 N. Highway 99W, Dundee, 503-538-7970; www.innatredhills.com

To live up to its name, Farm to Fork sources all of its ingredients within a 200-mile radius of the restaurant, so you know you're eating local, fresh-from-the-farm food here. Plus, charcuterie like pork and duck rillettes and wild boar terrine are made in-house. For the main course, go for the wild Oregon albacore doused with hazelnut romesco or the Dungeness crab pot pie. Since you know you're eating fresh, wholesome food, you won't feel too bad ending with the brandied almond cake with Meyer lemon cream, ricotta mousse and almond tuile. If you are doing your own wine-tasting tour, pick up road-trip provisions at the restaurant's deli, which is stocked with local cheeses, charcuterie and salads.

American. Breakfast, lunch, dinner, Sunday brunch. $16-35

EUGENE

OREGON ELECTRIC STATION
27 E. Fifth Ave., Eugene, 541-485-4444; www.oesrestaurant.com

Listed on the National Register of Historic Places, this restaurant originally was a train depot when it was built in 1912. The restaurant keeps to the locomotive vibe with a wine cellar converted from an old train car as well as dining rooms and lounges that transport you to old-time elegant railroad dining cars. Climb aboard and order the signature slow-roasted prime rib with creamed horseradish, or the seafood fettuccine with salmon, tuna, halibut, scallops and rock shrimp smothered in Mornay sauce.

American. Lunch (Monday-Friday), dinner. Reservation recommended. Outdoor seating. Children's menu. Bar. $16-35

WHAT ARE THE WILLAMETTE VALLEY'S BEST WINE BARS?

Dundee Bistro & Wine Bar

With Oregon wine country trailblazers the Ponzis at the helm of this bistro and bar, you know it's a must-stop on your wine tour of the region.

La Rambla

This tapas and wine bar received accolades from Wine Spectator for its collection of local and Spanish bottles. Come taste what all the fuss is about.

MCMINNVILLE
BISTRO MAISON
729 N.E. Third St., McMinnville, 503-474-1888;
www.bistromaison.com

Tucked away in wine country, this French bistro cooks up rich, hearty fare. Start off with the white truffle fondue, made with a cheese blend that includes local Tillamook cheddar. Don't miss the delicious coq au vin, a perfect dish to have in wine country.

French. Lunch (Wednesday-Friday, Sunday), dinner. Closed Monday-Tuesday. $16-35

GOLDEN VALLEY BREWERY & PUB
980 N.E. Fourth St., McMinnville, 503-472-2739;
www.goldenvalleybrewery.com

If you prefer brews over Burgundy, Golden Valley will give you a break from the wine-centric restaurants and bars in the Willamette Valley. The restaurant offers typical pub grub, but it gets elevated thanks to fresh local ingredients, some of it coming from the kitchen's own garden and the owners' Angus Springs Ranch. For example, the popular nachos have daily-made salsa using home-grown tomatoes and peppers as well as Tillamook cheddar and sour cream from local dairies. Order the Hardy Havarti burger with avocado, honey-cured ham, mushrooms, Havarti cheese and pesto mayo on ciabatta. Pair it with a pint of the Muddy Valley Oatmeal Stout, a full-bodied beer that's brewed using roasted black barley and chocolate malts.

American. Lunch, dinner. Bar. $15 and under

LA RAMBLA
238 N.E. Third St., McMinnville, 503-435-2126;
www.laramblaonthird.com

You can't miss this tapas bar, with its cozy-looking maroon façade. Inside is just as inviting with a mahogany, copper-topped bar and dangling hand-blown glass lighting fixtures. As far as food is concerned, you have your choice between tapas or large plates. The cuisine hails from the Iberian Peninsula, though you'll find Northwest influences in tapas like the crab and bay shrimp cakes with braised fennel, leeks and lemon aioli, and the albacore tuna empanadas. Pair your tapas with one of the 350 Oregon and Spain selections from the award-winning wine list.

Spanish. Lunch, dinner. Bar. $15 and under

SALEM
BENTLEY'S GRILL
The Grand Hotel in Salem, 291 Liberty St. S.E., 503-779-1660; www.bentleysgrill.com

This downtown restaurant, adjacent to the Grand Hotel and the Salem Conference Center, is a good place to sip some vino in the wine lounge before a business meeting. Or bring your clients along to win them over during a dinner of pan-seared filet mignon in a red wine demi-glace or the grilled Oregon snapper with spicy shrimp. Finish with the Konditorei Milky Way Mosaic torte, layered with chocolate ganache, fudge and caramel topped with crème anglaise and berry sauce.
American. Lunch, dinner. Bar. $16-35

WILD PEAR
372 State St., Salem, 503-378-7515; www.wildpearcatering.com

Wild Pear may be a breakfast-and-lunch joint, but its inventive dishes would be stars on any dinner menu. There are the requisite salads, a tasty option is the Wild Pear chicken salad with candied pecans, pears and blue cheese with mixed greens and a roasted pear vinaigrette. For heavier fare, try the panko-battered Dungeness crab cakes with roasted red pepper-jalapeño aioli.
American. Breakfast, lunch. Outdoor seating. Children's menu. Bar. $15 and under

CENTRAL OREGON

Outdoorsy types head to Central Oregon to do everything from skiing on Mount Bachelor to teeing off at one of the 25 golf courses to fishing in the region's 150 rivers and lakes. Tourists come to Bend year-round for its streams, lakes, mountains, great pine forests, ski slopes and golf courses. There is also much of interest to geologists and rock hounds in this area. It's also a great dining area and it's known for its abundance of top-notch breweries. Mount Hood National Forest is a popular getaway for Portland residents who come to hike, ski and enjoy the mountains that dot this expansive forest.

WHAT TO SEE

BEND
DESCHUTES NATIONAL FOREST
1001 S.W. Emkay Drive, Bend, 541-383-5300; www.fs.fed.us

The Deschutes National Forest encompasses 1.6 million acres of rugged wilderness, with snow-capped mountains, craggy volcanic formations, old-growth forests and deep rivers running through high-desert canyons. Established as a national forest in 1908, Deschutes has become one of the Pacific Northwest's most popular year-round tourist destinations, attracting more than 8 million visitors annually. The winter months bring hordes of skiers and snowmobilers. Oregon's largest ski resort can be found alongside the 9,065-foot-high Mt. Bachelor. Hikers arrive after the spring thaw, eager to take advantage of the area's 1,388 miles of trails. Paddlers head to the Deschutes River, which has been designated both a National Scenic River and a National Recreational River. Anglers are drawn to the forest's 157 trout-filled lakes and reservoirs.

HIGHLIGHTS

WHAT ARE SOME OF THE BEST PLACES FOR OUTDOOR FUN IN CENTRAL OREGON?

GET SPORTY AT DESCHUETES NATIONAL FOREST
This is one of the Pacific Northwest's most popular tourist attractions because its slopes and river provide lots of opportunities for outdoor sports.

LGO SKIING AT THE MOUNT BACHELOR SKI AREA
In the winter, skiers come to this scenic spot to tackle the 9,065-foot Mount Bachelor and its 56 miles of cross-country trails.

VISIT THE NEWBERRY NATIONAL VOLCANIC MONUMENT
Check out an active volcano at this monument. You'll get a chance to see Central Oregon's Lava Lands with 50,000-plus acres of lakes, lava flows and more.

HIT UP THE MOUNT HOOD NATIONAL FOREST FOR ACTIVE PURSUITS
The more than 1 million-acre forest is a perfect place for skiing, swimming, mountain climbing, golfing, horseback riding and the list goes on.

HIGH DESERT MUSEUM
59800 S. Highway 97, Bend, 541-382-4754; www.highdesertmuseum.org
A regional museum with indoor and outdoor exhibits featuring live animals and cultural history of the intermountain northwest arid lands, the High Desert Museum offers hands-on activities and ongoing presentations. The galleries house wildlife, Western art and Native American artifacts. Walk-through dioramas depict the opening of the American West. The desertarium showcases seldom-seen bats, burrowing owls, amphibians and reptiles.
Admission: May-October, adults $15, seniors $12, children5-12 $9, children 4 and under free; November-April, adults $10, seniors $9, children 5-12 $6, children 4 and under free. May-October, daily 9 a.m.-5 p.m.; November-April, daily 10 a.m.-4 p.m.

LAPINE STATE PARK

15800 State Recreation Road, Bend, 541-536-2071, 800-551-6949; www.oregonstateparks.org

A 2,333-acre park on the Deschutes River in the Ponderosa pine forest, LaPine offers scenic views, swimming, a bathhouse, fishing, boating, picnicking and trailer campsites.

LAVA BUTTE AND LAVA RIVER CAVE

11 miles south on Highway 97, 541-593-2421; vulcan.wr.usgs.gov

Lava Butte is an extinct cinder cone. A paved road to the top provides a view of the Cascades and there are interpretive trails through the pine forest and lava flow. One mile south, Lava River Cave features a lava tube 1.2 miles long. The visitor center has audiovisual shows.

May-September, daily.

MOUNT BACHELOR SKI AREA

22 miles southwest on Southwest Century Drive/Cascade Lakes Scenic Byway (Highway 46), Bend, 541-382-2442, 800-829-2442; www.mtbachelor.com

Panoramic views of forests, lakes and Cascade Range await visitors to Mount Bachelor, with facilities at a base of 6,000 feet. With 56 miles of cross-country trails, the area has 10 chairlifts, ski patrol, school, rentals, cafeterias, concession areas, bars, lodges and a day care. The longest run is 1 1/2 miles with the steepest vertical drop at 3,365 feet.

Mid-November-May, daily.

NEWBERRY NATIONAL VOLCANIC MONUMENT

24 miles south on Highway 97, then 14 miles east on Forest Road 21, in Deschutes National Forest, 541-383-5300; www.fs.fed.us

This monument, an active volcano, has a wide range of volcanic features and deposits similar to those of Mount Etna such as obsidian flow and pumice deposits. On the same road are East and Paulina lakes, both of which have excellent fishing.

PILOT BUTTE STATE SCENIC VIEWPOINT

Pilot Butte Summit Drive, off Highway 20, Bend, one mile east on Highway 20, 800-551-6949; www.oregonstateparks.org

A 101-acre park noted for a lone cinder cone rising 511 feet above the city, the summit at the Pilot Butte affords an excellent view of the Cascade Range.

PINE MOUNTAIN OBSERVATORY

26 miles southeast via Highway 20, Bend, 541-382-8331; pmo-sun.uoregon.edu

Visitors to the University of Oregon's astronomical research facility may view stars, planets and galaxies through telescopes.

Memorial Day-September, Friday-Saturday, evenings only.

TUMALO

5 1/2 miles northwest off Highway 20, Bend, 541-382-3586, 800-551-6949; www.oregonstateparks.org

A 320-acre park situated along the banks of the Deschutes River, Tumalo offers hiking, tent and trailer campsites, solar-heated showers and swimming and fishing nearby.

WHITEWATER RAFTING
Sun Country Tours, 531 S.W. 13th St., Bend, 541-382-6277, 800-770-2161;
www.suncountrytours.com

Thrill seekers can choose from two-hour or all-day rafting trips or try canoeing.
May-September.

HOOD RIVER
BONNEVILLE LOCK & DAM
U.S. Army Corp of Engineers Bonneville Lock & Dam, 23 miles west on I-84, Cascade
Locks, 541-374-8442; www.corpslakes.usace.army.mil

The dam consists of three parts, one spillway and two powerhouses. It has
an overall length of 3,463 feet and extends across the Columbia River to
Washington. It was a major hydroelectric project of the U.S. Army Corps of
Engineers. On the Oregon side is a five-story visitor center with underwater
windows into the fish ladders and a new navigation lock with viewing facilities,
which offer audiovisual presentations and tours of fish ladders and the original
powerhouse. The state salmon hatchery is adjacent, and fishing is allowed in
salmon and sturgeon ponds.

MOUNT HOOD SCENIC RAILROAD
110 Railroad Ave., Hood River, 541-386-3556, 800-872-4661; www.mthoodrr.com

This historic railroad makes 44-mile round-trip excursions. Dinner, brunch,
murder mystery and comedy excursions are available. Reservations are recommended.
March-December, schedule varies.

MADRAS
COVE PALISADES STATE PARK
7300 S.W. Jordan Road, Madras, 541-546-3412, 800-551-6949; www.oregonstateparks.org

This 4,130-acre park is on Lake Billy Chinook behind the Round Butte Dam.
It features a scenic canyon and spectacular views of the confluence of the
Crooked, Deschutes and Metolius rivers forming Lake Billy Chinook in a steep
basaltic canyon.

RICHARDSON'S ROCK RANCH
6683 N.E. Haycreek Road, Madras, 541-475-2680, 800-433-2680;
www.richardsonrockranch.com

The highlight of the rock ranch is its famous agate beds, which are studded with
thunder eggs and ledge agate material.
Daily 7 a.m.-5 p.m. Closed November-March.

MOUNT HOOD NATIONAL FOREST
MOUNT HOOD MEADOWS
11 miles northeast of Government Camp on Highway 35, 503-337-2222; www.skihood.com

Skiing enthusiasts will find a quad; triple and double chairlifts; a ski school and
rentals; a restaurant; a cafeteria; concessions; a bar; a day care; and two day
lodges at Mount Hood. The longest run is three miles and the highest vertical
drop is 2,777 feet. The area also features 550 acres of expert canyon skiing,
groomed and ungroomed cross-country trails and night skiing.
November-May.

MOUNT HOOD NATIONAL FOREST

16400 Champion Way, Sandy, 503-668-1700; www.fs.fed.us

Mount Hood is the natural focal point of this more than 1 million-acre forest with headquarters in Sandy. Its white-crowned top, the highest point in Oregon, can be seen for miles on a clear day. It is also popular with skiers, who know it has some of the best slopes in the Northwest. There are five winter sports areas. Throughout the year, however, you can take advantage of the surrounding forest facilities for camping, hunting, fishing, swimming, mountain climbing, golfing, horseback riding, hiking and tobogganing. The Columbia Gorge, which cuts through the Cascades here, has many spectacular waterfalls, including Multnomah. There are nine routes to the summit, which has fumed and smoked several times since the volcanic peak was discovered. Only experienced climbers should try the ascent and then only with a guide.

RIVER CRUISE

45 miles east of Portland via Interstate 84, 503-224-3900, 800-224-3901; www.sternwheeler.com

Take a two-hour narrated cruise of Columbia Gorge aboard the 599-passenger *Columbia Gorge*, an authentic sternwheeler.

Mid-June-September, three departures daily; reservations required for dinner cruise.

TIMBERLINE LODGE

Timberline Ski Area, six miles north of Highway 26, on Timberline Highway, 503-622-7979; www.timberlinelodge.com

Timberline Lodge features quads; triple and double chairlifts; a ski school and rentals; a restaurant; a cafeteria; a bar; and lodge. The longest run is more than two miles and the peak vertical drop is 3,580 feet.

WHERE TO STAY

HOOD RIVER

★★★SKAMANIA LODGE

1131 S.W. Skamania Lodge Way, Stevenson, 509-427-7700, 800-221-7117; www.skamania.com

Tucked among the mountain peaks, waterfalls and canyons of the Columbia River Gorge 45 minutes north of Portland, this resort offers many onsite recreational opportunities, such as golf, basketball, hiking trails and tennis. The guest rooms and suites pay tribute to the area's Native American heritage with lodge-style décor, and some feature fireplaces. Try to reserve a room with a view of the towering Cascade Mountains.

254 rooms. Restaurant, bar. Fitness center. Pool. Spa. Golf. Tennis. $61-150

★★★HOOD RIVER HOTEL

102 Oak St., Hood River, 541-386-1900, 800-386-1859; www.hoodriverhotel.com

Each room at this historic hotel is uniquely decorated with antique reproductions and artwork illustrating the hotel's history, which dates to 1913. You'll see four-poster beds and floral patterns in most of the rooms. The onsite restaurant, Cornerstone Cuisine, specializes in organic and locally grown Pacific Northwest dishes.

41 rooms. Restaurant, bar. Complimentary breakfast. Fitness center. $151-250

MADRAS

★★★KAH-NEE-TA LODGE

1-250 Highway, Highway 26 north to Warm Springs, Warm Springs, 541-553-1112, 800-554-4786; www.kahneeta.com

Overlooking the Warm Springs River, this resort gives a view of the sunrise from each room. But there are a slew of activities that'll prevent you from spending much time in there. Take a dip in the double Olympic-sized hot springs mineral pool, which also has a 140-foot and 184-foot slides, or stay dry and play a round of golf. Head to the spa for a soak in the hot mineral springs on the property, or try to win it big in the casino. Authentic Native American dances are featured on Sundays from May to September.

139 rooms. Restaurant, bar. Fitness center. Pool. Spa. Pets accepted. Casino. Golf. Tennis. $61-150

MOUNT HOOD NATIONAL FOREST

★★★THE RESORT AT THE MOUNTAIN

68010 E. Fairway Ave., Welches, 503-622-3101, 800-669-7666; www.theresort.com

A resort has operated at this spot since 1882, but the inn you'll find here today is anything but old-fashioned. A complete refurbishment in 2009 left guest rooms light and modern, with plenty of earth tones and natural materials, including stone fireplaces. Down duvets top the beds and flat-screen TVs hang on the walls. The resort includes a new full-service spa and casual, contemporary restaurants such as Altitude, which serves dishes made from fresh and local ingredients.

160 rooms. Restaurant, bar. Pool. Golf. Tennis. $61-150

RECOMMENDED

BEND

MOUNT BACHELOR VILLAGE RESORT

19717 Mount Bachelor Drive, Bend, 800-547-5204; www.mtbachelorvillage.com

If you plan on planting yourself on Mount Bachelor for a ski vacation, this resort is in a convenient place to stay. It's on the road to the mountain, and the resort provides shuttles to the Mount Bachelor Ski Area. Mount Bachelor Village Resort also offers gorgeous views, since it is perched on a ridge overlooking the Deschutes River. The resort is made up of condos, which is good for families or large groups. If you're not a skier, check out the 13-acre athletic club, where you can take free yoga and body sculpting classes.

160 rooms. Restaurant, bar. Business center. Fitness center. Spa. Tennis. $151-250

THE OXFORD HOTEL

10 N.W. Minnesota Ave., Bend, 877-440-8436; www.oxfordhotelbend.com

Located in downtown Bend, the Oxford Hotel's sleek décor makes going green chic. The hotel goes above and beyond to be eco-friendly; pillows are made of recycled bottles, room floors are cork, natural mattresses are built of latex and soy, guests are encouraged to partake in the in-room recycling program and valet is free for hybrid vehicles. But the hotel doesn't sacrifice design in all of the earthy details. The rooms embrace the nature theme with warm browns and creams, tree trunks serve as bases for floor lamps and branch sculptures adorn the walls. Rooms also come with French presses and organic teas, microwaves, mini-fridges, free Wi-Fi and two 42-inch TVs. There's also an onsite restaurant that serves regional food, most of which is locally sourced and organic, of course.

59 rooms. Restaurant, bar. Business center. Fitness center. Pets accepted. $151-250

THE RIVERHOUSE
3075 N. Highway 97, Bend, 541-389-3111, 866-453-4480; www.riverhouse.com

The Riverhouse offers a beautiful respite along the Deschutes River. It's a central location if you want to be near downtown and Mount Bachelor. It's within walking distance to boutiques; a family fun center with an arcade mini golf and go-karts; and restaurants. But you don't need to leave the property to play tennis, do some hiking or swim in the outdoor and indoor pools. The rooms have all of the conveniences of home, including microwaves, refrigerators and DVD players.

220 rooms. Restaurant. Complimentary breakfast. Business center. Fitness center. Pool. Spa. Pets accepted. Golf. Tennis. $61-150

WHAT TO EAT

BEND

900 WALL
900 N.W. Wall St., Bend, 541-323-6295; www.900wall.com

This casual eatery serves upscale pub food like your favorite neighborhood joint. Begin with the potato and chorizo fritters with aioli and manchego or the beef carpaccio with truffle oil. While there are sophisticated dishes like the halibut and maitake mushrooms drenched in a caramelized onion broth, nothing beats the delicious stone-oven pizzas. The pies come with untraditional topping combos like rotisserie chicken, bacon, Gorgonzola and thyme, or fennel, guanciale and ricotta. If you're in the mood for a tipple, the Thai Bloody Mary has some kick, thanks to the addition of cilantro and Thai chiles.

Contemporary American. Lunch, dinner. Bar. $16-35

BEND BREWING CO.
1019 N.W. Brooks St., Bend, 541-383-1599; www.bendbrewingco.com

Bend is a favorite brewpub, not least because of its great view of the river and Mirror Pond. Order the fish and chips, which are dredged through an Outback Ale batter. Pair it with a pint of the Outback, a malty beer with notes of raisins and caramel.

American. Lunch, dinner. Outdoor seating. Bar. $16-35

> **WHAT IS THE BEST PLACE TO STAY NEAR MOUNT BACHELOR?**
>
> You'll hit **Mount Bachelor Village Resort** on your way up the mountain, which makes it a good place to stay. Even better, the resort offers free shuttles to the popular Mount Bachelor Ski Area, which is only 18 miles away.

WHICH CENTRAL OREGON RESTAURANTS HAVE THE BEST OUTDOOR DINING?

Bend Brewing Company:
People fill the patio in warm weather to gaze at the Deschutes River and Mirror Pond while sipping an ice-cold beer.

Greg's Grill:
Take a seat at the patio for vistas of both the Deschutes River and the Cascade mountain range while you nosh on your prime rib.

THE BLACKSMITH RESTAURANT

211 N.W. Greenwood Ave., Bend, 541-318-0588;
www.bendblacksmith.com

Inside this intimate exposed-brick space with pumpkin-colored walls and deep brown furniture, you'll find fun dishes that give classic comfort food an upgrade. Try the lobster corndog; the Border Cheesesteak with roasted verde sauce, grilled onion, manchego and sweet potato enchiladas; or the Not Your Mother's Meatloaf, made-to-order loaves glazed with ketchup and fire-roasted tomato demi-glace. For a dessert that's equally clever and comforting, go for the Wonka Bar, a brownie with chocolate mousse, peanut butter ice cream, cocoa-nut rice crispies and a rich salted caramel sauce.
Steak. Dinner. Bar. $36-85

DESCHUTES BREWERY BEND PUB

1044 N.W. Bond St., Bend, 541-382-9242;
www.deschutesbrewery.com

Deschutes' handcrafted ales have earned it the reputation of being best brewery in the city. Order a pint of the Green Lakes Organic Ale, a crisp certified organic brew, or the popular Bachelor Bitter, which has a malt body. The same attention is paid to the food. The restaurant makes everything from the sausages to the mustards and breads in house. The appetizers get kicked up a notch with beer: The drunken buffalo prawns are tossed in the Mirror Pond Pale Ale and the housemade pretzels are made using the spent grain from the brewing process. The roasted garlic burger, piled high with whole cloves on a malt-cracked bun, is a local favorite. For something a little different, try the elk stroganoff with Black Butte Porter gravy.
American. Lunch, dinner. Bar. $15 and under

GREG'S GRILL

395 S.W. Powerhouse Drive, Bend, 541-382-2200;
www.gregsgrill.com

When you peer out of Greg's Grill's floor-to-ceiling windows, you'll see fabulous views of the Deschutes River and the Cascade Mountains. The interior is almost just as stunning, an airy light-wood-filled space with cozy curved booths that point toward the windows. When it comes time to order, go for the beefy dishes, like the flat-iron steak topped with blue cheese or the favorite slow-roasted prime rib served au jus with horseradish cream. If you're looking to make it a night on the town, the restaurant is in the historic Old Mill District amid galleries, theaters and more.
American. Lunch, dinner. Outdoor seating. Bar. $16-35

ZYDECO KITCHEN & COCKTAILS
919 Bond St., Bend, 541-312-2899; www.zydecokitchen.com

When you crave a bit of the South, try out Zydeco. The restaurant serves contemporary American food with a Southern touch. You'll taste it in dishes like the barbecue shrimp appetizer, which comes with grit cake. For the main course, go for the filet medallions with sea salt and green peppercorns or the blackened catfish with Dungeness crab. If you happen to be traveling with Fido, ask for an order of the complimentary house-made doggie biscuits. There's no reason that Fido can't enjoy a taste of the South, too.

Contemporary American, Southern. Lunch (Monday-Friday), dinner. Outdoor seating. Bar. $16-35

SOUTHERN OREGON

Natural beauty abounds in Southern Oregon. Whether it's Rogue River National Forest with its dense thicket of Douglas fir and ponderosa pine trees, Klamath Falls' fish-filled lakes or Oregon Caves National Monument's halls of marble, the scenery gets the spotlight.

But the Oregon Shakespeare Festival in Ashland deservedly takes center stage when it kicks off each season of its award-winning plays. The company's shows are a big draw for theater lovers.

WHAT TO SEE

ASHLAND
LITHIA PARK
E. 59 Winburn Way, Ashland, 541-488-5340 (band shell performances), 541-482-3486 (nature walks); www.nps.gov

Adjacent to City Plaza, the park has 93 acres of woodlands and ponds along with nature trails, tennis, concerts, picnicking, sand volleyball, and rose and Japanese gardens.

Daily.

MOUNT ASHLAND SKI AREA
693 Washington St., Ashland, eight miles south on I-5, then nine miles west on access road, 541-482-2897; www.mtashland.com

The ski area has two triple and two double chairlifts, a school, rentals and a cafeteria and bar. The longest run is one mile and the highest vertical drop is 1,150 feet.

Thanksgiving-April.

OREGON CABARET THEATRE
241 Hargadine St., Ashland, 541-488-2902; www.oregoncabaret.com

The Oregon Cabaret Theatre presents musicals, revues and comedies in a dinner club setting.

February-December, schedule varies.

OREGON SHAKESPEARE FESTIVAL
15 S. Pioneer St., Ashland, 541-482-4331, 800-219-8161; www.orshakes.org

From its humble beginnings with a 1935 staging of *Twelfth Night,* this repertory

HIGHLIGHT

WHAT ARE SOME OF THE TOP THINGS TO DO IN SOUTHERN OREGON?

SEE A PLAY AT THE OREGON SHAKESPEARE FESTIVAL

The Tony Award-winning OSF is one of the oldest and largest nonprofit theaters in the country. Catch everything from *Hamlet* to *Cat on a Hot Tin Roof* on its stages.

EXPLORE OREGON CAVES NATIONAL MONUMENT

Take a guided tour through one of the few marble caves in the world. "The Marble Halls of Oregon" are tucked into the wooded slopes of the Siskiyou Mountains.

SOLVE THE MYSTERY AT THE OREGON VORTEX

Why do balls roll uphill and people's heights change at the Oregon Vortex? Find out for yourself with a visit to the House of Mystery.

TAKE A DRIVE THROUGH ROGUE RIVER NATIONAL FOREST

Hop on the Rogue-Umpqua National Forest Scenic Byway to see breathtaking panoramas of the area's mountains, rivers and forest.

theater has evolved in size and scope, earning a reputation for excellent productions and making Ashland a must-stop destination for drama lovers. The festival features a variety of drama, from Shakespeare to Tennessee Williams. OSF actually consists of three separate theaters: the New Theatre, Angus Bowmer Theatre and the open-air Elizabethan Stage.
February-early November.

CAVE JUNCTION
OREGON CAVES NATIONAL MONUMENT
20 miles east of Cave Junction on Highway 46, 541-592-2100; www.nps.gov

This area was discovered in 1874, when hunter Elijah Davidson's dog followed a bear into the cave. After a visit in 1907, frontier poet Joaquin Miller called this "The Marble Halls of Oregon." In 1909, the cave and 480 acres of the Siskiyou Mountains were made a national monument. The cave has many chambers, including Paradise Lost, Joaquin Miller's Chapel and Ghost Room; guide service is required. On the surface, the area is covered with a beautiful old-growth forest with abundant wildlife, birds, wildflowers and an interesting variety of trees and shrubs. A maintained and marked system of trails provides access to these areas.

GRANTS PASS
GRANTS PASS MUSEUM OF ART
229 S.W. G St., Grants Pass, 541-479-3290; www.gpmuseum.com

The Museum of Art features permanent and changing exhibits of photography, paintings and art objects.

Admission: free. Tuesday-Saturday noon-4 p.m.

HELLGATE JETBOAT EXCURSIONS
966 S.W. Sixth St., depart from Riverside Inn, Grants Pass, 541-479-7204, 800-648-4874; www.hellgate.com

Take an interpretive jet boat trip down the Rogue River. You have your choice of cruise types: two-hour scenic excursions, four-hour country dinner excursions, five-hour whitewater trips or four-hour champagne brunch excursions.

ROGUE RIVER RAFT TRIPS
8500 Galice Road, Merlin, 800-826-1963; www.rogueriverraft.com

Serious rafting enthusiasts can take three- to four-day whitewater trips through the wilderness past abandoned gold-mining sites with overnight lodges or camping en route.

SISKIYOU NATIONAL FOREST
2164 N.E. Spalding Ave., 541-471-6500; www.fs.fed.us

Covering more than 1 million acres, Siskiyou is famous for salmon fishing in the lower Rogue River gorge and its early-day gold camps. Many species of trees and plants are relics of past ages. An 84-mile stretch of the Rogue River between Applegate River and Lobster Creek Bridge is designated a National Wild and Scenic River, nearly half of which is in the forest.

JACKSONVILLE
OREGON VORTEX
4303 Sardine Creek L Fork Road, Gold Hill, 541-855-1543; www.oregonvortex.com

At this self-dubbed House of Mystery, seemingly unexplainable things occur, like a ball rolling uphill by itself or people whose heights change depending where they stand. The Vortex is actually a spherical field of force half above the ground, half below. Natural, historical, educational and scientific phenomena are found in a former assay office and surrounding grounds. Skeptics and believers alike visit to try to unlock the mystery.

March-October, daily.

KLAMATH FALLS
COLLIER MEMORIAL STATE PARK AND LOGGING MUSEUM
46000 Highway 97, Chiloquin, 541-783-2471, 800-551-6949;
www.oregonstateparks.org

A 655-acre park at the confluence of Spring Creek and Williamson River, Collier includes an open-air historic logging museum with a display of tools, machines and engines; various types of furnished 1800s-era pioneer cabins; and a gift shop.

JACKSON F. KIMBALL STATE RECREATION SITE
46000 Highway 97, Chiloquin, 541-783-2471, 800-551-6949;
www.oregonstateparks.org

A 19-acre pine- and fir-timbered area, the recreation site is at the headwaters of the Wood River, which is noted for its transparency and deep-blue appearance. *Mid-April-October.*

KLAMATH COUNTY BALDWIN HOTEL MUSEUM
31 Main St., Klamath Falls, 541-883-4207; www.co.klamath.or.us

This restored turn-of-the-century hotel contains many original furnishings and offers guided tours.

Admission: adults $10, seniors and students $8, children 5-12 $8. Wednesday-Saturday 10 a.m.-4 p.m.

KLAMATH COUNTY MAIN MUSEUM
1451 Main St., Klamath Falls, 541-883-4208; www.co.klamath.or.us

The museum features local geology, history, wildlife and Native American displays and a research library with books on the history, natural history and anthropology of the Pacific Northwest.

Admission: adults $5, seniors and students $4, children 5-12 $3. Tuesday-Saturday 9 a.m.-5 p.m.

WINEMA NATIONAL FOREST
2819 Dahlia St., Highway 62 or Highway 140, Klamath Falls, 541-883-6714;
www.fs.fed.us

This forest stretches across more than 1 million acres and includes the former reservation lands of the Klamath Tribe, the high country of Sky Lakes, portions of Pacific Crest National Scenic Trail, and recreation areas in Lake of the Woods, Recreation Creek, Mountain Lakes Wilderness and Mt. Theilson Wilderness.

MEDFORD
CRATER ROCK MUSEUM
2002 Scenic Ave., Central Point, 541-664-6081; www.craterrock.com

The museum features gem and mineral collections, Native American artifacts, fossils, geodes and crystals. Check out the collection of glass work by well-known artist Dale Chihuly and his students.

Admission: adults $4, seniors and students $2, children free. Tuesday-Saturday 10 a.m.-4 p.m.

ROGUE RIVER NATIONAL FOREST
333 W. Eighth St., Medford, 541-858-2200; www.fs.fed.us

This national forest has 632,045 acres with extensive stands of Douglas fir, ponderosa pine and sugar pine. Rogue-Umpqua National Forest Scenic Byway offers a day-long drive through southern Oregon's dramatic panorama of mountains, rivers and forest viewpoints. A part of the Pacific Crest National Scenic Trail and portions of three wilderness areas are included in the forest. For fishermen, the upper reaches of the Rogue River and other streams and lakes yield rainbow, cutthroat and brook trout. Union Creek Historic District is on Highway 62 near Crater Lake National Park.

TOUVELLE STATE RECREATION SITE

Three miles northeast on I-5, then six miles north on Table Rock Road, 541-582-1118, 800-551-6949; www.oregonstateparks.org

The 51-acre TouVelle State Recreation Site features fishing on the Rogue River, swimming, hiking, bird-watching and picnicking.

WHERE TO STAY

ASHLAND

★★★THE WINCHESTER INN & RESTAURANT

35 S. Second St., Ashland, 541-488-1113, 800-972-4991; www.winchesterinn.com

Located one block from downtown Ashland and two blocks from the site of the Oregon Shakespeare Festival, this restored Victorian house once served as the area's first hospital. The individually decorated rooms feature antiques and feather beds, as well as flat-screen TVs, free Wi-Fi and fireplaces. Some bathrooms have claw foot tubs, and others have Jacuzzi tubs and separate showers. In the morning, you'll get a two-course breakfast, and when you need a mid-afternoon snack, you'll find pastries delivered to your door. When you want a drink, head down to the award-winning wine bar, which specializes in Ashland and Southern Oregon bottles.

19 rooms. Restaurant, bar. Complimentary breakfast. $151-250

CRATER LAKE

★★★CRATER LAKE LODGE

565 Rim Village Drive, Crater Lake, 541-594-2255, 888-774-2728; www.crater-lake.com

This grand lodge has been welcoming guests to its rustic lakeside location—it's actually in Crater Lake National Park—since 1915. The Great Hall's massive stone fireplace is a center point for the historic lodge. The peaceful lodge is a place to get away from it all, which is why guest rooms are without TVs and phones. Instead, go outside to do some hiking, rock-climbing, biking and more, all on the park grounds.

71 rooms. Restaurant. Closed mid-October-mid-May. $61-150

KLAMATH FALLS

★★★THE RUNNING Y RANCH RESORT

5500 Running Y Road, Klamath Falls, 541-850-5500, 888-850-0275; www.runningy.com

This 3,600-acre resort is set among wooded hills and open meadows at the edge of the Cascade Range. The Running Y Ranch overlooks Klamath Lake, the largest natural lake in the Northwest. The resort's lodge has comfortably appointed rooms with golf course views. Take advantage of the resort's fitness center, pool complex and Sandhill Spa. An onsite Arnold Palmer-designed golf

WHICH SOUTHERN OREGON HOTEL HAS THE BEST ROOM AMENITIES?

The historic **Ashland Springs Hotel** goes the old-fashioned route with its amenities: A lavender tea sachet is placed on your pillow, rooms come with French presses and vintage greeting cards are given out to celebrate that special occasion.

course is the among the best public links in the nation. *350 rooms. Restaurant, bar. Fitness center. Pool. Spa. Golf. $61-150*

RECOMMENDED

ASHLAND
ASHLAND SPRINGS HOTEL
212 E. Main St., Ashland, 541-488-1700, 888-795-4545; www.ashlandspringshotel.com

Built in 1925, this hotel harkens back to that time with old-fashioned hospitality. Lavender tea bath sachets that arrive on your pillow are a thoughtful touch. And if you are celebrating a special occasion, the hotel will attach the appropriate vintage greeting card to your door with a Victorian brass clip. Inside the bright apricot-, melon- and pear-colored rooms, there are French-style botanical toile quilts, lampshades made from natural cotton rag paper with imprints of leaves and 19th-century pressed French herbs in frames. The rooms also come outfitted with flat-screen TVs, mini-fridges and Gilchrist & Soames toiletries.

70 rooms. Restaurant, bar. Complimentary breakfast. Business center. Spa. Pets accepted. $151-250

CHANTICLEER INN
120 Gresham St., Ashland, 541-482-1919, 800-898-1950; www.ashland-bed-breakfast.com

This 1920s Craftsman bed and breakfast is convenient to area attractions such as the Shakespeare Festival, Cascade volcanoes and Oregon Caves. English country-style rooms are individually decorated with antiques. To get some fresh air, visit the inn's secluded garden and relax near the koi pond or on the hammock. The two-course breakfasts feature fruit, veggies and herbs from the onsite garden. When you want to snack between meals, fresh baked cookies, as well as port and sherry, await in the common area.

6 rooms. Complimentary breakfast. No children under 10. $151-250

COUNTRY WILLOWS BED & BREAKFAST INN
1313 Clay St., Ashland, 541-488-1590, 800-945-5697; www.willowsinn.com

This restored 1890s farmhouse is surrounded by 5 acres of farmland in the Siskiyou and Cascade mountains. Take breakfast out on the veranda so that you can nibble on your spiced pumpkin waffles while admiring the bucolic gardens and scenery. When you need a pick-me-up later in the day, head back down to the breakfast station for homemade cookies, biscotti or fruit, along with lemonade, hot cocoa or local teas. No two rooms are alike, though you'll see antiques in all of them.

9 rooms. Complimentary breakfast. Pool. No children under 12. $151-250

GRANTS PASS
WEASKU INN

5560 Rogue River Highway, Grants Pass, 541-471-8000, 800-493-2758; www.weasku.com

A secluded setting on the Rogue River amid towering pine trees lends this 1924 inn an air of tranquility. All rooms feature pine furnishings and beamed ceilings with ceiling fans. Guests enjoy an evening wine-and-cheese reception, nightly milk and cookies and summertime barbecues.

17 rooms. Complimentary breakfast. $151-250

MEDFORD
ROGUE REGENCY INN & SUITES

2300 Biddle Road, Medford, 541-770-1234;
www.rogueregency.com

The basic rooms at Rogue Regency are imbued with emerald green, dark brown and cream. They also come with microwaves, free Wi-Fi and refrigerators, while suites have hot tubs and fireplaces. On Friday and Saturday nights, head to the onsite Chadwicks Pub & Sports Bar to see touring comedians yuk it up.

212 rooms. Restaurant, bar. Business center. Fitness center. Pool. Spa. $61-150

WHERE TO EAT

JACKSONVILLE
★★★GARDEN BISTRO & WINE BAR

McCully House Inn, 240 E. California St., Jacksonville, 541-899-1942, 800-367-1942; www.mccullyhouseinn.com

Housed in a historic Gothic Revival mansion—one of the first houses built in town—that is now the McCully House Inn, the Garden Bistro features contemporary Pacific Northwest cuisine. Try the pan-seared quail with Madeira wine, shallots, wild mushrooms and a bit of cream or the grilled lamb loin with cucumber-mint relish and yogurt. Be sure to ask your server about wine to pair with your meal.

American. Dinner. Outdoor seating. Bar. $16-35

WHICH SOUTHERN OREGON RESTAURANTS ARE THE BEST FOR LARGE GROUPS?

The sharable small-plates menu at **Elements Tapas Bar & Lounge** practically requires that you come in with a big group. More people means more plates, and more fun you'll have trying dishes like cinnamon-cherry duck.

RECOMMENDED

ASHLAND
CHATEAULIN
50 E. Main St., Ashland, 541-482-2264; www.chateaulin.com

Situated at the entrance to the Oregon Shakespeare Festival, Chateaulin is a perfect dinner spot before catching a play. Though the French bistro cuisine is no mere secondary player. Among the appetizers, try the escargots or the Brie mousseline with toast points, almonds and dried apricots. Then move on to the cocoa nib-rubbed rack of lamb with black trumpet mushroom sauce or the bouillabaisse. Be sure to peruse the wine menu and get a glass before the curtain goes up.

French. Dinner. Closed Monday-Tuesday in winter. Reservations recommended. Bar. $36-85

LARKS HOME KITCHEN CUISINE
Ashland Springs Hotel, 12 E. Main St., Ashland, 541-488-5558; www.larksrestaurant.com

When you get a hankering for comfort food, try out Larks' upscale version. Southern fried chicken breast comes with Yukon Gold mashed potatoes and a drizzle of bacon pan gravy. A maple-balsamic-glazed double-cut pork chop is accompanied by apple compote and rosemary-roasted sweet potatoes. Obviously, no comfort meal is complete without a decadent dessert. Get a sweet, satisfying ending with the warm chocolate cake and a scoop of the housemade salted caramel ice cream.

American. Lunch (Monday-Friday), dinner, Saturday-Sunday brunch. Outdoor seating. Bar. $16-35

THE WINCHESTER RESTAURANT
Winchester Inn, 35 S. Second St., Ashland, 541-488-1113, 800-972-4991; www.winchesterinn.com

You have your choice of small plates or regular-sized entrées at this esteemed eatery. If you choose the former, go for the mini beef Wellingtons with port wine sauce and the seared scallops with mango and sofrito. If you're really hungry, try an entrée like the braised wild boar osso bucco with kaffir lime leaves and yucca gnocchi. The restaurant carries a good selection of South Oregon wines; ask the sommelier for a recommendation.

International. Dinner, Sunday brunch. Closed January; Sunday, Monday February-March. Reservations recommended. Outdoor seating. Bar. $16-35

MEDFORD
ELEMENTS TAPAS BAR & LOUNGE
101 E. Main St., Medford, 541-779-0135; www.elementsmedford.com

Bring the whole gang to this tapas bar. The exposed-brick walls and mix of high-top tables, wrap-around booths and oversized chocolate-colored chairs and ottomans give off a casual vibe where mingling is encouraged. The shareable food does the same thing. Divvy up tapas that are traditional—the house paella—and untraditional—a flight of lamb meatballs, one stuffed with blue cheese, another wrapped in Serrano ham and filled with chorizo, and a peach-stuffed ball with a spiced peach glaze. It'll be hard to choose among the long list of tapas, but since you're with a group, you'll have the chance to order half the menu. To keep everyone happy, make sure that all the glasses stay filled with one of the restaurant's Spanish wines.

Spanish. Dinner, late-night. Bar. $15 and under

PORTERS RESTAURANT AND BAR

147 N. Front St, Medford, 541-857-1910; www.porterstrainstation.com

Step into this former train depot for a flashback of a meal. The dining room retains a dining car feel with high-backed red and gold upholstered wooden booths sectioned off with curtains. Reproduced Craftsman-style chandeliers light up the room, and an original ticket-taking machine is on display. The menu is more modern-day with sesame and black pepper ahi tuna with wasabi-lime cream and a grilled rack of lamb with a mint-balsamic glaze. But if you want to be transported back to that classic time, order from the aperitif and cigar menu for a pre-meal sherry and smoke.

International, steak. Dinner. Outdoor seating. Bar. $16-35

REDROCK ITALIAN EATERY & BARRA

17 W. Fourth St., Medford, 541-773-6840; www.redrockitalianeatery.com

Classics rule the menu at this Italian eatery, whose cozy red walls match the housemade marinara. Signature dishes include the spaghetti and meatballs—which are crafted with a blend of Italian sausage, ground beef, Romano cheese and herbs—and a housemade pesto sauce with sun-dried tomatoes that pairs with your choice of pasta. This being an old-school Italian joint, both dishes come with a hunk of garlic bread. There's also a selection of stone-oven pizzas with dough made from scratch. Try the Capone, a meaty pie with pepperoni, ground beef, salami, onions and tomatoes.

Italian. Dinner. Bar. $36-85

WELCOME TO WASHINGTON

WASHINGTON STATE IS CHARACTERIZED BY DRAMATIC mountain ranges, expansive forests and inviting harbors. Here are the majestic spectacles of mighty Mount Rainier—revered as a god by the Native Americans—and the Olympic Peninsula, where one of the wettest and one of the driest parts of the country are separated by a single mountain; also here is Puget Sound, a giant inland sea where 2,000 miles of shoreline bend into jewel-like bays.

Although British and Spanish navigators were the first Europeans to explore Washington's serrated shoreline, the first major discoveries were made in 1792, when American Captain Robert Gray gave his name to Gray's Harbor and the moniker of his ship, Columbia, to the great river. An Englishman, Capt. George Vancouver, explored and named Puget Sound and christened Mount Baker and Mount Rainier, which he could see far inland.

Fort Vancouver was the keystone of the British fur industry, dominating a Northwest empire. After conflicting U.S. and British claims were resolved, Americans surged into this area by ship and wagon train.

Today, the state retains 24 million acres of superb forests, and miracles of modern engineering have almost completely erased the wastelands through which the wagon trains of the pioneers passed on their way to the sea.

The mighty Columbia River meanders through the heart of northeast and central Washington, then runs for 300 miles along the Oregon-Washington border. Through a series of dams and the Grand Coulee Reclamation Project, the energies of the Columbia have been harnessed and converted into one of the world's greatest sources of water power. Irrigation and a vast supply of inexpensive power gave a tremendous push to Washington's economy, sparking new industries and making possible the state's production of huge crops of grains, vegetables and fruit.

Central Washington is the nation's apple barrel and dairying is a big industry

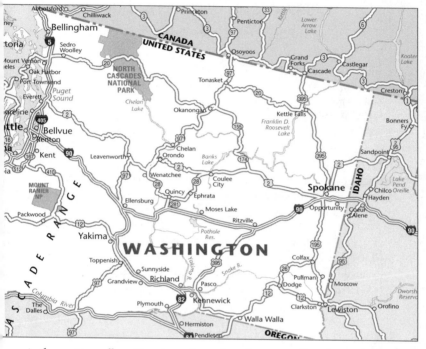

in the western valleys. Forestry and wood products, as well as the production of paper and allied products, are of major importance in the western and northern sections of the state; one-third of the state is covered by commercial forests. In recent years, Washington wines have enjoyed great popularity around the nation.

Since 1965, more than 25 percent of Washington's total manufacturing effort has been devoted to the production of transportation equipment, of which a large portion is involved in commercial jet aircraft. Along Puget Sound, industry means canning plants, lumber mills, and pulp and paper plants, but even here there is a new economic dimension: petroleum refineries of four major companies have a daily capacity of 366,500 barrels of crude oil and gasoline; biotechnology and software development are also growing industries. Tourism is the state's fourth-largest industry.

BEST ATTRACTIONS

WASHINGTON'S BEST ATTRACTIONS

LEAVENWORTH

This charming town warrants at least a day trip. The Bavarian-style architecture against an alpine setting makes it look like an Old World European village.

MOUNT RAINIER

One of the state's top tourist destinations, Mount Rainier attracts more than 2 million visitors each year. Come to see the breathtaking scenery or to take a hike.

PUGET SOUND

People visit Puget Sound to sample its amazing wineries. Washington is one of the largest U.S. wine regions, second only to California. Start your tippling here.

SEATTLE

The home of grunge and Starbucks, Seattle is the trend-setting city in the state. Come see the famous Space Needle, Pike Place Market and lots, lots more.

SEATTLE

Seattle has prospered from the products of its surrounding forests, farms and waterways, serving as a provisioner to Alaska and Asia. Since the 1950s, it has acquired a new dimension from the manufacture of airplanes, missiles and space vehicles which, along with tourism, make up the city's most important industries.

The Space Needle, which dominated Seattle's boldly futuristic 1962 World's Fair, still stands, symbolic of the city's forward-looking character. The site of the fair is now the Seattle Center, and many features of the fair have been made permanent. Seattle sits on Elliott Bay, nestled between Puget Sound—an inland-probing arm of the Pacific Ocean—and Lake Washington, a 24-mile stretch of fresh water. The city sprawls across hills and ridges, some of them 500 feet high, but all are dwarfed by the Olympic Mountains to the west and the Cascades to the east.

WHAT TO SEE

ACT THEATRE
700 Union St., Seattle, 206-292-7676; www.acttheatre.org

ACT Theatre presents contemporary (read: edgy and daring) pieces as well as classic plays and musicals. Performances are held in two main theaters in Kreielsheimer Place, a renovation of the historic Eagles Auditorium that was completed in 1996. The Allen, a theater in the round, was carved out of the old auditorium's floor; the top row of seats is actually at ground level. The Falls features a restored Joshua Green Foundation Vault, used by the Eagles as a bank vault.

ALKI BEACH
1702 Alki Ave. S.W., Seattle, 206-684-4075; www.seattle.gov

Skirting the northwestern waterfront of the South Seattle neighborhood, the 2 1/2-mile Alki Beach is a mecca for outdoor types of all kinds—joggers, divers, bicyclists, beach volleyball players, sunbathers and rollerbladers. The beach, administered by the Seattle Parks Department, runs from Duwamish Head to Alki Point on Elliot Bay and offers stunning views of Puget Sound and the city skyline. Facilities are a notch above the norm with scads of picnic tables, a playground, small boat access and a wide, multi-use path. At Alki Point (the southern end of the beach), there is a bathhouse/art studio, and a plaque commemorating the landing of the first settlers here in 1851. At Duwamish Head (the northern tip of the beach) are the sea-walled sites of a former amusement park and a miniature version of the Statue of Liberty. *April 15-October 1, daily 6 a.m.-11 p.m.; October 2-April 14, daily 4 a.m.-11:30 p.m.*

ARGOSY HARBOR CRUISES
Pier 55 Alaskan Way, Seattle, 206-622-8687, 800-642-7816; www.argosycruises.com

Boasting a 50-year history in Seattle's harbors, the family-owned Argosy Cruises has a fleet of nine cruise ships, ranging in size from the 36-foot Queen's Launch to the 180-foot Royal Argosy. The company operates from piers at the Seattle waterfront, Lake Union and suburban Kirkland (on the eastern shore

BEST ATTRACTIONS

WHAT ARE THE TOP THINGS TO DO IN SEATTLE?

VISIT THE EXPERIENCE MUSIC PROJECT/SCIENCE FICTION MUSEUM

Rock 'n' roll and science fiction cross paths in this museum, a remarkable Frank Gehry-designed structure. Music fans can see exhibits on native son Jimi Hendrix, while science-fiction fiends can check out the T-800 Terminator.

HANG OUT IN THE FREEMONT DISTRICT

The funky Fremont neighborhood has its own distinct flavor with eclectic coffee shops, secondhand stores and galleries. Don't miss the Fremont Troll sculpture, a massive monster under Aurora Bridge.

WALK AROUND PIKE PLACE MARKET

This famous market is known for its fishmongers, but there are also food stalls, fresh produce for sale, and arts and crafts displays in the indoor/outdoor market.

CHECK OUT PIONEER SQUARE

As the city's oldest neighborhood, Pioneer Square gives a glimpse of Seattle's past. Go beneath the streets to learn about the city before the Great Seattle Fire of 1889.

GO TO THE TOP OF THE SPACE NEEDLE

There's no other structure more synonymous with Seattle than the flying saucer-inspired Space Needle. You'll get amazing views of the city from the 605-foot tower.

SEE THE ANIMALS AT THE WOODLAND PARK ZOO

One of the biggest zoos in the country, Woodland Park is home to everything from Kodiak bears to elephants to a Komodo dragon.

of Lake Washington). The most basic Argosy outing is a one-hour Harbor Cruise, which explores Seattle's downtown shoreline and offers some nice skyline views. Longer options include the Locks Cruise, which meanders from Puget Sound to Lake Union via the Ballard Locks, and a pair of lake cruises that explore Lake Union and Lake Washington. Snacks and beverages are offered on every Argosy cruise, but food is not included in the ticket price—the exceptions being lunch and dinner trips on the Royal Argosy.

BAINBRIDGE ISLAND
Chamber of Commerce, 590 Winslow Way E., Bainbridge Island, 206-842-3700; www.bainbridgechamber.com

Reached via a half-hour ferry trip from downtown Seattle (ferries depart regularly throughout the day), Bainbridge Island is the size of Manhattan, but a world apart. In the late 1800s, the island boasted the world's largest sawmill and a substantial shipbuilding industry, but its economy stumbled. It has recently regained footing as a tourist destination. With about 20,000 residents, the city of Bainbridge Island is now known for its delightful Victorian architecture and abundant shops and galleries. Densely wooded and lush with greenery, the island also attracts outdoor enthusiasts of all stripes and boasts an active arts and entertainment scene. The Bainbridge Island Historical Museum (215 Ericksen Ave. N.E.; www.bainbridgehistory.org) is a great starting point, presenting displays on the island's geology, history and industry in a converted 1908 schoolhouse.

BALLARD LOCKS
2606 N.W. 58th St., Seattle, 206-783-7059; www.ci.seattle.wa.us

Popularly known as the Ballard Locks because of their location in Seattle's Ballard neighborhood, the Hiram M. Chittenden Locks are a marvel of engineering. Built in the early 20th century by the U.S. Army Corps of Engineers, the locks are part of the canal system that connects salty Puget Sound (and, by extension, the Pacific Ocean) to Seattle's freshwater, providing safe passage for watercraft. Salmon use a man-made fish ladder here to navigate their annual spawning migration past the locks. Underwater observation windows afford a firsthand look at the migrating fish (and the seals and sea lions that feast on them, which workers struggle to keep out), but only at certain times of the year; the coho and chinook runs peak in midsummer. A visitor center presents exhibits that detail the locks' history and ecology, and an impressively vibrant botanical garden is also onsite.

May-September, daily 7 a.m.-9 p.m.; October-April, Thursday-Monday 7 a.m.-8 p.m.

BURKE MUSEUM OF NATURAL HISTORY AND CULTURE
University of Washington, 17th Avenue N.E. and N.E. 45th Street, Seattle, 206-543-5590; www.washington.edu

The Burke Museum is Washington's official museum of natural and cultural history and a research hub for the entire Pacific Northwest. With its collections in anthropology, geology, zoology and botany, the museum possesses 5 million specimens. The facility houses a pair of notable permanent exhibits (in addition to a number of rotating temporary displays each year): "The Life and Times of Washington State," a look at the last 500 million years of the state's geology and biology (with fossils and skeletons galore), and "Pacific Voices," which delves into the rich melting pot of cultures present in the Pacific Northwest. Also onsite is the Erna Gunther Ethnobotanical Garden, alive with hundreds of plants used by the region's natives, as well as a café and gift shop.

Admission: adults $9.50, seniors $7.50, students and children 5-18 $6, children 4 and under free. Daily 10 a.m.-5 p.m., first Thursday of the month 10 a.m.-8 p.m.

CAPITOL HILL
12th Avenue to Boren Avenue and East Madison Street to Denny Way, Seattle; www.ci.seattle.wa.us

Melding metropolitan chic, Victorian elegance and urban grunge just east of downtown, Capitol Hill is one of Seattle's oldest and grandest neighborhoods and, today, is the nexus of the city's youth culture and gay scene. Broadway, the heart of Capitol Hill and one of the city's liveliest thoroughfares, has hip nightclubs, eateries and tattoo parlors to spare. The area also features an eclectic mix of stores that cater to fashion plates, tattooed punks, antique lovers and everyone in between. The primary shopping areas here are on Broadway (home to a bevy of youth fashion and resale shops, music retailers and unusual bookstores), 15th Street (plenty of home and garden stores with a more upscale slant than Broadway), and Pike and Pine streets (a mix of antique stores, florists, coffee shops and funky specialty retailers).

CENTER FOR WOODEN BOATS
1010 Valley St., Seattle, 206-382-2628; www.cwb.org

Located north of downtown on the southern tip of Lake Union, this is a hands-on maritime heritage museum with a focus on historic wooden sailboats, kayaks and canoes. You can learn time-tested boat-building skills from master craftsmen, take sailing lessons or rent a classic sailboat for a spin around the lake. The center also provides the setting for numerous annual festivals and boat shows.

Admission: varies by activity. Winter, daily 11 a.m.-5 p.m.; spring and fall, daily 10 a.m.-6 p.m.; summer, daily 10 a.m.-8 p.m.

CENTRAL LIBRARY
1000 Fourth Ave., Seattle, 206-386-4636; www.spl.org

The Central Library opened to much acclaim in 2004. The library was designed by famed Dutch architect Rem Koolhaas, winner of the 2000 Pritzker Prize, his profession's highest honor. With a transparent exterior of diamond-shaped panes of glass, the library stands as a marvel of contemporary architecture. The interior is equally amazing, highlighted by the Books Spiral, a series of tiers and ramps winding through four floors of book stacks. The library features more than 400 public computers and wireless Internet access is available throughout the facility. Built at a cost of $165.5 million, the 11-level library exemplifies Seattle's passion for books and learning.

Monday-Thursday 10 a.m.-8 p.m., Friday-Saturday 10 a.m.-6 p.m., Sunday noon-6 p.m.

CENTURY BALLROOM
915 E. Pine St., Seattle, 206-324-7263, 206-325-6500; www.centuryballroom.com

Home to one of Seattle's largest dance floors (2,000 square feet of refinished wood), the stylishly restored Century Ballroom is the place to go for swing and salsa dancing in the Emerald City. Many nights are themed (tango night, salsa night, swing night). For those with two left feet, lessons are offered; while most are multiweek endeavors, there are occasional one-shot workshops. With a full bar, seating at comfortable tables and a cavernous downtown location, the venue also hosts a number of concerts every month, mostly jazz acts and singer/songwriters. A popular restaurant here, The Tin Table, serves dinner and offers a great happy hour daily. The menu features local seasonal cuisine such as fresh seafood and meats. They offer an appealing wine list along with flights from nearby wineries as well as specialty cocktails.

Daily; hours vary by activity.

CHINATOWN INTERNATIONAL DISTRICT

Fourth Avenue to Interstate 5 and Yesler to South Dearborn Street; www.ci.seattle.wa.us

Southeast of downtown, the colorful International District is home to one of the largest and most vibrant Asian communities in the United States. It took root in the late 19th century, and the neighborhood is now home to one of the most diverse ethnic populations in the world. Asian markets and eateries of all kinds dot the streets. Top attractions include the Wing Luke Asian Museum, the Nippon Kan Theatre and Uwajimaya, a huge food market and cooking school.

DIMITRIOU'S JAZZ ALLEY

2033 Sixth Ave., Seattle, 206-441-9729; www.jazzalley.com

Widely considered the best jazz club in Seattle, the downtown venue originally opened in the University District in 1979, then moved downtown in 1985, and has seen performances by such names as Taj Mahal and Eartha Kitt. The atmosphere is refined, with chairs and tables surrounding the circular stage and a mezzanine overlooking it. A renovation in 2002 expanded Jazz Alley's capacity and bolstered the sound system while retaining the heralded ambiance. A restaurant serves an international menu with many Italian and Northwestern dishes.

Tuesday-Sunday; doors open Tuesday-Saturday 5:30 p.m., Sunday 4:30 p.m.

DISCOVERY PARK

3801 W. Government Way, Seattle, 206-386-4236; www.cityofseattle.net

An in-city wildlife sanctuary and nature preserve, the 534-acre Discovery Park is the largest park in Seattle. Located on the western shores of the swanky Magnolia neighborhood, it is centered on a tall bluff that formerly served as a post for the U.S. Army, making for great views of the Olympic Mountains to the west and the Cascades to the east and granting waterfront access to the north and west. An extensive trail system lures joggers, bikers and other fitness buffs from all over the city, but the educational program is at the heart of the park's mission; hence the "Discovery" tag. School buses and day campers frequent the park year-round, but the events calendar has something for every age and interest. A diverse population of flora and fauna calls the park's dunes, thickets, forests and tide pools home.

Tuesday-Sunday 8 a.m.-5 p.m.

DRUIDS GLEN GOLF COURSE
29925 207th Ave. S.E., Covington, 253-638-1200; www.druidsglengolf.com

Completed in June 2003, Druids Glen offers affordable prices and the backdrop of Mount Rainier. The second hole offers a view of the mountain from the tee box. Several holes require difficult shots over water right off the tee or on the approach to the green. Four different pros are available for private lessons, and the practice facility is unblemished.

EXPERIENCE MUSIC PROJECT/SCIENCE FICTION MUSEUM
325 Fifth Ave. N., Seattle, 206-770-2700, 877-367-7361; www.empsfm.com

Forty years after his death, legendary rock guitarist Jimi Hendrix remains Seattle's favorite native son, and this thoroughly modern museum is a tribute to the huge impact of his short life. Financed by Microsoft cofounder and Hendrix fanatic Paul Allen, the $200 million museum opened in 2000. The striking architecture's sharp angles, contrasting textures and bright hues evoke the image of a smashed guitar and the rhythms of rock 'n' roll. The facilities within are similarly cutting-edge, from the grand hall/ musical venue dubbed the "Sky Church" to Crossroads, an exhibit space that meshes historical artifacts with multimedia to present the history of American music. The Science Fiction Museum offers interactive exhibits that will make you geek out, including Capt. Kirk's command chair and the T-800 Terminator, and traveling exhibits that focus on fanboy favorites like Battlestar Galactica. Food and drink (and live music) are available at the contemporary Revolution Bar & Grill.

Admission: adults $15, seniors children 5-17 $12, children 4 and under free. Daily 10 a.m.-5 p.m.

FIFTH AVENUE THEATER
1308 Fifth Ave., Seattle, 206-625-1900, 888-584-4849; www.5thavenue.org

This historic theater, which opened as a vaudeville house in 1926, now features musicals, concerts, films and lectures. Its ornate interior, modeled after some of China's architectural treasures, may well distract you from whatever's taking place onstage.

FREEWAY PARK
700 Seneca St., Seattle, 206-864-4075; www.seattle.gov

This 5-acre park features dramatic water displays.

Daily 6 a.m.-11:30 p.m.

FREMONT DISTRICT
Bounded by Fremont Avenue and 46th Street, Seattle; www.ci.seattle.wa.us

Undoubtedly Seattle's funkiest neighborhood, Fremont wears its eccentricity like a badge: The self-proclaimed "Center of the Universe" went as far as to declare facetious independence from Seattle in 1994. North of downtown and the Lake Washington Ship Canal, the former lumber-mill center is now an artists' paradise, well known for such public sculptures as a towering statue of Vladimir Lenin, a post-Cold War import from the former Soviet Union; the Fremont Troll gobbling a VW Beetle under Aurora Bridge; and Waiting for Interurban, six cast aluminum figures waiting for the bus. The area is also home to a high concentration of brewpubs, coffee shops, secondhand stores and galleries. Typical shopping strips line Fremont Avenue, Fremont Place and 34th and 35th streets.

FRYE ART MUSEUM

704 Terry Ave., Seattle, 206-622-9250; www.fryeart.org

In a city where abstract and postmodern art are the norm, the conservative Frye Art Museum bucks the trend by focusing solely on representational art: contemporary and classic landscapes and portraits. The works are both dark and bright (in both tint and theme) and are all bathed in natural light in simple, classic settings. Among the artists represented here are Winslow Homer and Andrew Wyeth. The café and the bookstore here are both excellent and worth a visit.

Admission: free. Tuesday-Sunday 11 a.m.-5 p.m.,Thursday 11 a.m.-7 p.m.

GAS WORKS PARK

2101 N. Northlake Way, Seattle, 206-684-4075; www.seattle.gov

A former gas-processing plant on the north side of Lake Union, the 20-acre Gas Works Park is a model for urban renewal and a magnet for kite flyers. The plant's facilities have been nicely converted for recreational use: the boiler house is now a picnic area and the exhauster-compressor building is now the Play Barn, a brightly painted playground for kids. The 12 1/2-mile Burke-Gilman trail begins here, offering a paved route north to suburban Kirkland for joggers and bikers.

Daily 4 a.m.-11:30 p.m.

GOLDEN GATE PARK

8498 Seaview Place N.W., Seattle, 206-684-7254; www.seattle.gov

Nestled on the bluffs that front Puget Sound in Seattle's Ballard neighborhood, Golden Gardens Park attracts sunbathers and fishermen to its beach and pier and all sorts of outdoor buffs to its myriad recreational opportunities. The park's trail system connects the beach with the forested bluffs above with a leash-optional dog park at the summit. A teen center on the beach called the Brick House features concerts and other events year-round.

GOLF CLUB AT NEWCASTLE

15500 Six Penny Lane, Newcastle, 425-793-4653; www.newcastlegolf.com

Some of the best views in the Seattle area can be found at Newcastle, which includes sightlines of the city's skyline and Mount Rainier. There are two courses, the Coal Creek and the China Creek, with the latter being the more difficult of the two. There is a putting course and a practice facility for warming up before your round and a good restaurant and bar for afterward.

GREEN LAKE PARK

7201 E. Green Lake Drive N., Seattle, 206-684-4075; www.seattle.gov

Ground zero for jogging in fitness-crazy Seattle, Green Lake is the heart of a bustling 320-acre park of the same name. Two paved trails encircle the lake and see a good deal of use from a cross-section of ages and speeds. Each trail is about three miles around the lake and there are separate lanes for bikers, walkers and runners. Trails aside, the lake itself is a recreation destination: a private company provides boat rentals and the Green Lake Small Craft Center offers rowing, sailing and canoe classes and organizes several annual regattas. The lush park surrounding Green Lake is home to a pitch-and-putt golf course and an indoor pool, as well as a community center, tennis courts, picnic tables and a children's playground.

JEFFERSON PARK GOLF CLUB
4101 Beacon Ave. S., Seattle, 206-762-4513; www.seattlegolf.com

Seattle's Jefferson Park is a short, par-70 layout, but it doesn't cost quite as much as other courses in the area. There is also a par-three course on the grounds, but it's the big course people come for, with a hilly layout that is challenging at times but still playable for just about any golfer. Go for the views as much as the golf.

KLONDIKE GOLD RUSH NATIONAL HISTORIC PARK
319 Second Ave. S., Seattle, 206-220-4240; www.klondikegoldrushwa.areaparks.com

The 1897 gold strike in the Canadian Yukon triggered an influx of tens of thousands of prospectors to Seattle and its commercial district, Pioneer Square. Motivated by dreams of riches, they arrived here to purchase food, equipment and pack animals in preparation for the arduous six-month trip into the frozen wilderness of the Klondike Gold Fields. While the gold rush provided an economic boost to the city, it was an economic failure for nearly all of the prospectors. Only a handful struck it rich. Most discovered no gold, and many lost their lives during the trek across the steep, snow-covered trail leading to the Klondike. The stampede of prospectors spurred commercial development in Pioneer Square, where the Klondike Gold Rush National Historical Park is located. The National Historical Park offers exhibits, audiovisuals and ranger programs that document the gold rush and its impact on Seattle.

Daily 9 a.m.-5 p.m.

LAKE WASHINGTON CANAL
Seen from Seaview Avenue N.W. or N.W. 54th Street; www.nws.usace.army.mil

Chittenden Locks raises and lowers boats to link saltwater and freshwater anchorages. More than 400,000 passengers and 6 million tons of freight pass through annually. Commodore Park and a salmon ladder with viewing windows are on the south side.

MARION OLIVER MCCAW HALL
305 Harrison St., Seattle, 206-684-7200; www.seattlecenter.org

The Opera House is home to the Seattle Opera Association, Pacific Northwest Ballet and Seattle Symphony. Bagley Wright Theatre is home to Seattle Repertory Theatre.

THE MUSEUM OF FLIGHT
9404 E. Marginal Way S., Seattle, 206-764-5720; www.museumofflight.org

As a major hub for plane-maker Boeing, Seattle is the ideal location for this impressive air and space museum. The facility is highlighted by the soaring

Great Gallery, home of more than 50 vintage aircraft, many of which are suspended in formation six stories above the ground. On display here are the original presidential Air Force One and a replica of the Wright Brothers' biplane from Kitty Hawk, N.C., alongside mint-condition models of the first fighter jet (a 1914 Caproni Ca 20) and the first jumbo jet (a prototype Boeing 747). Many planes are open for visitors to sit in the cockpit or explore the hold. Located near Seattle-Tacoma International Airport in southern Seattle, the museum is also home to the restored Red Barn, where the Boeing Company was founded nearly a century ago, and several space-themed exhibits.

Admission: adults $15, military personnel $11, children 5-17 $8, children 4 and under free. Daily 10 a.m.-5 p.m. First Thursday of each month 10 a.m.-9 p.m. and free after 5 p.m.

MUSEUM OF HISTORY AND INDUSTRY

2700 24th Ave. E., Seattle, McCurdy Park, 206-324-1126; www.seattlehistory.org

The showcase of the Seattle Historical Society, this excellent facility (popularly known as MOHAI) tracks the people and events that have shaped Seattle over its 150-year history. With a collection of more than a million photographs and historical artifacts, MOHAI gives visitors a comprehensive look into the social and economic roots of the Puget Sound area. The Great Seattle Fire is documented by an exhibit complete with a historic fire engine, murals and other relics of the disaster that razed the city in 1889; a mock-up of an 1880s street scene gives visitors a glimpse into the prefire Emerald City. Another highlight is the comprehensive collection of souvenirs from the 1962 World's Fair.

Admission: adults $8, seniors, students and military personnel $7, children 5-17 $6, children 4 and under free. Daily 10 a.m.-5 p.m. Free first Thursday of month 10 a.m.-8 p.m.

NORTHWEST OUTDOOR CENTER

2100 Westlake Ave. N., Seattle, 206-281-9694, 800-683-0637; www.nwoc.com

A 20-year-old Seattle institution on the docks of Lake Union, the Northwest Outdoor Center is a major hub for the Pacific Northwest's paddling community. At this combination school/store/guide service, more than 100 kayaks are available for rental and a full slate of whitewater and sea kayaking classes, ranging from a 2 1/2-hour session to a six-day immersion, are offered. The center's guided tours include day trips spent sea kayaking in Puget Sound and multiday wildlife-watching adventures that take participants to the San Juan Islands and beyond. A bit off the beaten path, sunset and nighttime excursions explore Lake Union and the Lake Washington Ship Canal and the water elevator known as the Ballard Locks. The Northwest Outdoor Center is also the best source of paddling information and advice in the city.

PACIFIC SCIENCE CENTER

200 Second Ave. N., Seattle, 206-443-2001; www.pacsci.org

With subject matter that balances cutting-edge technology and natural history, the center features such permanent exhibits as an indoor butterfly house, a room-sized model of Puget Sound and "Dinosaurs: A Journey Through Time," complete with seven robotic dinosaurs; on the other side of the science spectrum is Tech Zone, where you can challenge a robot to a game of tic-tac-toe. Beyond the permanent and seasonal exhibits, movies are shown on a pair of giant IMAX screens (one of which is coupled with a 3-D projector) and there are astronomy demonstrations in the onsite planetarium and dazzling light displays with rock 'n' roll soundtracks in the Adobe Laser Dome.

Admission: adults $14, seniors $12, children 6-15 $9, children 3-5 $7, children 2 and under free. Monday, Wednesday-Friday 10 a.m.-5 p.m., Saturday-Sunday 10 a.m.-6 p.m.

PARAMOUNT THEATER

911 Pine St., Seattle, 206-467-5510; www.theparamount.com

This more than 80-year-old theater brings a wide range of entertainment to Seattle: Broadway plays and musicals, ballet and modern dance performances, jazz and rock 'n' roll concerts and comedy acts. It also shows silent films and hosts family-oriented entertainment. Checkout the Publix theater organ, one of only three remaining, which has been magnificently restored.

PIKE PLACE MARKET

First Avenue and Pike Street, 206-682-7453;
www.pikeplacemarket.com

Farmers established the Pike Place Market in 1907 because they were tired of middlemen taking more than their fair share. Today, the indoor/outdoor market is a Seattle landmark and a cornucopia for the senses, with burly guys tossing fresh fish back and forth; bin after bin of fresh, colorful fruits, vegetables and flowers; the sounds and sights of street performers; and the wares of hundreds of artists on display. Pike Place Market also has dozens of restaurants and food stands, a day spa, a barbershop and a tattoo parlor onsite. Just two blocks east of the waterfront, the market is a quick walk from the center of downtown and surrounded by eateries and bars. Guided tours are available Wednesday to Sunday year-round.

Monday-Saturday 10 a.m.-6 p.m., Sunday 11 a.m.-5 p.m.

PIONEER SQUARE

Bounded by First Avenue, James Street and Yesler Way, Seattle, 206-667-0687;
www.pioneersquare.org

Seattle's oldest neighborhood, the original Pioneer Square saw its beginnings in the early 1850s but soon met a blazing fate in the Great Seattle Fire of 1889. Today's Pioneer Square was built atop the scorched remains, resulting in a ghostlike underground beneath the city streets. (The Underground Tour allows you to explore this buried history.) The area boomed again after the lure of gold began attracting miners during the following decade, and a seedy underbelly (that remains to this day) followed in their wake. Now dominated by the stately Victorian and Romanesque red bricks above cobblestone squares, the neighborhood is a commercial and social hub: a melting pot of offices, stores, galleries, restaurants and nightclubs wedged between downtown and a pair of major stadiums, Safeco Field (baseball) and Qwest Field (football).

ROCK BOTTOM BREWERY

1333 Fifth Ave., Seattle, 206-623-3070;
www.rockbottom.com

This brewpub in the heart of downtown Seattle is one of the flagships of the Rock Bottom chain, which consists of about 30 breweries in the United States. At any given time, at least six beers are on tap, all of which are brewed onsite with Washington-grown hops. The menu is varied, with burgers, pizzas, salads and steaks served inside in an upstairs dining room and a downstairs bar/poolroom or outside on a breezy patio.

SEATTLE AQUARIUM

1483 Alaskan Way, Seattle, 206-386-4300; www.seattleaquarium.org

A waterfront mainstay at Pier 59 since 1977, the Seattle Aquarium is an engrossing educational experience for curious minds of all ages. The top facility of its kind in the region, the aquarium is home to nearly 400 species of fish, birds, marine mammals and other sea life. The staff has celebrated several breakthroughs over the years, including the first live births of sea otters in North American captivity, which has happened six times here, and the rearing of a giant Pacific octopus to adulthood, another first. Another highlight is the underwater dome, which allows guests to immerse themselves in a transparent bubble on the bottom of a fish-filled, 400,000-gallon tank. An IMAX theater is adjacent, charging separate entry fees.

Admission: adults $17, children 4-12 $11, children 3 and under free. Daily 9:30 a.m.-5 p.m.

SEATTLE ART MUSEUM

1300 First Ave., Seattle, 206-625-8900; www.seattleartmuseum.org

Its entrance guarded by an animated, 48-foot-tall sculpture named Hammering Man, the Seattle Art Museum (known locally as SAM) is the premier facility of its kind in the Pacific Northwest. There is something for everybody here, from ancient Greek sculpture to modern Russian decorative art. Held in particularly high regard are the collections of contemporary art (with pieces by Andy Warhol, Jackson Pollock and Roy Lichtenstein) and Northwest Coast Native American art (composed of nearly 200 masks, sculptures and household items). Temporary exhibitions are similarly diverse. A dynamic events calendar helps distinguish the museum; it offers up a bevy of concerts, films, lectures, demonstrations, family programs and classes. Admission is waived on the first Thursday of every month, and a restaurant and two gift shops are onsite.

Admission: adults $15, seniors and military personnel $12, students and children 13-17 $9, children 12 and under free. Wednesday-Sunday 10 a.m.-5 p.m., Thursday-Friday 10 a.m.-9 p.m.

SPACE NEEDLE

400 Broad St., Seattle, 206-905-2180, 800-937-9582; www.spaceneedle.com

First a sketch on a placemat, then the centerpiece of the 1962 World's Fair and now Seattle's face to the world, the Space Needle is one of the most distinctive structures in the United States. Capping the 605-foot tower, the flying saucer-inspired dome is symbolic of both the Seattle World's Fair's theme—"Century 21"—and the coinciding national push into space. The dome houses an observation deck, with super city views, and SkyCity, a revolving restaurant that goes full circle every 48 minutes. There is also a banquet facility 100 feet above street level and a gift shop at the tower's base, where visitors board an elevator for the 43-second journey to the top. The Space Needle is the setting for one of the West Coast's premier New Year's Eve celebrations.

Admission: adults $18, military personnel $16, children 4-13 $11, children 3 and under free. Observation deck and store: Monday-Thursday 10 a.m.-11 p.m., Friday-Saturday 9:30 a.m.-11:30 p.m., Sunday 9:30 a.m.-11 p.m.

SPECIAL EVENTS

BUMBERSHOOT

Seattle Center, 305 Harrison St., Seattle, 206-281-7788; www.bumbershoot.com
This annual four-day music fest is the largest of its kind on the West Coast. Legendary artists and rising stars alike ranging from Bob Dylan to the Black Eyed Peas perform in more than 30 different indoor and outdoor venues, stages and galleries. Bumbershoot also features poetry, dance, comedy and contemporary art exhibits.
Labor Day weekend.

CHILLY HILLY BICYCLE CLASSIC

Bainbridge Island, Seattle, 206-522-3222; www.cascade.org
This 33-mile course on Bainbridge Island attracts thousands of cyclists for a one-day organized ride in February. The course starts at the ferry dock and makes many gains and losses in elevation (with 2,700 feet of elevation change in all) before skidding to a stop at a finish-line festival with a huge chili feast.
Late February.

FREMONT OKTOBERFEST

Fremont District, 35th Avenue and Fremont Avenue N., Seattle;
www.fremontoktoberfest.org
The eccentric Fremont neighborhood puts its own stamp on the traditional Bavarian beer-drinking festival with a rambunctious chainsaw pumpkin-carving contest, a street dance, polka-dancing lessons and live bands that run the gamut from mainstream to bizarre. Held in the shadows of the Aurora Avenue Bridge, this street fair is considered one of the top Oktoberfest festivals outside of Germany, taking place over the course of the third weekend in September. The rowdy beer garden here is quite a sight, serving up a wide variety of beers (including root beer for kids) with an emphasis on local micro-brews. The street fair is free and open to all, but admission is charged to enter the beer garden; six beer tokens and a souvenir cup are included.
Late September.

OPENING DAY REGATTA

1807 E. Hamlin St., Seattle, 206-325-1000; www.seattleyachtclub.org
A Seattle tradition since the 1910s, the opening day of yachting season takes place every year on the first Saturday in May with such featured events as a boat parade and a rowing regatta. Most of the action is centered on the Montlake Cut, which links Lake Washington and Lake Union, and there are a number of great viewpoints on and near the campus of the University of Washington.

SEATTLE INTERNATIONAL FILM FESTIVAL

Various venues throughout Seattle, 206-324-9996; www.seattlefilm.com

Held annually from late May to mid-June, Seattle's top-notch film fest is one of the largest cinema showcases in the United States. While the content tends toward documentaries and international independent films, Hollywood is also well represented.

SEATTLE MARATHON

Downtown, Seattle, 206-729-3660; www.seattlemarathon.org

Held annually in late November, the Seattle Marathon is open to runners and walkers of all skill levels and registers more than 10,000 entrants each year. Much of the hilly, scenic route runs along the Lake Washington shoreline, taking entrants from the Seattle Center to Seward Park in southeast Seattle and back again. A kids' marathon, a half marathon and a marathon walk are also held.

Late November.

SEATTLE REP

155 Mercer St., Seattle, 206-443-2222, 877-900-9285; www.seattlerep.org

Short for Seattle Repertory Theatre, the award-winning Seattle Rep is one of the top regional nonprofit theater companies in the United States. Two stages host six to 10 productions a year with the emphasis on presenting challenging dramatic works and time-tested classics injected with fresh perspectives.

September-June.

SEATTLE TO PORTLAND BICYCLE CLASSIC

Seattle, 206-522-3222; www.cascade.org

This 200-mile road race draws up to 8,000 riders each year for a one- or two-day tour through Washington and Oregon's forests and farmlands starting at the University of Washington.

SUR LA TABLE

Pike Place Market, 84 Pine St., Seattle, 206-448-2244; www.surlatable.com

In the 1970s, Seattle spawned this clearinghouse for hard-to-find kitchen gear, and it soon became known as a source for cookware, small appliances, cutlery, kitchen tools, linens, tableware, gadgets and specialty foods. Sur La Table has since expanded to include cooking classes, chef demonstrations and cookbook author signings, as well as a catalog and online presence. Cooking connoisseurs discover such finds as cool oven mitts, zest graters, copper whisks, onion soup bowls and inspired TV dinner trays.

TEATRO ZINZANNI

222 Mercer St., Seattle, 206-802-0015; www.zinzanni.org

An avant-garde dinner theater with a sister facility in San Francisco, Teatro ZinZanni offers entertainment like nothing else in town: a hyper-imaginative circus/nightclub act hybrid of music, comedy, trapeze, Kabuki and magic.

UNDERGROUND TOUR

608 First Ave., Seattle, 206-682-4646; www.undergroundtour.com

A fun and funny look at Seattle's colorful past, Bill Speidel's Underground Tour takes you on a journey under the streets of Pioneer Square, where remnants of the frontier town that met its fiery end in 1889 still remain. The tour begins in a bar (Doc Maynard's Public House) and lasts about an hour and a half. Advance reservations are recommended.

Daily.

VICTORIA CLIPPER CHARTERS

2701 Alaskan Way, Pier 69, Seattle, 206-448-5000, 800-888-2535, 250-382-8100 (Victoria, B.C.); www.victoriaclipper.com

This tour company operates a fleet of high-speed, passenger-only ferries on routes among Seattle, the San Juan Islands in Puget Sound, and Victoria, Canada. The trip to Victoria takes about two hours, and VCC offers many packages that integrate hotel stays, recreational excursions and other transportation. There are also narrated whale-watching cruises, and the clippers have basic cafés and duty-free shops on board.

WEST SEATTLE GOLF COURSE

4470 35th Ave. S.W., Seattle, 206-935-5187; www.seattlegolf.com

This public course, designed by course architect H. Chandler Eagan and opened in 1940, has drawn good reviews over the years. You can usually get on for less than $30, and early-bird specials make it even cheaper.

WING LUKE ASIAN MUSEUM

407 Seventh Ave. S., Seattle, 206-623-5124; www.wingluke.org

An apt counterpart to the Seattle Asian Art Museum, the Wing Luke Asian Museum in Seattle's busy International District illuminates the Asian-American experience in a historical and cultural light. A collection of diverse artifacts details the 200-year history of Asians in the Pacific Northwest. Another permanent exhibit, the Densho Project, allows you to access oral histories recorded by Japanese Americans who were detained in World War II-era internment camps.

Admission: adults $12.95, seniors and students 13-18 $9.95, children 5-12 $8.95, children 5 and under free. Tuesday-Sunday 10 a.m.-5 p.m.

WOODLAND PARK ZOO

5500 Phinney Ave. N., Seattle, 206-548-2500; www.zoo.org

One of the biggest and best zoos in the country sits in the park of the same name in north Seattle. The exhibits focus on ecosystems instead of single species: the Alaska enclosure is home to Kodiak bears that catch live trout out of a stream; Tropical Asia inhabitants include elephants, tapirs and orangutans; and the African Savannah features giraffes, hippos and zebras. There is also a Komodo dragon display, a petting zoo, Bug World (with such denizens as millipedes, scorpions and tarantulas), and an enclosed aviary housing hawks, falcons and owls. The special events calendar is dense and varied with breakfasts and over-nighters for kids, as well as lectures, festivals and holiday happenings.

Admission: May-September, adults $16.50, children 3-12 $11, children 2 and under free; October-April, adults $11, children 3-12 $8, children 2 and under free. May-September, daily 9:30 a.m.-6 p.m.; October-April, daily 9:30 a.m.-4 p.m.

WHERE TO STAY

★★★ALEXIS

1007 First Ave., Seattle, 206-624-4844, 866-356-8894; www.alexishotel.com

This luxury boutique hotel has been in operation since the turn of the 20th century, making it as much a Seattle landmark as the Space Needle. The mid-century-tinged rooms feature Aveda bath products, plush terrycloth bathrobes and soft Egyptian cotton linens. There's also evening turndown service with chocolates, complimentary morning coffee and an evening wine reception. The Library Bistro, a 1940s-style supper club, offers American cuisine in a cozy, bookstore-like setting, while the Bookstore Bar is the perfect spot to sample a cocktail at the end of the day.

109 rooms. Restaurant, bar. Spa. $151-250

★★★★THE FAIRMONT OLYMPIC HOTEL

411 University St., Seattle, 206-621-1700, 800-257-7544; www.fairmont.com

The Fairmont is conveniently located in Rainier Square, only minutes from the city's top attractions. The guest rooms and suites are tasteful retreats with floral draperies, soft pastel colors and period furnishings. Traditional high tea service in the onsite restaurant is a treat worth making time for. The bounty of the Pacific Northwest is the focus at the excellent Georgian, while Shuckers is a popular oyster bar at which Seattle's famous microbrews are served, and a selection of cocktails is available at The Terrace.

450 rooms. Restaurant, bar. Fitness center. Pool. Spa. Pets accepted. $251-350

★★★★FOUR SEASONS HOTEL SEATTLE

99 Union St., Seattle, 206-749-7000; www.fourseasons.com

Seattle's newest luxury hotel is a sophisticated, urbane retreat housed in a modern glass tower close to the Seattle Art Museum. That the service is top-notch and attentive goes without saying—staff here attend to whatever you need with a laid-back, friendly but confident flair that's hard to duplicate.

Rooms are bright and contemporary, with the hotel brand's signature pillow-top beds and luxury linens, as well as spacious bathrooms with extra-deep soaking tubs, rain showers and L'Occitane bath products. The Pool Terrace, with its rooftop pool, outdoor fire pit and views of Elliott Bay, is a great spot for lounging or sipping a glass of locally produced wine. The onsite restaurant ART, serves organic Northwest cuisine (think wild king salmon with lobster mashed potatoes) in a sleek, contemporary setting.

147 rooms. Restaurant, bar. Fitness center. Pool. Spa. $251-350

★★★GRAND HYATT SEATTLE

721 Pine St., Seattle, 206-774-1234, 888-591-1234; www.grandseattle.hyatt.com

This downtown hotel is loaded with technological treats, from the wired public spaces to the in-room digital concierges and iPod docking stations. The earth-toned guest rooms have streamlined blond wood furnishings and extra-large baths with marble tubs. Amenities include a comprehensive fitness center and a variety of dining options, from Starbucks to Ruth's Chris Steakhouse.

425 rooms. Restaurant, bar. Fitness center. Spa. $351 and up

★★★HOTEL ÄNDRA

2000 Fourth Ave., Seattle, 206-448-8600, 877-448-8600; www.hotelandra.com

This boutique hotel combines Northwest and Scandinavian design influences and has a prime location in Seattle's vibrant Belltown neighborhood. Guests are greeted with a dramatic lobby fireplace built from split-grain granite and bookended by a pair of golden maple bookcases. Rooms include such luxuries as 300-thread-count cotton linens, goose-down pillows and alpaca headboards.

119 rooms. Restaurant, bar. Fitness center. Spa. $151-250

★★★HOTEL MAX

620 Stewart St., Seattle, 206-728-6299, 866-986-8087; www.hotelmaxseattle.com

This boutique hotel offers unique features, such as a spiritual menu, a pillow menu, and creative Asian fusion cuisine in its Red Fin restaurant. Decorated with more than 350 original paintings and photos, the hotel's contemporary design includes teak wood furniture. Rooms are small but come stocked with pillow-top mattresses, Aveda bath amenities, Torrefazione coffee and Tazo tea.

165 rooms. Restaurant, bar. Business center. Fitness center. Pets accepted. $151-250

★★★HOTEL MONACO

1101 Fourth Ave., Seattle, 206-621-1770, 800-715-6513; www.monaco-seattle.com

This hip hotel is centrally located near the waterfront, Pike Place Market, the Seattle Art Museum, convention centers and shops. The contemporary rooms feature duvet-topped beds, L'Occitane bath products and even all-hours yoga on the in-room TV. The complimentary evening wine reception in the two-story lobby is the perfect place to relax in front of the fireplace. Pets are accepted, and the hotel offers a temporary pet goldfish for lonely pet owners who miss their animal companions.

189 rooms. Restaurant, bar. Spa. Pets accepted. $251-350

★★★HOTEL VINTAGE PARK

1100 Fifth Ave., Seattle, 206-624-8000, 800-853-3914;
www.vintagepark.com

Built in 1922, this beautifully renovated hotel offers
elegantly decorated guest rooms, each named after
a local winery or vineyard, drenched in reds and
golds with cherry wood furnishings. The lobby and
its fireplace are the meeting spot for nightly tastings
of local wines and microbeers—a complimentary
reception is held every night. After the reception,
stop in at Tulio Ristorante, the in-house Italian
restaurant that serves housemade pastas.

126 rooms. Restaurant, bar. Fitness center. Pets accepted.
$151-250

★★★THE INN AT EL GAUCHO

2505 First Ave., Seattle, 206-728-1337, 866-354-2824;
www.elgaucho.com

Seattle's hip Belltown district is the setting for the
swank Inn at El Gaucho. Cozy chocolate-and-tan-
colored rooms are equipped with luxe amenities,
including pillow-top beds with Egyptian cotton
linens, rainfall showerheads, L'Occitane bath
products, oversized Egyptian cotton towels, plasma
TVs and CD players. In-room dining—with bedside
preparation—is provided by the downstairs El
Gaucho steak house.

18 rooms. Restaurant, bar. Complimentary breakfast.
$151-250

★★★INN AT HARBOR STEPS

1221 First Ave., Seattle, 206-748-0973, 888-728-8910;
www.innatharborsteps.com

Guests of this inn on Seattle's waterfront will find
themselves near all of the city's top attractions,
including shops, galleries, cafés, Harbor Steps Park,
Woodland Park Zoo and Pike Place Market. Rooms
are elegant yet urban with floral-patterned bed
spreads and furniture, fireplaces, garden views and
sitting areas, as well as wet bars and refrigerators.

28 rooms. Complimentary breakfast. Fitness center. Pool.
$151-250

★★★INN AT THE MARKET

86 Pine St., Seattle, 206-443-3600, 800-446-4484;
www.innatthemarket.com

This boutique hotel has a prime location at Pike
Place Market, overlooking Elliott Bay. The spacious
and stylish rooms have Tempur-Pedic mattresses;
in-room massages and spa treatments are available.

WHAT ARE THE BEST BOUTIQUE HOTELS IN SEATTLE?

Alexis:
This chic hotel has mid-
century flourishes in
the rooms. Bibliophiles
will adore dining in
the Library Bistro and
hanging out in the
Bookstore Bar.

Hotel Ändra:
The Belltown hotel has
Scandinavian influences
in its design and has
warm touches like an
alpaca headboard, slate
blue chenille covers and
minimalist warm wood.

Hotel Max:
You'll find more than
350 original paintings
and photos peppered
throughout this arty
hotel. It also pampers
with services like a
spiritual menu and
pillow menu.

Hotel Vintage Park:
A wine theme flows
throughout this hotel,
whose rooms are named
after local winery and
vineyards. Don't miss the
free nightly tastings of
local wines.

The Inn at El Gaucho:
The comfy-cozy
chocolate and cream
rooms invite you to stay
awhile with perks like
L'Occitane soaps, Philip
B hair products, Bose
stereos and Egyptian
cotton towels.

The rooftop garden, with views of the bay and market below, is a great spot for sipping a glass of local wine. Other treats include privileges at the Seattle Club's state-of-the-art fitness facility and in-room dining provided by Café Campagne.
70 rooms. Restaurant, bar. Pets accepted. $251-350

★★★MARRIOTT SEATTLE AIRPORT

3201 S. 176th St., Seattle, 206-241-2000, 888-236-2427; www.marriott.com

This airport hotel has updated rooms with plush beds and ample workspaces. The indoor enclosed pool and renovated fitness center are good diversions; the two-story lobby bar has a stone fireplace and plenty of cozy, overstuffed leather couches and chairs for lounging.
459 rooms. Restaurant, bar. Fitness center. Pool. $151-250

★★★MAYFLOWER PARK HOTEL

405 Olive Way, Seattle, 206-623-8700, 800-426-5100; www.mayflowerpark.com

The historic Mayflower Park Hotel first opened in 1927 as The Bergonian and has since been renovated to recapture its original grandeur. Queen Anne-style rooms are luxuriously appointed with rich fabrics, large-screen televisions, fluffy bathrobes and Baudelaire bath amenities. The hotel's bar, Oliver's, consistently comes out on top in Seattle's annual Martini Classic Challenge.
171 rooms. Restaurant, bar. $151-250

★★★PAN PACIFIC SEATTLE

2125 Terry Ave., Seattle, 206-264-8111; www.panpacific.com

Located in Seattle's South Lake Union neighborhood, this contemporary, upscale hotel is close to the city's best shopping. Rooms are modern and stylish, with luxury linens, large plasma TVs, DVD players and free wireless Internet access. The hotel is connected to a shopping area that includes everything from a day spa to Starbucks, Whole Foods and several restaurants.
160 rooms. Restaurant, bar. $251-350

★★★RENAISSANCE SEATTLE HOTEL

515 Madison St., Seattle, 206-583-0300, 888-236-2427; www.renaissancehotels.com

Located in downtown Seattle, this hotel combines contemporary décor of marble and glass with earth-toned colors. The tower in which the hotel is located stretches to the 25th floor, where the indoor pool is situated. Nearly everything that defines Seattle is less than a mile away: Pike Place Market, the waterfront, Pioneer Square, Safeco Field (home of the Mariners) and Qwest Field.
558 rooms. Restaurant, bar. Pool. Pets accepted. $151-250

★★★SEATTLE MARRIOTT WATERFRONT

2100 Alaskan Way, Seattle, 206-443-5000, 800-455-8254; www.marriott.com

This waterfront hotel affords great views of the city skyline, the Olympic Mountains, Mount Rainier and Elliott Bay. Common areas feature modern touches like colorful blown-glass displays and eclectic mosaic tile floors, while guest rooms feature CD players, luxurious bedding with down comforters and pillows, and complimentary Starbucks coffee service. The onsite restaurant, Fish Club, offers seafood-focused dishes with a Mediterranean influence along with a beautiful atmosphere, which includes floor-to-ceiling windows, chandeliers and floral arrangements.

358 rooms. Restaurant, bar. Fitness center. Pool. $251-350

★★★THE SHERATON SEATTLE HOTEL
1400 Sixth Ave., Seattle, 206-621-9000, 800-325-3535; www.sheraton.com

In downtown Seattle, this hotel offers a great location near many of the city's attractions, including KeyArena and Seattle Center. Earth-toned guest rooms feature a host of amenities, including flat-screen TVs and Sheraton's signature Sweet Sleeper Bed.

1,258 rooms. Restaurant, bar. Fitness center. Pool. Pets accepted. $151-250

★★★SORRENTO HOTEL
900 Madison St., Seattle, 206-622-6400, 800-426-1265; www.hotelsorrento.com

Drawing on its namesake Italian village for inspiration, the Sorrento has a Mediterranean theme and friendly service. Rooms have marble baths, Egyptian cotton linens and stereos with CD players. Home to the Hunt Club, one of Seattle's revered landmarks, dining options also include the cozy Fireside Room and the seasonal outdoor Café Palma.

76 rooms. Restaurant, bar. Pets accepted. $251-350

★★★W SEATTLE HOTEL
1112 Fourth Ave., Seattle, 206-264-6000, 888-625-5144; www.whotels.com

The W Seattle Hotel combines cutting-edge style with top-notch comfort and cute and quirky touches like a candy necklace in the in-room munchies box. Since this hotel is designed for tech-savvy business travelers, rooms offer well-equipped workstations. The lobby and adjacent bar are popular spots with locals for after-work cocktails.

426 rooms. Restaurant, bar. Pets accepted. $351 and up

RECOMMENDED

ACE HOTEL
2434 First Ave., Seattle, 206-448-4721; www.acehotel.com

The ultra-hip Ace Hotel bills itself as the ultimate lodging for the urban nomad on a mission of experience. Modeled after European hotels, Ace presents stylish décor with modern furnishings and clean white walls throughout. Rooms feature exposed brick walls, lofted ceilings and hardwood floors. Half of the hotel's accommodations have private bathrooms, while the other half utilize shared facilities. Each private bathroom is entered through a revolving door that's hidden in the wall. All rooms include a sink and vanity.

28 rooms. Pets accepted. $151-250

ARCTIC CLUB HOTEL
700 Third Ave., Seattle, 206-340-0340, 800-600-7775; www.hilton.com

Listed on the National Register of Historic Places, the building used to house the Arctic Club, whose members were part of the Alaskan gold rush. You see traces of its Klondike gold rush past everywhere, from photos of the old-time members cramming the walls and columns in the lobby to decorations like Alaska Yukon Pacific Exposition memorabilia and walrus head sculptures. The taupe-drenched rooms have fun touches like porthole mirrors, bedside tables that look like old trunks and a beveled glass door with the word Bath stenciled on it leading to the restroom. The Northern Lights-inspired Dome Room is gorgeous, with a stained-glass and gilt dome ceiling, and is the perfect place for a special event.

120 rooms. Restaurant, bar. Business center. Fitness center. $151-250

HOTEL DECA

4507 Brooklyn Ave. N.E., Seattle, 206-634-2000, 800-899-0251; www.hoteldeca.com

This hip boutique hotel, set in the University District, offers modern art-deco-themed rooms. The headboards are an artsy focal point in the room; some almost reach the ceiling in bold hues like mustard, and others have a red, white and gray checkerboard pattern. They also come equipped with DVD players and microwaves. Head to the inviting lobby and plunk down on the dark brown velvety sofas or lime-green armchairs to warm up by the fire or admire the oversized art on the walls.

158 rooms. Restaurant, bar. Complimentary breakfast. Fitness center. $151-250

THE PARAMOUNT

724 Pine St., Seattle, 206-292-9500, 800-716-6199; www.coasthotels.com

This European-inspired hotel resides in downtown Seattle. Its muted rooms are outfitted with 37-inch LCD televisions, free Internet access, soundproofed walls and windows, and Portland Roasting Coffee and Tazo Tea. For dinner or drinks, visit the Dragonfish Asian Café, where you can watch the chefs in action in the open kitchen as they whip up your dim sum.

146 rooms. Restaurant, bar. Business Center. Fitness center. $151-250

WHERE TO EAT

★★★AL BOCCALINO

1 Yesler Way, Seattle, 206-622-7688; www.seattleslittleitaly.com

This intimate Italian restaurant in Pioneer Square features soft antique lighting and candlelit tables that set the stage for many marriage proposals. The owner, Carlos Tager, is a nightly fixture and greets each guest. The menu features dishes from northern and southern Italy, like lasagna layered with crimini mushrooms, caramelized onions and fontina cheese drenched in béchamel sauce, or pillows of three-cheese ravioli swimming in a pistachio cream sauce. But diners in the know come Sunday through Thursday to indulge in the five-course dinner-for-two offerings.

Italian. Lunch, dinner. Reservations recommended. Outdoor seating .Bar. $16-35

★★★ANDALUCA

407 Olive Way, Seattle, 206-382-6999; www.andaluca.com

Take a trip through the Mediterranean with Andaluca's fare. Sit down in the intimate dining room and partake in mains like the crusted-beef tenderloin with Spanish blue cheese, grilled pears, and idiazabal mashed potatoes with a marsala demi-glace. There's also a selection of pintxos, tapas-sized portions of dishes like Medjool dates stuffed with chorizo and doused in a blood-orange dressing. Top it off with a rich feta cheesecake with a phyllo crust, and a merlot dried cherry sauce.

Mediterranean. Breakfast, lunch, dinner. Reservations recommended. Children's menu. Bar. $16-35

★★★ASSAGGIO RISTORANTE
2010 Fourth Ave., Seattle, 206-441-1399;
www.assaggioseattle.com
Diners feel like family at this Belltown Italian restaurant, where the executive chef and owner Mauro Golmarvi welcomes every diner. The décor is Renaissance style with Michelangelo replica murals, wood booths, soft sconce lighting and intimate tables. The restaurant's authentic Italian cuisine emphasizes the North Central Adriatic region of Italy, and Mauro takes numerous trips to Italy each year to replenish his wine offerings. Go for pasta dishes like the pappardelle with wild boar ragu or the penne with pancetta, peppercorns and green onions drowning in a tomato-vodka cream sauce.
Italian. Lunch, dinner. Closed Sunday. Reservations recommended. Outdoor seating. $16-35

★★★BRASA
2107 Third Ave., Seattle, 206-728-4220; www.brasa.com
Seattle's foodies gather at Brasa to indulge in chef Tamara Murphy's robust, Mediterranean-inspired fare. Two of the signature dishes show off the kitchen's culinary brilliance: the roasted suckling pig and the mussels and clams served oven-steamed in a cataplana (a double-domed copper pot). All dishes are layered with the bold flavors of Spain, Portugal, France and Brazil. Brasa serves wonderful food that dazzles the palate and the eye and expertly balances the rustic and the sophisticated.
Mediterranean. Dinner. Reservations recommended. Bar. $36-85

★★★BRASSERIE MARGAUX
Warwick Seattle Hotel, 401 Lenora St., Seattle, 206-777-1990; www.margauxseattle.com
This French brasserie adjacent to the Warwick Seattle Hotel has good views of the city skyline, making it a great choice for special occasions. The dining room is decorated with warm dark woods, upholstered chairs and candlelit tables. The menu specializes in Northwest cuisine with French influences, like a pork loin with a mushroom-apple demi-glace. The restaurant also carves prime rib tableside.
Pacific Northwest, French. Breakfast, lunch, dinner, weekend brunch. Bar. $36-85

WHAT ARE THE BEST ITALIAN RESTAURANTS IN SEATTLE?

Al Boccalino:
The Pioneer Square restaurant's menu draws from northern and southern Italy. Don't miss the lasagna stuffed with crimini mushrooms and caramelized onions.

Assaggio Ristorante:
The staff at this Belltown restaurant welcomes guests like family. You'll feel right at home when you sit down to dishes like pappardelle with wild boar ragu.

Tavolàta:
The city's chic masses come to this industrial-looking eatery to chat over linguine with clams at the 30-foot-long communal table.

Tulio Ristorante:
You know this Italian restaurant is dedicated to using fresh organic ingredients when eco-activist Al Gore gives it a thumbs-up. The former vice-president has eaten here.

★★★CAFÉ FLORA

2901 E. Madison St., Seattle, 206-325-9100; www.cafeflora.com

There are people who believe that the words delicious and innovative could never be used to describe vegetarian cuisine, but Café Flora proves them wrong. Since 1991, this Seattle gem has been turning out perfect plates of fresh and nutritious fare that consistently receives raves from both vegetarians and omnivores alike. Herbs from the restaurant's own garden are used in seasonal dishes like mushroom asparagus risotto with artichoke bottoms, pine nuts, scallions, mascarpone and parsley oil.

Vegetarian. Lunch, dinner, Saturday-Sunday brunch. Reservations recommended. Children's menu. $16-35

★★★CAMPAGNE

Inn at the Market, 86 Pine St., Seattle, 206-728-2800; www.campagnerestaurant.com

This charming French restaurant is at the Inn at the Market in Pike Place Market. Its delicious menu focuses on the regions of southern France and features entrées such as boneless rib-eye steak with green peppercorn sauce; roasted leg of lamb on tomato, basil and marrow bean ragout with lamb jus, and pan-roasted brined duck breast served on ratatouille. The majority of its ingredients are supplied from the local farmers market.

French. Dinner. Bar. Reservations recommended. Outdoor seating. $36-85

★★★CANLIS RESTAURANT

2576 Aurora Ave. N., Seattle, 206-283-3313; www.canlis.com

This contemporary dining room with floor-to-ceiling windows delivers views of Lake Union and the Cascade Mountains. Ingredients are sourced locally, and only the freshest seasonal choices appear on the menu in dishes such as Dungeness crab cakes with Granny Smith apples, cilantro and curry.

American, Pacific Northwest. Dinner. Closed Sunday; December. Reservations recommended. Jacket required. Bar. $86 and up

★★★CHEZ SHEA

94 Pike St., Seattle, 206-467-9990; www.chezshea.com

Tucked into Pike Place Market is Chez Shea, an Old World charmer featuring the freshest ingredients of the Northwest prepared with French technique, like the Muscovy duck leg confit with huckleberry demi-glace. The candlelit dining room offers views of the Puget Sound, and the four-course prix fixe menu features hearty, home-style regional fare. The chocolate torte and the harvest apple cake are worth the splurge. An eight-course chef's tasting menu is also available.

French bistro. Dinner, late-night. Closed Monday. Reservations recommended. Bar. $36-85

★★★DAHLIA LOUNGE

2001 Fourth Ave., Seattle, 206-682-4142; www.tomdouglas.com

James Beard Award-winning chef/owner Tom Douglas and his wife, Jackie Cross (both also of Palace Kitchen and Etta's Seafood), oversee this fun, artsy eatery in the heart of downtown. Red walls, yellow pillars, glass sconces and chandeliers, and upholstered booths create a colorful, playful backdrop for boldly flavored Pacific Northwest cuisine. The daily changing menu offers diners a variety of inventive beef, seafood and poultry dishes. Sample the Washington king salmon with farro, pan-roasted chanterelles and red wine pickled huckleberries. Diners with a sweet tooth can visit the Dahlia Bakery next door for take-home treats.

American, Pacific Northwest. Lunch, dinner. Reservations recommended. Bar. $36-85

★★★EARTH AND OCEAN

W Seattle, 1112 Fourth Ave., Seattle, 206-264-6060; www.earthocean.net

A chic crowd matches this downtown restaurant's hip décor and fusion cuisine. Multicolored mosaic floors and candles decorate the room, and artfully prepared and dishes under the categories of "Earth" and "Ocean" make up the tasting-style menu. Try the roasted pork with lacinato kale and ricotta gnocchi. Located in the W Seattle hotel, this downtown restaurant is also a great people-watching spot.

American, Pacific Northwest. Breakfast, lunch, dinner, Saturday-Sunday brunch. Reservations recommended. Bar. $16-35

★★★EL GAUCHO

2505 First Ave., Seattle, 206-728-1337; www.elgaucho.com

Located just a few minutes from the center of downtown, this swanky, nostalgic restaurant—a former union hall for merchant sailors—is known mainly for its martinis and meat. Order up tableside preparations of Caesar salad, Châteaubriand and bananas Foster, or settle in and check out the nightly piano music. The lively lounge area is good spot for a before- or after-dinner cocktail.

Steak. Dinner, late-night. Reservations recommended. Bar. $36-85

★★★ETTA'S SEAFOOD

2020 Western Ave., Seattle, 206-443-6000; www.tomdouglas.com

This casual seafood house is just half a block from the popular Pike Place Market and is named after the owners' daughter, Loretta. Its large windows overlook the farmers market, which supplies a majority of the fresh ingredients on the menu. The menu ranges from fish and chips to juicy crab cakes and Oregon country beef rib-eye steak.

Seafood. Lunch, dinner, Saturday-Sunday brunch. Reservations recommended. Children's menu. Bar. $36-85

★★★FLYING FISH

2234 First Ave., Seattle, 206-728-8595; www.flyingfishseattle.com

At this Belltown seafood house, you'll find Asian-influenced fish dishes that are artfully presented in a fun and casual environment. The décor is eclectic with glass chandelier "tubes" hanging from a "popcorn" ceiling and various fish sculptures dotting the room. Chef/owner Christine Keff is committed to using fresh, organic ingredients. The fish served here comes directly from Puget Sound, and the organic produce is supplied by a farm in the Green River Valley.

Seafood. Lunch, dinner, late-night. Reservations recommended. Outdoor seating. Bar. $16-35

★★★★THE GEORGIAN

Fairmont Olympic Hotel, 411 University St., Seattle, 206-621-7889; www.fairmont.com

The Fairmont Olympic Hotel houses one of the most acclaimed restaurants in the Pacific Northwest. Executive chef Gavin Stephenson brought his culinary expertise to the restaurant after honing his skills first at the Savoy Hotel in London and then as personal chef to Saudi Prince Alwaleed Bin Talal Alsaud. While expressing a mastery of all plates related to seafood, Stephenson also excels with such dishes as carpaccio of artichokes and spring asparagus, ashed goat cheese and tomato mousseline, filet of Kobe beef topped with shallot and oxtail braisage and double chocolate napoleon.

American, French, Northwest. Breakfast, lunch, dinner. Reservations recommended. Children's menu. Bar. $86 and up

★★★THE HUNT CLUB
Hotel Sorrento, 900 Madison St., Seattle, 206-343-6156; www.hotelsorrento.com

This cozy restaurant located inside the Hotel Sorrento is a popular choice for pre-theater dining thanks to its downtown location. The menu includes dishes made from fresh, local and organic ingredients, such as flat-iron steak with Yukon Gold potatoes and Swiss chard, or Alaskan halibut with local vegetables. Chef Matthew Mina's specialty is pastry and baking, and his seasonal dessert menus are a special treat.

International. Breakfast, lunch, dinner, Saturday-Sunday brunch. Reservations recommended. Children's menu. Bar. $36-85

★★★IL TERRAZZO CARMINE
411 First Ave. S., Seattle, 206-467-7797; www.ilterrazzocarmine.com

This Pioneer Square restaurant serves authentic Italian fare in a classic setting. The menu includes authentic takes on dishes such as osso bucco (served with fettuccine or saffron risotto), ciopinno, and linguine with clam sauce. The desserts and ice cream are made fresh, and the wine list spotlights bottles from Italy's top wine-growing regions.

Italian. Lunch, dinner. Closed Sunday. Reservations recommended. Outdoor seating. Bar. $36-85

★★★LAMPREIA RESTAURANT
2400 First Ave., Seattle, 206-443-3301; www.lampreiarestaurant.com

Not content with serving what many typically identify as Italian food, chef Scott Carsberg takes the highest-quality ingredients and lets them shine in contemporary, visually appealing preparations that carry a slight Italian influence. Fresh fava beans come enveloped by a sheet of squid ink pasta, for example, while pan-seared halibut is served with different preparations of heirloom oranges. Numerous tableside presentations by the charming service staff add a sense of flair to the dining room.

International. Dinner. Closed Sunday-Monday. Reservations recommended. $36-85

★★★LOLA
2000 Fourth Ave., Seattle, 206-441-1430; www.tomdouglas.com

Located in Belltown and adjacent to the Hotel Ändra, this Mediterranean restaurant is sister to the many restaurants helmed by Tom and Jackie Douglas (Dahlia Lounge is just across the street, while Etta's is a downtown favorite). The modern dining room is welcoming with warm brown tones, floor-to-ceiling windows, high-backed booths and hand-painted chandeliers.

The menu includes everything from eight different variations on traditional kebabs (including squid or portobello mushroom) to a unique lamb burger with chickpea fries.

Greek, Mediterranean. Breakfast, lunch, dinner, late-night, Saturday-Sunday brunch. Reservations recommended. Outdoor seating. Children's menu. Bar. $16-35

★★★MADISON PARK CAFÉ

1807 42nd Ave. East, Seattle, 206-324-2626; www.madisonparkcafe.ypguides.net

This French bistro is in a charming residential neighborhood across the street from a beautiful park—lending an atmosphere that's distinctly Parisian. The interior space has a cozy feel with its fireplace, and yellow-washed walls hung with works from local artists. The dinner menu offers French favorites such as onion soup, cassoulet and steak au poivre. There are no reservations taken for brunch, so come early.

French. Dinner, Saturday-Sunday brunch. Closed Monday. Reservations recommended. Outdoor seating. Bar. $16-35

★★★PALACE KITCHEN

2030 Fifth Ave., Seattle, 206-448-2001; www.tomdouglas.com

Located under the monorail at Fifth and Lenora in Belltown, this saloon, owned by Tom and Jackie Douglas, caters to a drinking crowd in search of imaginative rustic food, served late into the night in small-plate portions. A horseshoe-shaped wooden bar is the focal point of the space. Although the menu changes daily, a rotisserie dish prepared over an applewood grill is always available and is a good choice.

American. Dinner, late-night. Reservations recommended. Bar. $36-85

★★★PALISADE

Elliott Bay Marina, 2601 W. Marina Place, Seattle, 206-285-1000; www.palisaderestaurant.com

Palisade is set on the Magnolia Marina with waterfront views of the Seattle skyline and the yachts that fill the harbor. Locals line up for Sunday brunch, which features a sprawling raw bar stocked with fresh shrimp, oysters and crab. At dinner, menu highlights include made-to-order shellfish chowder and fresh local Dungeness crab stuffed with black tiger prawns.

American, seafood. Lunch, dinner, Sunday brunch, late-night. Reservations recommended. Outdoor seating. Children's menu. Bar. $36-85

★★★PALOMINO

1420 Fifth Ave., Seattle, 206-623-1300; www.palomino.com

This attractive restaurant is on the third floor of the City Centre Mall—a great spot for people-watching. Tuscan colors, blown-glass chandeliers and sconces and an open kitchen add to the cozy atmosphere. The menu features Italian-inspired American cuisine, including brick-oven pizzas and Gorgonzola fries.

American, Italian. Lunch, dinner. Reservations recommended. Children's menu. Bar. $36-85

★★★PLACE PIGALLE

81 Pike St., Seattle, 206-624-1756; www.placepigalle-seattle.com

This charming and casual bistro, tucked into Pike Place Market, has great waterfront views and a menu that makes the most of fresh market ingredients.

Sample dishes such as grilled octopus with lavender and fennel sausage, or organic chicken with smoked bacon roulade, and settle in with a glass of one of the many wines sourced from the Pacific Northwest.

American, Pacific Northwest. Lunch, dinner. Closed Sunday. Reservations recommended. Outdoor seating. Bar. $36-85

★★★PONTI SEAFOOD GRILL
3014 Third Ave. N., Seattle, 206-284-3000; www.pontiseafoodgrill.com

A charming courtyard with a terra cotta fountain is at the entrance of Ponti Seafood Grill. Dine on the outside patio, which has views of Lake Union, or inside the cozy dining room. Menu offerings include house-smoked Alaskan black cod, Ponti shellfish paella and Parmesan and spinach-stuffed chicken.

Seafood. Lunch (December only), dinner. Reservations recommended. Outdoor seating. Children's menu. Bar. $16-35

★★★RAY'S BOATHOUSE
6049 Seaview Ave. N.W., Seattle, 206-789-3770; www.rays.com

Located in quaint Ballard, this upscale yet casual seafood house is situated about 20 minutes from downtown. Dine on fresh Alaskan red king crab legs or smoked sablefish on the outside deck (with warm blankets provided by Ray's), or in the waterfront dining room, and watch the boats pass as they leave the Ballard Locks on the way to Elliott Bay and the Pacific Ocean.

American, seafood. Dinner. Reservations recommended. Outdoor seating. Children's menu. Bar. $36-85

★★★★ROVER'S
2808 E. Madison St., Seattle, 206-325-7442; www.rovers-seattle.com

A small white clapboard cottage in Madison Park houses Rover's, an intimate restaurant serving innovative contemporary cuisine. Thierry Rautureau, the chef and owner, stays true to the regional ingredients of the Northwest while paying homage to precise French technique. Take the Wagyu beef with corn flan and huckleberry gastrique or the foie gras mousse with citrus clafouti, honey and sauternes crème fraîche. Presented like works of art, the portions are perfect in size, taste and appearance. The restaurant offers five- and eight-course tasting menus in addition to a five-course vegetarian menu; an à la carte menu is also available.

Contemporary American, Pacific Northwest. Lunch (Friday only), dinner. Closed Sunday-Monday. Reservations recommended. $86 and up

★★★RUTH'S CHRIS STEAK HOUSE
727 Pine St., Seattle, 206-624-8524, 800-544-0808; www.ruthschris.com

Aged prime Midwestern beef is broiled to order and served on a heated plate, sizzling in butter at this outpost of the national steak house chain. Ample portions of classic sides such as creamed spinach and fresh asparagus with hollandaise accompany the meats. Choose from seven different preparations of spuds, from a one-pound baked potato to au gratin potatoes with cream sauce and topped with cheese.

Steak. Breakfast, lunch, dinner. Reservations recommended. Children's menu. Bar. $36-85

★★★SAZERAC

Hotel Monaco, 1101 Fourth Ave., Seattle, 206-624-7755; www.sazeracrestaurant.com

Sazerac, adjacent to the Hotel Monaco, serves reliable, satisfying, Southern-inspired food, like wood-fired pizzas dotted with hunks of andouille sausage or more upscale fare like cider-jalapeño-glazed pork back ribs. The interior features a vibrant, eclectic décor that's a hit with the happy-hour crowd. Dine at the counter seating of the rotisserie grill and pizza oven or at tables or booths.

Southern. Breakfast, lunch, dinner, late-night, Saturday-Sunday brunch. Reservations recommended. Outdoor seating. Children's menu. Bar. $16-35

★★★SHUCKERS

Fairmont Olympic Hotel, 411 University St., Seattle, 206-621-1984; www.fairmont.com

This casual pub, with clubby, traditional décor, is inside the Fairmont Olympic Hotel. The menu features hearty dishes such as applewood-smoked salmon and garlic-and-rosemary-roasted Dungeness crab with roasted potatoes. Shuckers earned its rep from its wide selection of oysters—13 at last count. They can be prepared a myriad of ways, including house-smoked, baked, Olympic, Rockefeller, Kilpatrick, Provençal, pan-fried, barbecue or half-shell.

Seafood. Lunch, dinner. Reservations recommended. Children's menu. Bar. $36-85

★★★SZMANIA'S MAGNOLIA

3321 W. McGraw St., Seattle, 206-284-7305; www.szmanias.com

Guests at this favorite neighborhood hangout can always see the German chef at work in the open kitchen, which features counter seating. A one-of-a-kind glass mural is at the front of the restaurant, and paintings by a local artist hang throughout. The bistro menu draws from whatever is fresh and seasonal, evidenced in dishes such as wild salmon with corn barley risotto and wilted greens.

German. Lunch (Friday), dinner. Closed Monday. Reservations recommended. Children's menu. Bar. $16-35

★★★TAVOLÀTA

2323 Second Ave., Seattle, 206-838-8008; www.tavolata.com

An industrial-chic vibe draws a stylish crowd to chef Ethan Stowell's Belltown bistro, where diners gather around the centerpiece 30-foot-long communal table made of reclaimed wood to sample creative Italian dishes such as olive oil-poached halibut with fingerling potato chips and prosecco vinaigrette. The handmade pastas are the stars of the menu, including spicy spaghetti with anchovies, chili, roasted peppers and hazelnuts, or linguine with local clams.

Italian. Dinner. Bar. $36-85

★★★TULIO RISTORANTE

Hotel Vintage Park, 1100 Fifth Ave., Seattle, 206-624-5500; www.tulio.com

This downtown trattoria is adjacent to the Hotel Vintage Park, and offers straightforward Italian dishes made from fresh organic ingredients. Menu standouts include pappardelle with fava beans, pancetta, ricotta salata and mint, and whole roasted branzino with caramelized fennel, olives and lemon.

Italian. Breakfast, lunch, dinner. Reservations recommended. Outdoor seating. Children's menu. Bar. $36-85

HIGHLIGHT

THE BUZZ ON SEATTLE'S CAFFEINE CULTURE

For most of the 20th century, Seattle was regarded as a great place to partake in fresh fish, not fresh coffee. The emergence of Seattle's caffeine scene corresponded with the spectacular success of a local company bearing a now familiar name, Starbucks. Founded in 1971, **Starbucks'** first coffeehouse opened in the city's **Pike Place Market**. Not until the mid-1980s, when Starbucks employee Howard Schultz convinced the company's founders to develop a coffee bar culture similar to that found in Milan's espresso bars, did Starbucks' fortunes take off. It soon became a cultural and commercial phenomenon in Seattle and around the globe. Attempting to take advantage of the coffee craze, the likes of **Seattle's Best Coffee** and **Tully's** opened numerous Seattle locations, and now it's almost impossible to walk a city block without passing a franchise coffeehouse.

To appreciate Seattle's coffee culture fully, you should visit a few of the city's many independent shops, one of the best being **Espresso Vivace Roasteria** (*901 E. Denny Way; www.espressovivace.com*). Situated on Capitol Hill near the Seattle Center, Espresso Vivace has made espresso preparation an art form, having spent 15 years perfecting the roasting process for its signature beverage. Espresso Vivace even offers an intensive three-day espresso preparation course.

Artists like to gather downtown at the stylish and hip **Zeitgeist Coffee** (*171 S. Jackson St.; www.zeitgeistcoffee.com*). Zeitgeist is particularly crowded on the first Thursday of each month, when the art galleries in and around Pioneer Square stay open late and hundreds of art lovers congregate in the area. Coffee is not the only thing on the menu; Zeitgeist also serves fresh pastries and grilled sandwiches.

Visitors to the Queen Anne neighborhood should stop by **Uptown Espresso** (*525 Queen Anne Ave. N.; www.uptownespresso.net*). Weekends are particularly crowded at this casual coffeehouse situated at the bottom of Queen Anne Hill. Uptown Espresso's velvet foam lattes are a local favorite. The coffeehouse features vintage décor and the artwork of local painters.

★★★WILD GINGER

1401 Third Ave., Seattle, 206-623-4450; www.wildginger.net

Housed in a landmark 1926 building, this long-standing restaurant serves creative Asian fusion cuisine in a streamlined, contemporary dining room. The satay bar features more than a dozen variations on this classic Asian snack, while the dinner menu has riffs on panang beef curry, kung pao chicken and black pepper scallops. An extensive vegetarian menu goes beyond tofu to spotlight fresh, locally sourced vegetables served in curries and noodle dishes.

Pan-Asian. Lunch, dinner, late-night. Reservations recommended. Bar. $36-85

RECOMMENDED

CAFÉ LAGO

2305 24th Ave. E., Seattle, 206-329-8005; www.cafelago.com

This Montlake neighborhood Italian trattoria takes its cuisine seriously, making fresh pasta every morning. Don't miss the signature lasagna, one of the best in town, with its delicate layers of thin pasta, ricotta, béchamel and tomato sauce. There's also a tempting list of appetizers, from the pomodori al forno, San Marzano tomatoes slow-roasted until they caramelize and served with goat cheese and crostini, to the antipasti plate teeming with eggplant, bruschetta, mozzarella, capicola and more.

Italian. Dinner. Children's menu. Bar. $36-85

IL BISTRO

93A Pike St., Seattle, 206-682-3049; www.ilbistro.net

This popular spot is nestled underneath Pike Place Market, where the chef regularly shops for ingredients for that evening's traditional Italian meals. Sample the fig-and-Gorgonzola-stuffed ravioli in a hazelnut cream sauce, or the cioppino with Dungeness crab, white prawns, mussels, calamari and clams in a tomato broth. The great daily happy hour is a big draw: goat cheese and other crostini go for only $2.95, pasta dishes like rigatoni Bolognese are $3.95, and glasses of wine are only $3.

Italian. Dinner, late-night. Reservations recommended. Outdoor seating. Bar. $36-85

MAXIMILIEN FRENCH CAFÉ

81A Pike St., Seattle, 206-682-7270; www.maximilienrestaurant.com

The reason to dine here are the beautiful views of the Puget Sound, Elliott Bay and the Olympic Mountains from the restaurant's big-picture windows. Located in Pike Place Market, Maximilien is at a central spot for tourists. The food isn't an afterthought; try pan-seared beef tenderloin doused in a truffle and Armagnac sauce. Or come by during the Monday-to-Saturday happy hour, which features $2.95 appetizers like steamed mussels and goat cheese mousse as well as cheap specialty drinks like $4 martinis and $5 absinthes.

French. Lunch, dinner. Sunday brunch. Reservations recommended. Children's menu. Bar. $36-85

THE PINK DOOR

1919 Post Alley, Seattle, 206-443-3241; www.thepinkdoor.net

Dining at the Pink Door is quite the experience, and not only because of comfy Italian dishes like pappardelle ragu Bolognese or spicy fennel sausages atop polenta. The restaurant is a cabaret, with a trapeze artist contorting herself 20 feet in the air, tarot readings, tap-dancing saxophone players and risqué burlesque shows. It's like dinner and a show wrapped up all in one.

American, Italian. Lunch, dinner, late-night. Reservations recommended. Outdoor seating. Bar. $16-35

QUEEN CITY GRILL

2201 First Ave., Seattle, 206-443-0975; www.queencitygrill.com

The brick and dark-wood-filled dining room with high-backed wooden booths and soft lighting creates a cozy setting that's perfect for a slab of juicy steak or the braised short ribs. But the house specialty is the fish, like the Northwest halibut with tomato beurre blanc and a paprika aioli drizzle. Whatever you choose, pair it with a selection from the lengthy wine list.

Seafood, steak. Dinner. Reservations recommended. Outdoor seating. Bar. $16-35

SERAFINA

2043 Eastlake Ave. E., Seattle, 206-323-0807; www.serafinaseattle.com

The ochre walls in this neighborhood Italian restaurant are supposed to evoke the Tuscan countryside. But the menu does that job quite nicely, with penne and veal meatballs covered in a tomato sauce studded with green olives and topped with ricotta salata, or thin slices of eggplant rolled with ricotta, basil and Parmesan. The Sunday jazz brunch is a must; it's the only live jazz brunch in the city. Plus, it offers creative Italian takes on typical brunch items, like baskets of Black Forest ham filled with polenta, mushrooms and poached eggs.

Italian. Lunch, dinner, late-night, Sunday brunch. Reservations recommended. Outdoor seating. Children's menu. Bar. $16-35

SPAS

★★★★SPA AT FOUR SEASONS SEATTLE

Four Seasons Seattle, 99 Union St., Seattle, 206-749-7000; www.fourseasons.com

This spa inside the Four Seasons Seattle is a sybaritic, streamlined retreat that offers more than just traditional spa services. Whether you book an emerald rain massage (a massage that begins with drops of essential oils that simulate rain and progresses to bodywork designed to soothe the spine) or rejuvenating facial, you can use the spa's extensive relaxation lounge, eucalyptus steam room, sauna and rain showers for as long as you like. Settle in for a pampering pedicure and try one of the "spa-tinis," a nonalcoholic concoction that makes the experience even more of a treat. Or book the couples' room for your treatment, which comes complete with views of the Puget Sound, a private soaking tub and a rain shower.

WHERE TO SHOP

ALDERWOOD MALL

3000 184th St. S.W., Lynnwood, 425-771-1211; www.alderwoodmall.com

The largest shopping center in north Seattle, the Alderwood Mall is a retail and entertainment destination with shops in an indoor village and on outdoor terraces, as well as a 16-screen movie theater. Of the 120-plus stores, Alderwood's anchors include Nordstrom and Macy's. Other shops include White House/Black Market, Helly Hansen, Swarovski, Gap, Sephora, Pottery Barn, L'Occitane and New Balance.

Monday-Saturday 10 a.m.-9 p.m., Sunday 10 a.m.-7 p.m.

DOWNTOWN SHOPPING DISTRICT

First to Seventh avenues and Madison and Pine streets, Seattle, www.downtownseattle.com

Prime window-shopping corridors include First and Second avenues, populated by fashionable boutiques, upscale galleries and a few quirky curiosities to boot, and Fifth and Sixth Avenues, brimming with jewelers, kitchen stores and clothing stores ranging from small boutiques to mega-sized versions of national staples. There are also two malls on Pine Street: Westlake (between Fourth and Fifth avenues), a fairly typical enclosed shopping center, and the ritzy Pacific Place Mall, downtown Seattle's newest (and most stylish) retail destination. The centerpiece of the whole shopping district is Nordstrom (500 Pine St.), the flagship of the Seattle-based department store chain.

UNIVERSITY VILLAGE SHOPPING
45th Street N.E., Seattle, 206-523-0622; www.uvillage.com

Located near the University of Washington campus in northeast Seattle, University Village has a rare balance of national and local establishments. Stores range from Barnes & Noble to Crate & Barrel, with plenty of dining options.

OLYMPIC PENINSULA

The Olympic Peninsula's main attraction is Olympic National Park and Olympic National Forest, but along the coast are a few charming small towns. Sitting atop the Olympic Peninsula, Port Angeles has the Olympic Mountains at its back and the Juan de Fuca Strait at its shoreline; just 17 miles across the strait is Victoria, British Columbia. Ediz Hook, a sandspit, protects the harbor and helps make it the first American port of entry for ships coming to Puget Sound from all parts of the Pacific. Located on the Quimper Peninsula at the northeast corner of the Olympic Peninsula, Port Townsend was once a busy port city served by sailing vessels and sternwheelers. Today Port Townsend is a paper mill town with boat building and farming.

WHAT TO SEE

PORT ANGELES
JOYCE DEPOT MUSEUM
16 miles west of Port Angeles on Highway 112, 360-928-3568; www.joycewa.com

The museum is in a former railroad station. You can browse through general store items from the 1920s through the 1940s, logging equipment and historical railroad tools. Old photos of the area have been preserved, as well as articles from the former City of Port Crescent newspaper.

JOYCE GENERAL STORE
16 miles west of Port Angeles on Highway 112, 360-928-3568; www.joycewa.com

Built in the early 1900s, the Joyce General Store still has the original false front, beaded ceiling, oiled wood floors and fixtures. Much of the interior came from the Markham House Hotel, which stood in the now-extinct town of Port Crescent. Joyce's namesake, Joe Joyce, transported much of what was used to build the store from Port Crescent (now Crescent Bay) to its present location. The store has been in the same family for more than 48 years.

HIGHLIGHT

WHAT IS THE BEST WAY TO EXPLORE NATURE?

Head to Olympic National Park and Forest. In these 1,442 square miles of rugged wilderness are such contrasts as the wettest climate in the contiguous United States (averaging 140-167 inches of precipitation a year) and one of the driest. There are also seascapes and snow-cloaked peaks, glaciers and rain forests, elk and seals. With Olympic National Forest, much private land and several Native American reservations, the national park occupies the Olympic Peninsula due west of Seattle and Puget Sound.

In 1774, the Spanish explorer Juan Perez was the first European to spot the Olympic Mountains. However, the first major western land exploration did not take place until more than a century later. Since then, generations of adventurous tourists have rediscovered Mount Olympus, the highest peak (7,965 feet), several other 7,000-foot peaks and hundreds of ridges and crests between 5,000 and 6,000 feet high. The architects of these ruggedly contoured mountains are glaciers, which have etched these heights for thousands of years. About 60 glaciers are still actively eroding these mountains; the largest three are on Mount Olympus.

From approximately November through March, the west side of the park is soaked with rain and mist, while the northeast side is the driest area on the West Coast except Southern California. The yearly deluge creates a rain forest in the western valleys of the park. Here Sitka spruce, western hemlock, Douglas fir and western red cedar grow to heights of 250 feet with 8-foot diameters. Mosses carpet the forest floor and climb tree trunks. Club moss drips from the branches.

Some 50 species of mammals inhabit this wilderness, including several thousand elk, Olympic marmots, black-tailed deer and black bears. On the park's 60-mile strip of Pacific coastline wilderness, deer, bears, raccoons and skunks can be seen; seals sun on the offshore rocks or plow through the water beyond the breakers. Mountain and lowland lakes sparkle everywhere; Lake Crescent is among the largest. Some roads are closed in winter.

MERRILL AND RING TREE FARM INTERPRETIVE TOUR

Highway 112, Port Angeles, 800-998-2382; www.nps.gov

Merrill and Ring Tree Farm and Forestry Trail offers self-guided tours. Along the trail are interpretive resources explaining resource management and reforestation, providing an opportunity to educate visitors about the clear-cuts along the SR 112 corridor. The Merrill and Ring Tree Farm also offers a bit of history, as the site still has the original cabins built by Merrill and Ring to house its loggers in the early 1900s.

WHERE TO STAY

PORT LUDLOW

★★★INN AT PORT LUDLOW

1 Heron Road, Port Ludlow, 360-437-7000, 877-805-0868; www.portludlowresort.com

This inn, located on the shores of the Olympic Peninsula, offers updated rooms with duvet-topped beds and working fireplaces. Built to resemble an estate in Maine, the inn offers free wireless access and can arrange in-room spa services such as massages and facials.

39 rooms. Restaurant. Complimentary breakfast. $151-250

RECOMMENDED

PORT ANGELES

DOMAINE MADELEINE

146 Wildflower Lane, Port Angeles, 360-457-4174, 888-811-8376; www.domainemadeleine.com

The guest rooms at this intimate bed and breakfast are individually decorated. The grounds offer nice views of Victoria, British Columbia and the San Juan Islands. The rooms have panoramic views, fireplaces and two-person Jacuzzis.

5 rooms. Complimentary breakfast. No children under 12. $151-250

RED LION HOTEL

221 N. Lincoln St., Port Angeles, 360-452-9215, 800-733-5466; www.redlion.com

This comfortable hotel overlooking the Port Angeles harbor provides all of the vacation amenities a family needs just outside Olympic National Park and only a block from downtown Port Angeles. The hotel offers free shuttle service to the airport, as well as a nearby casino. If you're in the mood for crab, the onsite restaurant is the place to feast.

186 rooms. Restaurant, bar. Business center. Fitness center. Pool. Pets accepted. $61-150

TUDOR INN BED & BREAKFAST

1108 S. Oak St., Port Angeles, 360-452-3138, 866-286-2224; www.tudorinn.com

This Tudor-style bed and breakfast offers a historical location from which to enjoy the Pacific Northwest. You can relax in the living room, the wood-burning fireplace-equipped library or the inn's natural surroundings while enjoying the view of the Strait of Juan de Fuca. Breakfast, a spread of homemade pastries, egg dishes and fruit, is served by candlelight each morning.

5 rooms. Complimentary breakfast. No children under 12. $61-150

SOL DUC HOT SPRINGS RESORT

12076 Sol Duc Hot Springs Road, Port Angeles, 360-327-3583, 866-476-5382; www.visitsolduc.com

This cozy cabin resort boasts reasonable rates, three hot spring pools and a freshwater pool, and makes a convenient base for hiking, fishing, beachcombing and wildlife watching. To help you get away from it all, there are no phones or TVs in the rooms.

32 rooms. Closed late October-late March. Restaurants. Complimentary breakfast. Pool. Pets accepted. $61-150

WHAT ARE THE BEST PLACES TO ENJOY A MEAL?

C'est Si Bon:
Enjoy authentic Gallic cuisine at this eclectic dining room.

The Fireside:
Cozy up by the fireplace at this upscale but casual restaurant where you can sample local dishes such as fresh steamed mussels or just-shucked oysters.

PORT TOWNSEND

JAMES HOUSE

1238 Washington St., Port Townsend, 800-385-1238; www.jameshouse.com

Built in 1889, this grand Victorian mansion sits on a bluff overlooking Puget Sound and mountains. Rooms feature fine woodwork, furnishings and some have fireplaces.

12 rooms. Complimentary breakfast. No children under 12. $61-150

WHERE TO EAT

PORT ANGELES

★★★C'EST SI BON

23 Cedar Park Road, Port Angeles, 360-452-8888; www.cestsibon-frenchcuisine.com

Look past the somewhat fussy pink and green dining room to take in the thing that most come to this French restaurant for: the authentic Gallic cuisine. The menu includes classic dishes such as roasted rack of lamb with fresh herbs, French onion soup and peppercorn steak.

French. Dinner. Closed Monday. Reservations recommended. Outdoor seating. Bar. $36-85

★★★TOGA'S INTERNATIONAL CUISINE

122 W. Lauridsen Blvd., Port Angeles, 360-452-1952

The menu at this quaint, intimate restaurant shows influences from all over Europe while highlighting ingredients unique to the Pacific Northwest. The dining room is located in a remodeled 1943 home and boasts beautiful views of the Olympic Mountain Range. The carrot soup (yes, carrot soup) wins raves.

International. Dinner. Closed Sunday-Monday; September. Reservations recommended. Outdoor seating. Children's menu. Bar. $16-35

PORT LUDLOW

★★★THE FIRESIDE

1 Heron Road, Port Ludlow, 360-437-7000, 877-805-0868; www.portludlowresort.com

Not surprisingly, a huge double-sided fireplace is the focal point of this upscale but casual restaurant. Settle in and sample local dishes such as fresh steamed mussels or just-shucked oysters, and finish with entrées such as wild king salmon with leek and mushroom risotto.

Seafood. Dinner. Reservations recommended. Outdoor seating. Children's menu. Bar. $16-35

PORT TOWNSEND
★★★CASTLE KEY
Seventh and Sheridan streets, Port Townsend, 360-385-5750, 800-732-1281;
www.manresacastle.com

This century-old, European-inspired castle houses a casual dining room with spectacular views of the Olympic and Cascade Mountains. Dishes include pub classics such as panko-breaded halibut and chips, and peppercorn steak.
American. Dinner, Sunday brunch. Closed Monday. Reservation recommended. Bar. $16-35

RECOMMENDED

PORT ANGELES
BELLA ITALIA
118 E. First St., Port Angeles, 360-457-5442; www.bellaitaliapa.com

Twihards may recall that this restaurant is where Bella and Edward had their first date. You can mimic Bella and order the mushroom ravioli, or you can branch out and order the espresso-smoked duck breast or the cioppino seafood stew. One perk of not being Bella: You are old enough to order from the excellent wine list.
Italian. Dinner. Reservations recommended. Children's menu. Bar. $16-35

BUSHWHACKER
1527 E. First St., Port Angeles, 360-457-4113; www.bushwhackerpa.com

This is a traditional seafood restaurant in one of the best places for it. Order the cod Dungeness, baked filets stuffed with a crab-shrimp mixture and slathered with hollandaise sauce. Catering to vacationing families, the Bushwacker is a favorite of return travelers to the peninsula.
Seafood. Dinner. Bar. Children's menu. $16-35

SAN JUAN ISLANDS AND NORTHWEST WASHINGTON

The San Juan archipelago includes 700 islands and reefs. The islands are a popular local spot for a weekend getaway, though only four are accessible by ferry—Lopez, Orcas, San Juan and Shaw. San Juan Island was the last place the British flag flew within the territorial United States. On the eastern shore, Friday Harbor, the most westerly stop in the United States on San Juan Islands ferry tour, is the county seat of San Juan. It serves as a base for the salmon fleet and is the major commercial center of the islands. To access the islands, you have to head to Anacortes, in nearby Northwest Washington at the northwest tip of Fidalgo Island, to board the San Juan Islands ferries. You could also opt to travel by seaplane to reach these islands with rocky and sandy shores.

HIGHLIGHT

WHAT ARE THE TOP THINGS TO DO?

SEE THE SAN JUAN ISLANDS

Hop on a ferry from Anacortes to these beautiful and historic islands. You'll find secluded coves, giant trees, freshwater lakes, and fishing camps.

ENJOY BIRCH BAY STATE PARK

Head to these 190 acres, set up camp and enjoy picnicking, swimming, scuba diving, fishing, and more.

VISIT MOUNT BAKER-SNOQUALMIE NATIONAL FOREST

Head to this scenic destination to go skiing and snowboarding.

WHAT TO SEE

ANACORTES

DECEPTION PASS STATE PARK

41229 Highway 20, Anacortes, 360-675-2417; www.parks.wa.gov

More than 4,100 acres of sheltered bays and deep old-growth forests with fjord-like shoreline, Deception Pass offers four lakes that provide ample opportunities for swimming, scuba diving, fishing, clamming and boating. More than 170 varieties of feathered friends make this a popular bird-watching spot. You'll also find 38 miles of hiking trails, some accessible for the disabled.

Summer, 6:30 a.m.-dusk; winter, 8 a.m.-dusk.

SAN JUAN ISLANDS TRIP

360-293-3832

Ferries leave several times daily for Lopez Island, Shaw Island, Orcas Island, Friday Harbor and Sidney, British Columbia. Leave your car at the dock in Anacortes, or take your vehicle with you and disembark at any point and explore from paved roads.

SWINOMISH NORTHERN LIGHTS CASINO

12885 Casino Drive, Anacortes, 360-293-2691; www.swinomishcasino.com

The largest Washington casino north of Seattle has tables, machines, off-track betting and a large poker room. Lower-key gamblers can hit the bingo hall or keno lounge. The Starlight Lounge features live comedy; you'll also find pro boxing, musical entertainment and a family-style restaurant with both buffets and table service. Daily.

WASHINGTON PARK

6300 Sunset Ave., Anacortes, 360-293-1927; www.anacortes.org

With more than 100 species of birds, this 220-acre park is popular with bird-watchers; it also draws whale-watchers in season.

BELLINGHAM

MOUNT BAKER-SNOQUALMIE NATIONAL FOREST

2930 Wetmore Ave., Everett, 425-783-6000, 800-627-0062; www.fs.fed.us

The Mount Baker and Snoqualmie national forests were combined under a single forest supervisor in July 1974. Divided into five ranger districts, the combined forest encompasses nearly 2 million acres. The Snoqualmie section lies east and southeast of Seattle; the Mount Baker section lies east on Highway 542 and includes the Mount Baker Ski Area. The forest extends from the Canadian border south to Mount Rainier National Park and includes rugged mountains and woodlands on the western slopes of the Cascades, the western portions of the Glacier Peak and Alpine Lakes. Attractions include seven commercial ski areas and 1,440 miles of hiking trails. Mount Baker rises 10,778 feet in the north, forming a center for recreation all year, famous for deep-powder skiing and snowboarding. Snoqualmie Pass (via Interstate 90) and Stevens Pass (via Highway 2) provide year-round access to popular scenic destinations; Baker Lake offers excellent boating and fishing.

SEHOME HILL ARBORETUM

25th Street and McDonald Parkway, Bellingham, 360-676-6985; www.ac.wwu.edu

The 180-acre native plant preserve contains hiking and interpretive trails and scenic views of the city, Puget Sound, the San Juan Islands and mountains from an observation tower.

BLAINE

BIRCH BAY STATE PARK

5105 Helwig Road, Blaine, 360-371-2800; www.parks.wa.gov

Approximately 190 acres, Birch Bay features swimming, scuba diving, fishing, crabbing, clamming, picnicking and camping.

Daily, reservations advised Memorial Day-Labor Day.

SEMIAHMOO PARK

9261 Semiahmoo Parkway, Blaine, 360-733-2900; www.co.whatcom.wa.us

A cannery once located on this 1.5-mile-long spit was the last port of call for Alaskan fishing boats on Puget Sound. Restored buildings now house a museum, gallery and gift shop.

June-mid-September, Saturday and Sunday afternoons.

SAN JUAN ISLANDS

SAN JUAN ISLANDS

www.guidetosanjuans.com

These 172 islands nestled between the northwest corner of Washington and Vancouver Island compose a beautiful and historic area. Secluded coves, giant trees, freshwater lakes, fishing camps, modest motels, numerous bed and breakfasts, and plush resorts characterize the four major islands. More than 500 miles of paved or gravel roads swing through virgin woodlands and along lovely shorelines. The islands are accessible by ferry from Anacortes.

WHALE MUSEUM
62 First St. N., Friday Harbor, 360-378-4710; www.whale-museum.org

Art and science exhibits document the lives of whales and porpoises in this area. *Daily.*

WHERE TO STAY

BELLINGHAM
★★★THE CHRYSALIS INN & SPA
804 10th St., Bellingham, 360-756-1005, 888-808-0005; www.thechrysalisinn.com

This waterfront inn has rooms decorated in streamlined, contemporary Pacific Northwest style, with gas fireplaces, four-poster beds and window seats overlooking the water. The onsite spa offers a full menu of treatments, while the restaurant, Fino Wine Bar, is a casual spot to take in the views and nosh on fresh seasonal dishes such as pan-seared scallops with zucchini risotto.

43 rooms. Restaurant, bar. Spa. $151-250

★★★HOTEL BELLWETHER
1 Bellwether Way, Bellingham, 360-392-3100, 877-411-1200; www.hotelbellwether.com

This waterfront hotel features an onsite spa, the Harborside Bistro and access to the Coast Guard-operated Pacific Sea Taxi. Mahogany-filled rooms are comfortable and updated with luxury linens, DVD players, wireless Internet and deep soaking tubs. Check out the water view from your private balcony.

66 rooms. Restaurant, bar. Pets accepted. $151-250

BLAINE
★★★RESORT SEMIAHMOO
9565 Semiahmoo Parkway, Blaine, 360-318-2000, 800-770-7992; www.semiahmoo.com

This cottage-style resort, located on a wildlife preserve at the tip of a peninsula stretching into Puget Sound, enjoys one of the most scenic spots in the state. Rooms with blond wood furnishings and fireplaces offer views of snow-capped peaks, the Gulf Islands, Drayton Harbor or Semiahmoo Bay. Golf, water activities and a terrific spa compete for attention.

198 rooms. Restaurant, bar. Spa. Pool. Pets accepted. Golf. Tennis. $61-150

SAN JUAN ISLANDS
★★★ROSARIO RESORT
1400 Rosario Road, Eastsound, 360-376-2222, 800-562-8820; www.rosarioresort.com

Visitors land directly in front of the resort, located at the tip of Orcas Island in Washington's picturesque San Juan Islands, via a thrilling and scenic seaplane ride (less adventurous types may opt for the ferry). This resort is a veritable Eden for outdoor enthusiasts—activities range from whale-watching and sea kayaking to nature hikes in Moran State Park. Back at the resort, the Avanyu Spa has a full menu of treatments, and the four restaurants range from casual to fine dining. A recent renovation gave the rooms a smart new look with duvet-topped beds.

116 rooms. Restaurant, bar. Fitness center. Pool. Spa. $151-250

SPOKANE
★★★THE DAVENPORT HOTEL AND TOWER
10 S. Post St., Spokane, 509-455-8888, 800-899-1482;
www.thedavenporthotel.com

This grand downtown hotel opened in 1914 and has been restored it to its original grandeur. Guest rooms feature hand-carved mahogany furniture, imported Irish linens (made by the same company that supplied the hotel when it first opened) and travertine marble bathrooms with spacious walk-in showers. Some suites and deluxe rooms have fireplaces, wet bars and jetted tubs. The Palm Court Grill serves European cuisine with some Asian touches, while the Peacock Room serves cocktails. The hotel also offers a candy shop, a flower shop, an art gallery and an onsite spa.

283 rooms. Restaurant, bar. Fitness center. Pool. Spa. Pets accepted. $151-250

★★★HOTEL LUSSO
808 W. Sprague Ave., Spokane, 509-747-9750;
www.hotellusso.com

Lusso means "luxury" in Italian and that's what you see when you stay here. This Italian Renaissance building is in downtown Spokane, close to shops, restaurants and entertainment. The interior is decorated with marble, hardwood and warm Mediterranean colors, and guest rooms are comfortably appointed. The Cavallino Lounge is a good spot for an after-dinner drink.

48 rooms. Complimentary breakfast. Restaurant, bar. $151-250

RECOMMENDED

SAN JUAN ISLANDS
BIRD ROCK HOTEL
35 First St., Friday Harbor, 360-378-5848, 800-352-2632;
www.birdrockhotel.com

Located a short walk from this bed and breakfast are Friday Harbor's waterfront, town shops and restaurants. The property features limited-edition wildlife art, soundproof rooms and a large parlor. Take a swim in the heated indoor pool or borrow one of the free beach bikes and go explore the island.

15 rooms. Complimentary breakfast. Fitness center. Pool. $151-250

WHICH SPOKANE HOTEL HAS THE MOST HISTORICAL SIGNIFICANCE?

The Davenport Hotel and Tower:
This grand downtown hotel opened in 1914 and has been restored it to its original grandeur. When it opened, it was the first hotel with air conditioning and housekeeping carts.

WHICH SPOKANE RESTAURANT USES SEASONAL, SUSTAINABLE INGREDIENTS?

Luna:
With a commitment to going "green," Luna uses seasonal ingredients from its own garden as well as sustainable locally-grown foods. Everything is made in house, including bread and desserts.

TURTLEBACK FARM INN

1981 Crow Valley Road, Eastsound, 360-376-4914, 800-376-4914; www.turtlebackinn.com

The inn is a country farmhouse on Orcas Island overlooking the clear waters of the Puget Sound. It features spacious guest rooms decorated with antiques and contemporary pieces. Fine dining and unique shopping are nearby.

11 rooms. Complimentary breakfast. $151-250

WHERE TO EAT

SAN JUAN ISLANDS

★★★CHRISTINA'S

310 Main St., Eastsound, 360-376-4904; www.christinas.net

The cozy dining room at this bistro is a comfortable setting to sample locally sourced, seasonal Northwest cuisine. Entrées include pan-roasted chicken with chorizo bread pudding, and pan-seared cod with Italian farro. The bar serves a menu of small plates and creative cocktails.

Pacific Northwest. Dinner. Closed first three weeks in November. Reservations recommended. Outdoor seating. Children's menu. Bar. $36-85

SPOKANE

★★★LUNA

5620 S. Perry St., Spokane, 509-448-2383; www.lunaspokane.com

Located on Spokane's South Hill and a 10-minute drive from downtown, this Mediterranean restaurant is worth the drive. Locals come for breakfast, lunch, dinner and brunch, served in a warm and eclectic interior. The open kitchen provides views of entrées such as halibut with roasted orzo being made from scratch—everything here is, from the breads to the desserts.

Mediterranean. Breakfast, lunch, dinner, brunch. Reservations recommended. Outdoor seating. Children's menu. Bar. $36-85

★★★THE PALM COURT GRILL

Davenport Hotel, 10 S. Post St., Spokane, 509-789-6848, 800-899-1482; www.thedavenporthotel.com

This upscale restaurant, located inside the Davenport Hotel, serves steaks and seafood in elegant setting. Entrées include everything from cedar plank salmon to beef tenderloin with béarnaise sauce.

American. Breakfast, lunch, dinner, brunch. Reservations recommended. Children's menu. Bar. $16-35

PUGET SOUND

The Puget Sound region is named after the body of water that extends from the Pacific Ocean about 80 miles south into Washington. The area is home to the state capital, Olympia. As though inspired by the natural beauty that surrounds it—Mount Rainier and the Olympic Mountains on the skyline and Puget Sound at its doorstep—Washington's capital city is a carefully groomed, park-like community. Although concentrating on the business of government, Olympia also serves tourists and the needs of nearby military installations.

Also in the region is Redmond, which experienced dramatic change over the course of the 20th century, evolving from a sleepy logging town to a high-tech hub. The transformation was driven by the exponential growth of Microsoft, which is headquartered here. Situated at the northern tip of Lake Sammamish, Redmond has a public park system that covers 1,350 acres and more than 25 miles of trails. A wide variety of shops and restaurants can be found at Redmond Town Center.

In its gemlike setting on Puget Sound, midway between Seattle and Olympia, Tacoma is the nearest metropolitan center to Mount Rainier National Park, which makes it a good base for trips to Olympic National Park and Puget Sound.

The place that has won the region the most accolades is small-town Woodinville, which sits at the northern end of the Sammamish River Valley and is about 17 miles from downtown Seattle. The wine-making area hosts more than 35 of the state's 400-some wineries, making this a destination for oenophiles everywhere.

WHAT TO SEE

AUBURN
AUBURN GOLF COURSE
29630 Green River Road, Auburn, 253-833-2350; www.auburngolf.org

This excellent 18-hole public course abuts the Green River in Auburn, about 25 miles southeast of downtown Seattle. Well known for its lush vegetation and challenging greens, the course is alternately flat (the front nine) and hilly (after the turn). It is widely regarded as one of the best golf venues in the state and is accordingly crowded on weekends.

EMERALD DOWNS
2300 Emerald Downs Drive, Auburn, 253-288-7000; www.emdowns.com

The only live thoroughbred horse racing venue in the Seattle area, Emerald Downs features a full slate of races from spring to late summer. The esteemed Longacres Mile, an area tradition since the 1930s with an ever-growing purse, is the schedule's highlight, held in August. Built in 1996, the grandstand is thoroughly modern, with a wide range of seating on six levels and numerous food stands, restaurants and bars. The one-mile oval track hosts a number of special events and concerts, including an Independence Day celebration with fireworks. Sundays bring family fun days, with clowns, face painting, pony rides and other kid-friendly diversions.

MUCKLESHOOT CASINO

2402 Auburn Way S., Auburn, 800-804-4944; www.muckleshootcasino.com

Located between Seattle and Tacoma, Muckleshoot Casino sports a tropical theme and more than 2,000 gaming machines, as well as the usual array of Vegas-style tables. The distinguishing features here are a piano lounge and a sushi bar. Entertainment includes a Legends show, with impersonators aping Elvis, Madonna and other stars, and pro boxing matches on Saturday nights.

Saturday-Tuesday 24 hours, Wednesday-Friday 10 a.m.-5:45 p.m.

WHITE RIVER VALLEY MUSEUM

918 H St. S.E., Auburn, 253-288-7433; www.wrvmuseum.org

Situated in Les Gove Park, this historically rich museum celebrates the settlement of the White River Valley during the early part of the 20th century. You can explore a Japanese-American farmhouse, climb aboard a Northern Pacific caboose and tour a replica of downtown Auburn complete with a public market, drugstore and hat shop.

Admission: adults $2, children and seniors $1. Wednesday free. Wednesday-Sunday noon-4 p.m.

BELLEVUE

BELLEVUE BOTANICAL GARDEN

12001 Main St., Bellevue, 425-452-2750; www.bellevuebotanical.org

Bellevue Botanical Gardens features 36 acres of woodlands, meadows and display gardens, including the Waterwise Garden, Japanese Gardens and Fuchsia Display.

Admission: free. Dawn-dusk. Visitor Center 9 a.m.-4 p.m.

OLYMPIA

MIMA MOUNDS NATURAL AREA PRESERVE

I-5 South to exit 95, Olympia, 360-902-1004; www.dnr.wa.gov

Mounds 8 to 10 feet high and 20 to 30 feet in diameter spread across miles of meadows west of Olympia. Once thought to be ancient burial chambers, they are now believed to be the result of Ice Age freeze-thaw patterns. Trails wind through the 500-acre site.

WOLF HAVEN INTERNATIONAL

3111 Offut Lake Road, Tenino, 360-264-4695, 800-448-9653; www.wolfhaven.org

The 75-acre sanctuary is home to 40 wolves no longer able to live in the wild. Take a guided walking tour to visit these beautiful creatures in a natural habitat.

Tours: adults $9, seniors and military personnel $8, children 3-12 $7, children 2 and under free. April-September, Monday, Wednesday-Saturday 10 a.m.-3 p.m., Sunday noon-3 p.m.; October-January and March, Saturday 10 a.m.-3 p.m., Sunday noon-3 p.m. Tours are every hour on the hour.

YASHIRO JAPANESE GARDENS

1010 Plum Street, Olympia, 360-753-8380; www.ci.olympia.wa.us

A cooperative project between Olympia and its sister city, Yashiro, Japan, the gardens include a pagoda, bamboo grove, pond and waterfall.

Daily during daylight hours.

HIGHLIGHT

WHAT ARE THE BEST WINERIES?

BETZ FAMILY WINERY

If you prefer reds over whites, this winery is for you. The family-owned business specializes in Bordeaux varietals and knows what it's doing; owner Bob Betz is one of the few in the world to hold the Master of Wine title.

CHATEAU STE. MICHELLE

This 87-acre winery is the oldest in the state. Come and taste its heralded riesling, as it was among the first wineries in Washington to plant the grape. The chateau's grounds also host a number of outdoor summertime concerts.

JANUIK WINERY

Januik went against the traditional winery protocol and built a contemporary, sleek structure filled with concrete. But an outdoor fireplace adds some life into it, as do the chardonnay, merlot, syrah and cabernet sauvignon, the winery's specialties.

PORT GAMBLE

OF SEA AND SHORE MUSEUM

General Store Building, 3 Rainier Ave., Port Gamble, 360-297-2426; www.ofseaandshore.com

The Of Sea and Shore Museum features one of the largest shell collections in the country along with a gift and book shop.

Admission: free. Daily 9 a.m.-5 p.m.

PORT GAMBLE HISTORIC MUSEUM

3 Rainier Ave., Port Gamble, downhill from the General Store, 360-297-8074; www.portgamble.com

Exhibits trace the history of the area and the timber company with displays arranged in chronological order, including a replica of an old saw filing room and Forest of the Future exhibit.

Admission: adults $4, seniors, students, military personnel $3, children 6 and under free. May-October, daily 9:30 a.m.-5 p.m.; November-April, Friday-Sunday 9:30 a.m.-5 p.m.

REDMOND

BETZ FAMILY WINERY

13244 Woodinville Redmond Road N.E., Redmond, 425-861-9823; www.betzfamilywinery.com

If you're a fan of reds, a stop at Betz is a requirement—the winery specializes in the rich, dark purple stuff, particularly Bordeaux varietals like cabernet sauvignon and merlot. The patriarch of the family-run business, Bob Betz, is one of only 289 people in the world to hold the title of Master of Wine, and though you won't get much face time with the man (the winery doesn't have a tasting room or tours), try to visit during the Release Weekends in the fall (for Rhone-style wines) and late winter (Bordeaux-style wines). If you can, get your hands on the winery's 2005 Clos de Betz, a coveted vintage that's a blend of merlot, cabernet sauvignon, malbec and cabernet franc.

Call for Release Weekend details.

CELTIC BAYOU IRISH PUB & CAJUN CAFÉ

7281 W. Lake Sammamish Parkway N.E., Redmond, 425-869-5933; www.celticbayou.com

An Irish pub with a laid-back vibe, a Cajun menu and an in-house brewery, Celtic Bayou is a pleasant place to unwind with walls clad in mellow-toned wood, booths and tables and an outdoor beer garden. The place attracts its fair share of Microsoft employees and other tech types. Live music is featured on Saturday nights.

Sunday-Monday 11:30 a.m.-10 p.m., Tuesday-Thursday 11:30 a.m.-midnight, Friday-Saturday 11:30 a.m.-1 a.m.

MARYMOOR PARK

6046 W. Lake Sammamish Parkway, Redmond, 206-205-3661; www.metrokc.gov

Marymoor Park is the largest, and likely the busiest, park in metro Seattle. With 640 acres of parkland around a historic farmhouse, it is home to the area's only velodrome, as well as a climbing rock, a model airplane field and numerous sports fields. Marymoor is also home to a very popular off-leash dog park, about 40 acres of forest and meadow on the shores of a slow-moving river.

SAMMAMISH RIVER TRAIL

www.metrokc.gov

An 11-mile paved path running southeast from Bothell to Redmond, the Sammamish River Trail connects with the Burke-Gilman Trail, forming a 27-mile route that leads to Gas Works Park in Seattle. This peaceful, mostly level trail follows alongside the gentle current of the Sammamish River, passing through Woodinville, its two wineries and the Redhook Ale Brewery, a short jaunt off the trail. The trail is popular with joggers, walkers, cyclists and inline skaters. At the north end of the trail, start your journey at Bothell Landing Park (9919 N.E. 180th St.). Down south in Redmond, begin your trek at Marymoor Park (6046 W. Lake Sammamish Parkway N.E.).

WILLOWS RUN GOLF CLUB

10402 Willows Road N.E., Redmond, 425-883-1200; www.willowsrun.com

Willows Run offers an intriguing mix of golf getaway and closeness to civilization during your round. Much of the back nine is built next to an industrial park, but the course has few trees and resembles British Open layouts. There are two 18-hole tracks and a 9-hole par-three course as well. The holes are closely packed, but they are challenging, with plenty of water along either 18. The facility's signature hole is the 17th on the Eagle's Talon course, a long hole with a nearly island green that slopes to the front, assuring that those who do not hit the ball far enough will go fishing.

TACOMA

EMERALD QUEEN I-5 CASINO, EMERALD QUEEN CASINO HOTEL

2024 E. 29th St., Tacoma (Casino); 5700 Pacific Highway E., Fife (Hotel/Casino), 253-594-7777, 888-831-7655; www.emeraldqueen.com

The Emerald Queen Casino is big and bright, brimming with antiques and Vegas-style tables (including blackjack, Caribbean stud poker, roulette, craps and others), as well as more than 2,000 slots and video poker machines and live-action keno. The hotel/casino in Fife also has hundreds of machines and keno. Both locations have smoke-free gaming areas. The stage regularly attracts national rock and country acts, some of them household names. In addition to the requisite casino buffet, the Tacoma location has a casual deli and an Asian eatery; the hotel has a full-service restaurant.

Daily.

POINT DEFIANCE ZOO & AQUARIUM

5400 N. Pearl St., Tacoma, 253-591-5337; www.pdza.org

The zoo has a polar bear complex, a musk ox habitat, tundra waterfowl, elephants, beluga whales, walrus, seals and otters. The 38 perimeter displays show off hundreds of Pacific Northwest marine specimens. The South Pacific Aquarium features coral reefs and sharks; the North Pacific Aquarium includes a hands-on Marine Discovery Center.

Admission: adults $13.50, seniors $12.50, children 5-12 $9.50, children 3-4 $5.50. January-March and October-December, daily 9:30 a.m.-4 p.m.; April-late May, daily 9:30 a.m.-5 p.m.; mid-May-early September, daily 9:30 a.m.-6 p.m.; early-late September, daily 9:30 a.m.-5 p.m.; closed July 16.

SEATTLE MUSEUM OF GLASS

1801 E. Dock St., Tacoma, 253-284-4750, 866-568-7386; www.museumofglass.org

The only museum in the United States focusing on contemporary glass art, the Museum of Glass first opened its doors at the waterfront in downtown Tacoma in 2001. The collection includes works by some of the best-known glass artists in the world, including Dale Chihuly, whose 500-foot Chihuly Bridge of Glass here is one of the largest outdoor glass installations in existence. You can watch glass artists ply their trade at an onsite amphitheater.

Admission: adults $12, seniors $10, children 6-12 $5, children 5 and under free. Labor Day-Memorial Day, Wednesday-Saturday 10 a.m.-5 p.m., Sunday noon-5 p.m.; Memorial Day-Labor Day, Monday-Saturday 10 a.m.-5 p.m., Sunday noon-5 p.m. Third Thursday of month 10 a.m.-8 p.m. (free admission).

UNION STATION

1717 Pacific Ave., Tacoma, 253-863-5173; www.unionstationrotunda.org

Built in 1911 by Northern Pacific Railroad, the station, with its 98-foot-high dome, has been restored. Now home to the federal courthouse, the rotunda houses the largest single exhibit of sculptured glass by Tacoma native Dale Chihuly.

Monday-Friday.

WOODINVILLE

BRIAN CARTER CELLARS

14419 Woodinville-Redmond Road, Woodinville, 425-806-9463, www.briancartercellars.com

Brian Carter Cellars is working on opening a new winery with a heated outdoor courtyard, a private tasting library and a spacious public tasting room, complete with a full kitchen and two tasting bars. The new plans are an indicator of BCC's recent success, but in the meantime, its cozy, small yellow house tasting room offers samples of handcrafted European-style blends. Go there to imbibe on little-known local wines. The amiable staff will help you find some good bottles.

Admission: (tasting fees) $8. Tasting Room: Daily noon-5 p.m.

CHATEAU STE. MICHELLE

14111 N.E. 145th St., Woodinville, 425-488-1133, 800-267-6793; www.ste-michelle.com

Although it's the oldest winery in the state, Chateau Ste. Michelle doesn't show any wear and tear. The beautiful, pristine white chateau is surrounded by 87 acres of perfectly manicured grounds, and Ste. Michelle continues to churn out delicious wine. It was among the first in Washington to plant Riesling, and the winery is still an advocate for the grape, having created the yearly Riesling Rendezvous seminar to celebrate it. But the winery is also known for its chardonnay, merlot and cabernet. If you head over to the chateau, carve out time to browse the well-stocked shop and tasting room. Premium tastings are available for a nominal fee. Try to time your trip to coincide with one of the chateau's big outdoor summer concerts, which have included headliners such as Earth, Wind & Fire; Crosby, Stills & Nash; and B.B. King.

Daily 10 a.m.-5 p.m.

COLUMBIA WINERY

14030 N.E. 145th St., Woodinville, 425-482-7490, 800-488-2347; www.columbiawinery.com

Columbia Winery's humble beginnings can be traced back to a garage in the Seattle neighborhood of Laurelhurst. In that garage in 1962, the first bottles were vinted. Founded by 10 friends, the operation has grown steadily over the years, helping to launch Washington's wine industry, which now ranks only behind California's in premium wine production. On weekends, tours and tasting are available at the winery's Victorian-style manor in Woodinville.

Group tours: Saturday-Sunday, by appointment. Retail shop: daily 10 a.m.-7 p.m.

JANUIK WINERY

14710 Woodinville-Redmond Road N.E., Woodinville, 425-481-5502; www.januikwinery.com

Family-owned Januik is ushering in a new kind of winery. Instead of the rustic, Old World-style estate, Januik's state-of-the-art building is contemporary and sleek. Wood elements and an outdoor fireplace inject warmth into the endless concrete structures, whose linear design mimics rows of vineyards. If you need an extra dose of warmth, visit the tasting room, which Januik shares with the independent Novelty Hill winery, to sip the winery's limited-release bottles. Try Januik's acclaimed chardonnay, merlot, syrah and cabernet sauvignon. You can also take classes and hold private functions on the grounds.

Daily 11 a.m.-5 p.m.

MOLBAK'S

13625 N.E. 175th St., Woodinville, 425-483-5000, 866-466-5225; www.molbaks.com

Each year more than 1 million green thumbs pay a visit to Molbak's, a garden shop 20 miles northeast of Seattle. Egon and Laina Molbak emigrated from Denmark to Woodinville in 1956, purchasing a small greenhouse and becoming a wholesaler of cut flowers. Ten years later, the Molbaks expanded their business by opening a 700-square-foot retail shop. Their business has flourished ever since, and today Molbak's employs 200 people to oversee their garden, gift and floral shops, as well as a store selling Christmas items and patio furniture.

Sunday-Friday 10 a.m.-6 p.m., Saturday 9 a.m.-9 p.m.

PAGE CELLARS

19495 144th Ave. N.E., Woodinville, 253-232-9463; www.pagecellars.com

Owners Jim and Rothelle Page are passionate about their reds, as is evident from the 2004 Preface, a cabernet that starts out aromatic and deep, and finishes elegantly, or their 2005 Sauvignon Blanc, a crisp tipple reminiscent of Anjou pears and apples. It doesn't hurt that the winery doesn't shy away from fun names for their wines, such as the 2003 Libra de Carta (i.e., "Paperback Novel") and a syrah called Lick My Lips.

Saturday noon-4 p.m, Sunday 1-5 p.m.

REDHOOK ALE BREWERY

14300 N.E. 145th St., Woodinville, 425-483-3232; www.redhook.com

In the early 1980s, Paul Shipman and Gordon Bowker identified that import beers were becoming increasingly popular and that the Pacific Northwest held the nation's highest per-capita draft beer consumption. The pair responded by founding Redhook Brewing Company, producing their ale at a brewery in the Ballard area of Seattle. They sold their first pint in 1982. Sales took off with the 1984 release of Ballard Bitter, and Redhook grew to become one of the most successful microbreweries in the United States. To keep pace with demand, a brewery was built in Woodinville in 1994. For a mere $1, you can tour the brewery, sample several of Redhook's eight ales, receive a free tasting glass and learn about the company's history. After the tour, sidle up to the bar in the Forecasters Public House and partake of pub-style food and, of course, fresh Redhook ale.

Daily.

SILVER LAKE WINERY

15029 Woodinville-Redmond Road, Woodinville, 425-485-2437; www.silverlakewinery.com

A shared love of wine prompted three University of Washington professors and a local real estate investor to start Silver Lake Wines in 1987. Today, more than 1,200 wine enthusiasts are members of Washington's largest consumer-owned winery. Silver Lake uses Bordeaux, Rhone and Burgundian grape varietals from Roza Hills vineyard in Eastern Washington to produce its three collections: cask wines, reserve wines and grand reserve wines. After uncorking a few in the winery's tasting room, try to pop into one of the seminars, covering topics such as "How to Bottle Your Own Wine," "Red Wine & Chocolates" and "Wine Making 101."

Monday-Saturday 11 a.m.-5 p.m., Sunday noon-5 p.m.

HIGHLIGHT

WHAT IS THE BEST WAY TO TOUR DEFIANCE PARK?

One of Tacoma's preeminent attractions, this 700-acre park, flanked by the waters of Puget Sound, contains a wealth of gardens, the city zoo and aquarium, and a number of recreational and historical sites. The park includes 14 miles of hiking trails, which wind through groves of old-growth forests and lead to sheltered beaches.

The main paved road through the park is called Five Mile Drive; on Saturdays this scenic road remains closed to vehicles until 1 p.m., though it's open to cyclists, joggers and in-line skaters. Enter the park at Pearl Street and follow signs to the parking area at the Vashon Island Ferry. From here, watch as the ferries cross to and from Vashon Island, an agricultural island in the misty distance. Walk past the tennis courts and follow the path to the garden area. Formal gardens are abundant at Point Defiance Park and are maintained cooperatively by members of local garden clubs, with help from Tacoma's Metropolitan Park District. Park gardens include the Japanese Garden with a torii gate and Shinto shrine received as gifts from Kitakyushu, Tacoma's sister city in Japan. Also found here are iris gardens, dahlia test gardens, herb gardens and a rhododendron garden that is ablaze with color in May. Just past the zoo entrance on Five Mile Drive is the civic Rose Garden, established in 1895, with more than an acre of bushes, many of heirloom varieties. The Northwest Native Garden, located near the Pearl Street entrance, presents a collection of indigenous plants ranging from trees to grasses.

Just past the main garden area is the Point Defiance Zoo & Aquarium. Often considered one of the best in the United States, the Point Defiance Zoo is unusual in that it focuses primarily on species from the Pacific Rim, including polar bears, musk oxen and Arctic foxes. Peer at coastline mammals through the underwater windows at Rocky Shores. No fewer than 30 huge sharks swim among tropical fish and eels in the lagoon at Discovery Reef Aquarium. Elephants and apes and other zoo favorites are housed in the Southeast Asia complex.

From the zoo, follow trails north into the wild heart of the park. Point Defiance has been a public park for almost 125 years, and vast sections of it preserve old-growth forest and virgin meadowlands. Stop at Owens Beach to explore the shoreline or take in the sun along the sandy strand. Farther west, past a viewpoint onto Vashon Island, is Mountaineer Tree, a massive fir nearly 450 years old. The western edge of the park is at Gig Harbor Viewpoint, which overlooks the Tacoma Narrows, a constricted, surging strait between Point Defiance and the Kitsap Peninsula. Round the cap and walk south along the western flank of the park. From here, watch for vistas onto the Tacoma Narrows Bridge. At a mile, it is the fifth-longest span in North America. The present bridge replaced the infamous Galloping Gertie bridge that collapsed during a windstorm in 1940.

At the southwest corner of the park are a number of attractions. If you have kids in tow, they may enjoy Never Never Land, a 10-acre storyland theme park in an outdoor forest setting. Wooded paths lead to oversized sculpted figures of nursery-rhyme characters. On summer weekends, kids can meet living costumed characters.

Adjacent is Fort Nisqually Historic Site. In 1833, the Hudson Bay Company trading post at Fort Nisqually was established 17 miles south of Tacoma, near DuPont. This restoration of the original fort includes the factor's house, granary, trade store, blacksmith shop, laborer's quarters and stockade, all furnished to reflect life on the frontier in the 1850s. Docents in period clothing demonstrate blacksmithing, spinning, beadwork and black powder.

Walk back toward the main park entrance, stopping by Camp Six Logging Museum, an open-air logging museum and reconstruction of a pioneer logging camp. On spring and summer weekends, hitch a ride on a logging train with a steam locomotive. Back at the ferry terminal, refresh yourself with a stop at the Boathouse Grill, located above the marina with views over Vashon Island and the Olympic mountain peaks.

WHERE TO STAY

BELLEVUE

★★★BELLEVUE CLUB HOTEL

11200 S.E. Sixth St., Bellevue, 425-454-4424, 800-579-1110; www.bellevueclub.com

You instantly feel the hush of the Bellevue Club Hotel when you walk through its vine-covered entrance. While the Bellevue Club feels very private and exclusive, hotel guests are greeted with thoughtful touches and deluxe amenities. Each room comes complete with luxurious bedding and baths crafted of marble, limestone or granite. Stone fireplaces or private balconies are featured in some rooms.

67 rooms. Restaurant, bar. Business center. Fitness center. Pool. Spa. Pets accepted. Tennis. $151-250

★★★HYATT REGENCY BELLEVUE

900 Bellevue Way N.E., Bellevue, 425-462-1234, 800-233-1234, 425-646-7567; www.bellevue.hyatt.com

Located in the fashionable Eastside area and directly across from Bellevue Square Mall, this hotel is situated within Bellevue Place, a mixed-use development that includes retail stores, a fitness center and plenty of dining options. The hotel encourages guests to use the Bellevue Place Club (for a fee) and to dine at one of the many nearby restaurants (the hotel restaurant isn't open for dinner). The lobby is a welcoming space, with seating near a small live bamboo forest and lots of natural light. The rooms are inviting with dark wood and a chocolate and beige palette and oversized decorative pillows adorning the comfy beds.

381 rooms. Restaurant, bar. Fitness center. Pool. $151-250

KIRKLAND

★★★THE WOODMARK HOTEL ON LAKE WASHINGTON

1200 Carillon Point, Kirkland, 425-822-3700, 800-822-3700; www.thewoodmark.com

With Seattle's skyline only seven miles in the distance, the Woodmark Hotel sits on the shores of scenic Lake Washington. Guest rooms feature lake, marina or creek views. Rooms have 32-inch LCD televisions with surround sound, a make-your-own martini bar and complimentary "raid the pantry" access to grab midnight snacks like sandwiches, chips and desserts. Bathrooms are crafted in limestone and come with soaking tubs, rain showers and Molton Brown toiletries. The region's fresh ingredients are the highlight at Waters Lakeside Bistro, and the Library Bar serves afternoon tea, complete with a special menu and china service for children.

100 rooms. Restaurant, bar. Spa. Pets accepted. $151-250

TACOMA
★★★HOTEL MURANO
1320 Broadway Plaza, Tacoma, 253-238-8000, 877-986-8083; www.hotelmuranotacoma.com

This sleek, contemporary boutique hotel features a three-story, skylit lobby decorated with glasswork by world-renowned local artist Dale Chihuly. The stylish rooms feature flat-screen TVs, iPod docking stations and beds swathed in luxury linens. At the top of the hotel is Bite, a rooftop restaurant where you can enjoy contemporary cuisine and check out views of Mount Rainier and Commencement Bay.

319 rooms. Restaurant, bar. Spa. Pets accepted. $61-150

WOODINVILLE
★★★WILLOWS LODGE
14580 N.E. 145th St., Woodinville, 425-424-3900, 877-424-3930; www.willowslodge.com

Bordering the Sammamish River in Washington's western wine country, Willows Lodge is an exceptional getaway. Industrial chic meets Native American sensibilities at this former hunting lodge. Stained concrete, slate and sleek lines give a modern edge to the guest rooms (while Frette linens soften them up), and dynamic artwork crafted by Northwest Coast Native Americans showcases local pride. The grounds include landscaped gardens, and the herb and edible plant gardens inspire the menus at The Herbfarm and Barking Frog restaurants. The full-service spa offers a host of soothing treatments.

86 rooms. Restaurant, bar. Complimentary breakfast. Spa. Pets accepted. $251-350

WHERE TO EAT

KIRKLAND
★★★CAFÉ JUANITA
9702 120th Place N.E., Kirkland, 425-823-1505; www.cafejuanita.com

This charming bistro, helmed by chef Holly Smith, serves fresh, creative dishes with Northern Italian influences. The menu changes according to what's in season, but might include tagliatelle with Wagyu beef Bolognese or local lamb with olives and artichoke potato gratin. The wine list is a well-priced selection of bottles from Italy's top vino regions, as well as some wines from California and beyond.

Italian. Dinner. Closed Monday. $36-85

TACOMA
★★★BITE
Hotel Murano, 1320 Broadway Plaza, Tacoma, 253-591-4151; www.hotelmuranotacoma.com

This restaurant offers panoramic views of Puget Sound, Commencement Bay and Mount Rainier. The décor is streamlined and contemporary, and the menu is equally up-to-date, with dishes such as grilled tofu with miso vinaigrette served alongside classics like truffled mac and cheese.

Italian. Breakfast, lunch, dinner. Reservations recommended. Bar. $36-85

WHICH RESTAURANT OFFERS A UNIQUE DINING EXPERIENCE?

When dining at The **Herbfarm**, be sure to set aside four to five hours for a culinary feast. You'll work up a little bit of an appetite on a pre-dinner Garden Tour of the Willows Lodge property and then you'll dig right into a seasonal nine-course dinner paired with about six wines.

★★★CLIFF HOUSE

6300 Marine View Drive, Tacoma, 253-927-0400, 800-961-0401; www.cliffhouserestaurant.com

Northwest-influenced cuisine is served at this dusty rose and floral-accented dining room, which offers views of Mount Rainier and Puget Sound. Classics like shrimp linguine and pan-seared filet mignon are paired with wines from a list that includes bottles from around the world.

Northwest. Lunch, dinner. Reservations recommended. Bar. $36-85

★★★RUSTON WAY LOBSTER SHOP

4015 Ruston Way, Tacoma, 253-759-2165; www.lobstershop.com

This Commencement Bay restaurant has a nautical look, boat moorage and outdoor dining (during spring and summer). The menu is loaded with fresh seafood, from pan-seared oysters to oven-roasted Australian lobster tail.

Seafood, steak. Lunch, dinner, Sunday brunch. Outdoor seating. Children's menu. Bar. $36-85

WOODINVILLE

★★★BARKING FROG

Willows Lodge, 14580 N.E. 145th St., Woodinville, 425-424-2999; www.willowslodge.com

After a day touring nearby wineries, take a seat at this cozy, lodge-like bistro. A quaint and casual atmosphere of warm earth tones and exposed wood complements the rustic regional Northwest menu, which changes seasonally and features choices like organic chicken breast, Grand Marnier prawns and grilled New York strip.

American. Breakfast, lunch, dinner, brunch. Reservations recommended. Outdoor seating. Children's menu. Bar. $36-85

★★★★THE HERBFARM

Willows Lodge, 14590 N.E. 145th St., Woodinville, 425-485-5300; www.theherbfarm.com

A four-hour meal of nine courses and five perfectly paired wines. A flamenco guitarist strumming in the half-light of flickering candles in an antique-filled dining room. The sun setting over a fragrant garden lying just outside your window. If this were real life in the rural world, America's cities would be empty. Here, chef (and gentleman gardener) Jerry Traunfeld creates seasonal, themed meals based on the bounty of the restaurant's own gardens and farm, plus produce, meats and artisan cheeses sourced from local growers, producers, ranchers and fishermen. The result is a culinary treat: You'll gorge on dishes like paddlefish caviar on crisp salmon skin as well as sockeye and squash blossoms with lemon thyme.

American. Dinner. Closed Monday-Wednesday. Reservations recommended. $86 and up

RECOMMENDED

BELLEVUE
SEASTAR RESTAURANT AND RAW BAR
205 108th Ave. N.E., Bellevue, 425-456-0010;www.seastarrestaurant.com

As is evident from the restaurant's name, seafood is the star on this menu. A raw bar caters to those who want sushi—like a Washington roll with Dungeness crab, smoked salmon and tart apple—ceviche and oysters. There's a host of hot seafood entrées, including cedar-plank-roasted red king salmon and potato-chip-crusted halibut. Be sure to peruse the award-winning wine list for a glass or two.

American. Lunch, dinner. Bar. Reservations recommended. $36-85

WOODINVILLE
PURPLE CAFÉ AND WINE BAR
14459 Woodinville-Redmond Road N.E., Woodinville, 425-483-7129;www.thepurplecafe.com

For a low-key evening out, head to the Purple Café, which uses fresh, seasonal ingredients to craft its sandwiches, pizzas and pastas. The extensive wine menu devotes a page to Woodinville labels, so head here if you don't have time to check out all the vineyards in the area. Beginner wine lovers will make use of the glossary in the back of the menu to ensure they order the perfect bottle to pair with one of the café's many cheese flights.

American. Lunch, dinner. Reservations recommended. Children's menu. $16-35

WHERE TO SHOP

BELLEVUE
BELLEVUE SQUARE
575 Bellevue Square, Bellevue, 425-646-3660; www.bellevuesquare.com

One of the biggest and most posh shopping centers in metro Seattle, Bellevue Square is eight miles east of the city in suburban Bellevue, on the eastern shore of Lake Washington. Well-heeled locals love the place for its eye-catching design, climate-controlled corridors and 200 high-end stores: anchors such as Nordstrom and the Bon March, specialty shops like Pottery Barn and Williams-Sonoma, and eateries including P.F. Chang's China Bistro and Ruth's Chris Steak House. This is not to mention the non-shopping facilities and services, including a concierge, valet parking, a local shuttle bus and two play areas for kids. An Eastside institution since the 1940s, Bellevue Square underwent a major redevelopment in the 1990s that transformed it into the shoppers paradise it is today.

REDMOND
REDMOND TOWN CENTER
76th Street and 166th Avenue, Redmond, 425-867-0808; www.shopredmondtowncenter.com

This 120-acre, open-air shopping and entertainment hub includes national chains such as Gap, REI, Borders and Eddie Bauer. There are also a number of restaurants (including national chains) and an eight-screen movie theater. Every Saturday from May through October, a farmers market offers fresh produce and flowers, and on Tuesday evenings in summer, live music can be enjoyed. There are also a number of events for children on the Redmond Town Center calendar.

Monday-Saturday 10 a.m.-8 p.m., Sunday 11 a.m.-6 p.m.

CASCADE MOUNTAINS

The Cascade Mountains extend from British Columbia to California, but two of the range's most popular mountains, Mount Rainier and Mount St. Helens, are in Washington. The two spots are popular for recreation, including hiking, mountain climbing, camping and more.

Surrounded by the Cascade Mountains, Leavenworth has an Old World charm enhanced by authentic Bavarian architecture. Located less than three hours from Seattle, the village is a favorite stop for people who enjoy river rafting, hiking, bicycling, fishing, golf and skiing. A gateway to Mount Baker-Snoqualmie National Forest (Snoqualmie section), North Bend is also a favorite winter sports area.

WHAT TO SEE

LEAVENWORTH
EAGLE CREEK WINERY
10037 Eagle Creek Road, Leavenworth, 509-548-5401; www.eaglecreekwinery.com

This family-operated boutique winery sits at the base of the Cascade Mountains and turns out delicious pours like the fruity Raspberry D'Vine and several cabernet franc blends. Ask winemaker Ed Rutledge for a tour of his personal wine cellar and for some recommendations. Then take a seat on the patio overlooking the vineyards with a bottle and some local cheese. The winery also has a second Leavenworth location, d'Vinery (617 Front St., suite 4A).

May-October, Friday-Sunday 11 a.m.-5 p.m.

ICICLE RIDGE WINERY
8977 North Road, Peshastin, 509-548-7019; www.icicleridgewinery.com

There's no better setting for a winery. Located on the foothills of the Cascade Mountains and overlooking a lake, the tasting room is housed in a warm, rustic log cabin. It's warm for a reason; the log cabin is also the home of the winery's owners. Try to sample the Riesling here, especially the Huckleberry Riesling a slightly sweet concoction made with the winery's own hand-picked fruit. The winery also hosts winemaker dinners and outdoor concerts in warmer weather. The winery also has another tasting room in downtown Leavenworth (821 Front St., suite B).

Daily noon-5 p.m.

HIGHLIGHT

WHAT ARE THE BEST THINGS TO DO IN THE CASADE MOUNTAINS?

SPEND THE DAY IN LEAVENWORTH

This charming Bavarian alpine town is an idyllic spot against the Cascade Mountains. Peruse the Bavarian-style shops and go to the various tasting rooms to try out the local wines.

VISIT MOUNT RAINIER

More than 2 million people visit this majestic mountain each year. They come to hike, climb, picnic and just to soak in the amazing scenery; Mount Rainier soars 8,000 feet above the Cascade Range.

EXPLORE MOUNT ST. HELENS NATIONAL VOLCANIC MONUMENT

It's hard to believe that this volcano, the youngest in the Cascade Range, erupted in 1980. Now you can see trees, wildflowers and herds of elk and other animals all over the monument.

LEAVENWORTH NUTCRACKER MUSEUM

735 Front St., Leavenworth, 509-548-4573, 800-892-3989; www.nutcrackermuseum.com

Spanning the wall and floor space of a beautiful Bavarian-style house is the Nutcracker Museum, born out of Arlene Wagner's love of the Tchaikovsky ballet of the same name. Wagner now has more than 4,000 nutcrackers in her museum, having traveled the world over in search of the most exotic specimens. Some of the examples housed in the museum date as far back as the 15th century and detail the history of these very functional, yet ornamental, items. *Admission: adults $2.50, students $1, children 5 and under free. May-October, daily 2-5 p.m.; November-April, Saturday-Sunday or by appointment.*

MOUNT RAINIER NATIONAL PARK
CARBON RIVER

www.nps.gov

Located on the Pacific side of Mount Rainier, the Carbon River area receives the most rainfall and contains the most luxurious forests in Washington. In fact, much of the woodland here is considered temperate rain forest.

HIGHLIGHT

WHAT IS THERE TO SEE AT MOUNT RAINIER NATIONAL PARK?

Majestic Mount Rainier, towering 14,411 feet above sea level and 8,000 feet above the Cascade Range of Western Washington, is one of America's outstanding tourist attractions. More than 2 million people visit this 378-square-mile park each year to picnic, hike, camp, climb mountains or simply admire the spectacular scenery along the many miles of roads. The park's various "life zones," which change at different elevations, support a wide array of plant and animal life. Douglas fir, red cedar and western hemlock, some rising 200 feet into the air, thrive in the old-growth forests. In the summer, the subalpine meadows come alive with brilliant wildflowers. These areas are home to more than 130 species of birds and 50 species of mammals. Mountain goats, chipmunks and marmots are favorites among visitors, but deer, elk, bears, mountain lions and other animals can also be seen here.

Mount Rainier is the largest volcano in the Cascade Range, which extends from Mount Garibaldi in Southwestern British Columbia to Lassen Peak in Northern California. The eruption of Mount St. Helens in 1980 gives a clue to the violent history of these volcanoes. Eruptions occurred at Mount Rainier during the mid-1800s. Even today, steam emissions often form caves in the summit's ice cap and usually melt the snow along the rims of the twin craters.

A young volcano by geologic standards, Mount Rainier was once a fairly symmetrical mountain rising about 16,000 feet above sea level, but glaciers and further volcanic activity shaped the mountain into an irregular mass of rock. The sculpting action of the ice gave each face of the mountain its own distinctive profile. The glaciation continues today, as Mount Rainier supports the largest glacier system in the contiguous United States, with 35 square miles of ice and 26 named glaciers. Much of the park's beauty can be attributed to the glaciers, which at one time extended far beyond the park's boundaries. The moving masses of ice carved deep valleys separated by high, sharp ridges or broad plateaus. From certain vantages, the valleys accentuate the mountain's height. The glaciers are the source of the many streams in the park, as well as several rivers in the Pacific Northwest. The meltwaters also support the various plants and animals throughout the region.

Winters at Mount Rainier are legendary. Moist air masses moving eastward across the Pacific Ocean are intercepted by the mountain. As a result, some areas commonly receive 50 or more feet of snow each winter. At 5,400 feet in elevation, Paradise made history in the winter of 1971 to 1972, when it received 93 feet of snow, the heaviest snowfall ever recorded in this country. The three-story Paradise Inn is often buried up to its roof in snow. Since the mountain's summit is usually above the storm clouds, the snowfall there is not as significant.

The park's transformation from winter wonderland to summer playground is almost magical. Beginning in June or July, the weather becomes warm and clear, although the mountain is occasionally shrouded in clouds. The snow at the lower elevations disappears, meltwaters fill stream valleys and cascade over cliffs, wildflowers blanket the meadows and visitors converge on the park for its many recreational activities.

There are several entrances to the park. The roads from the Nisqually entrance to Paradise and from the southeast boundary to Ohanapecosh are usually open year-round but may be closed temporarily during the winter. Following the first heavy snow, around November 1, all other roads are closed until May or June. The entrance fee is $10 per vehicle.

HIGHLIGHT

WHAT IS THE MOUNT ST. HELENS NATIONAL MONUMENT?

In 1978, two geologists who had been studying Mount St. Helens warned that the youngest volcano in the Cascade Range could erupt again by the end of the century. On March 27, 1980, the volcano did just that, ending 123 years of inactivity. Less than two months later on May 18, a massive eruption transformed this beautiful snow-capped mountain and the surrounding forest into an eerie, desolate landscape with few signs of life.

Among the 57 people missing or killed by the eruption was 83-year-old Harry R. Truman, who for many years owned a lodge on Spirit Lake just north of the mountain. Truman refused to heed evacuation warnings, believing his "beloved mountain" would not harm him; he and his lodge are now beneath hundreds of feet of mud and water.

The Monument, established in 1982, covers 110,000 acres within the Gifford Pinchot National Forest and provides a rare natural laboratory in which scientists and visitors can view the effects of a volcanic eruption. Despite the destruction, the return of vegetation and wildlife to the blast zone has been relatively rapid. Within just weeks of the eruption, small plants and insects had begun to make their way through the ash. Today, herds of elk and other animals, as well as fir trees and wildflowers, have taken a strong foothold here.

Forest Service Road 25, which runs north to south near the eastern boundary, provides access to views of the volcano. The roads are usually closed from approximately November through May because of snow; some roads are narrow and winding.

You are advised to call ahead for current road conditions. Although volcanic activity at Mount St. Helens has decreased greatly in the last few years, some roads into the Monument could be closed if weather conditions dictate.

CRYSTAL MOUNTAIN RESORT

33914 Crystal Mountain Blvd., Crystal Mountain, 360-663-2265, 888-754-6199 (snow conditions); www.skicrystal.com

Located 75 miles south of Seattle in the shadow of Mount Rainier, Crystal Mountain is a ski resort with an impressive 3,100-foot vertical drop and equally impressive 340 inches of average annual snowfall. During the December-to-April ski season, 10 lifts service 1,300 acres of skiable terrain on Silver King Mountain with a nice balance of beginner, intermediate and advanced trails; an additional 1,000 acres of backcountry terrain is available for diehards. The place is known for its family-friendly perks, such as free children's passes with an adult purchase and a Kids Club that offers supervision, skiing classes and lunch while parents enjoy the slopes. The resort also encompasses several hotels and restaurants, as well as a rental shop, skiing and snowboarding school and day spa.

MOUNTAIN CLIMBING

360-569-2211; www.nps.gov

Mount Rainier has many opportunities for climbers; one of the most popular climbs is the two-day trek to the summit of Mount Rainier. The guide service at Paradise conducts various programs for new and experienced climbers. Climbs should be attempted only by persons who are in good physical condition and have the proper equipment; deep crevasses and unstable ridges of lava are dangerous. All climbers must register with a park ranger.

OHANAPECOSH

Mount Rainier National Park, southeast corner of park, 360-569-2211; www.nps.gov

A preserve of rushing waters and dense, old-growth forest, including some of the largest trees in the park—many more than 1,000 years old—are here. The Grove of the Patriarchs, a cluster of massive conifers on an island in the Ohanapecosh River, is reached by bridge along a popular trail that starts near the Steven's Canyon Entrance Station. At the Ohanapecosh Visitor Center exhibits tell the story of the lowland forest ecosystem, where Douglas fir, western hemlock and red cedar trees reign supreme.

MOUNT ST. HELENS

APE CAVE

Forest Service Road in southern part of monument, Amboy, 360-247-3900

At 12,810 feet in length, the cave is said to be one of the longest intact lava tubes in the continental United States. The downslope portion of the cave, extending approximately 4,000 feet, is the most easily traveled. The upslope portion, extending nearly 7,000 feet, is recommended only for those carrying the proper equipment. All visitors are advised to carry three sources of light and wear sturdy shoes or boots and warm clothing. The cave is a constant 42 degrees F.

JOHNSTON RIDGE OBSERVATORY

24000 Spirit Lake Highway, Mount St. Helens National Volcanic Monument, 360-274-2140

At 4,200 feet, state-of-the-art interpretive displays focus on the sequence of geological events that drastically altered the landscape and opened up a new era in the science of monitoring an active volcano and forecasting eruptions.
May-October, daily 10 a.m. to 6 p.m.

MOUNT ST. HELENS VISITOR CENTER

3029 Spirit Lake Highway, Castle Rock, 360-274-0962; www.parks.wa.gov

Outside the monument, the center houses exhibits that include a walk-through model of the volcano, displays on the history of the mountain and the 1980 eruption, and volcano monitoring equipment. A 10-minute slide program and a 22-minute movie are shown several times daily, and special programs are held throughout the year. Also here are volcano viewpoints and a nature trail along Silver Lake.
May-September, daily 9 a.m.-5 p.m.; October-April, daily 9 a.m.-4 p.m.

NORTH BEND
MOUNT SI GOLF COURSE
9010 Boalch Ave. S.E., Snoqualmie, 425-391-4926; www.mtsigolf.com

Mount Si used to be the world's largest field for growing beer hops before being turned into an 18-hole course in the 1930s. Since then, it has undergone several renovations, including in 1994, when eight of the holes were completely changed. The alteration upped the length of the course to more than 6,300 yards. The course has several leagues and sessions for younger golfers to learn the game, making it one of the better-organized courses in the Seattle area.

WHERE TO STAY

LEAVENWORTH
★★★MOUNTAIN HOME LODGE
8201 Mountain Home Road, Leavenworth, 509-548-7077, 800-414-2378; www.mthome.com

With its picturesque mountain setting, this unique lodge offers cabins and rooms with luxury touches like down duvets, wireless access and huge picture windows for taking in the miles of unspoiled scenery surrounding the property. The cabins offer even more seclusion, with wood-burning fireplaces and Jacuzzi tubs. The lodge includes a cozy restaurant where hearty breakfasts and full dinners are served in front of the fireplace.

12 rooms. Restaurant. Complimentary breakfast. Pool. No children allowed. Tennis. $251-350

NORTH BEND
★★★SALISH LODGE & SPA
6501 Railroad Ave., Snoqualmie, 425-888-2556, 800-272-5474; www.salishlodge.com

A lodge has existed in the Salish's unique location, overlooking the Snoqualmie Falls, since 1919. While the fireplace located in the restaurant's dining room is all that remains of the original building, this rustic lodge retains a historic feel. A recent renovation introduced down duvets and custom-built Pacific Northwest-inspired furnishings, but maintained the rooms' wood-burning fireplaces and jetted tubs. The onsite spa has a menu of treatments inspired by the lodge's surroundings, as well as a eucalyptus-filled steam room. Classes such as riverside yoga make the most of the nearby outdoors.

91 rooms. Restaurant, bar. Fitness center. Spa. $251-350

WINTHROP
★★★SUN MOUNTAIN LODGE
604 Patterson Lake Road, Winthrop, 509-996-2211, 800-572-0493; www.sunmountainlodge.com

Located on 3,000 acres in the mountains east of Seattle, this resort offers hiking, biking and fly-fishing in summer and cross-country skiing, ice-skating and sleigh rides in winter. Rooms feature working fireplaces and pillow-top beds, but no televisions. The onsite restaurant has a 5,000-bottle wine cellar and the grounds include a full-service spa.

102 rooms. Restaurant, bar. Pool. Spa. $151-250

RECOMMENDED

LEAVENWORTH
ALL SEASONS RIVER INN
8751 Icicle Road, Leavenworth, 509-548-1425, 800-254-0555;
www.allseasonsriverinn.com

Located 80 feet above the Wenatchee River, this bed and breakfast feels more like a private home than a hotel. Guest rooms lack TVs and telephones, but water views and Jacuzzi tubs provide their own form of entertainment. Passionate about antiques, the innkeeper has meticulously furnished each room with unique pieces. The inn makes bicycles available for the half-mile ride to downtown Leavenworth.

6 rooms. Complimentary breakfast. No children allowed. $151-250

BAVARIAN LODGE
810 Highway 2, Leavenworth, 888-717-7878;
www.bavarianlodge.com

If you're charmed by Bavarian-inspired Leavenworth, stay at this lodge, which overlooks the village center. It carries on the Bavarian theme with flower boxes of colorful blooms underneath the windows and art and antiques reminiscent of Old World Bavaria decorating the inside. Sage and maroon rooms come with floral-printed bedspreads, free Wi-Fi, and Starbucks and Tazo teas, because even though this is like a town in Bavaria, it is still Washington, after all.

7 Rooms. Complimentary breakfast. Pool. $151-250

ENZIAN INN
590 Highway 2, Leavenworth, 800-223-8511;
www.enzianinn.com

The Alps-inspired inn tries to deliver an authentic experience. In fact, during your complimentary hot breakfast, the owner will don his lederhosen and serenade you with the alphorn. Rooms have hand-painted or hand-carved imported Austrian furniture. And the property has a hutte, but this two-story "hut" outfitted with a microwave and dishwasher is much more chic than its German equivalents found in rustic spots. A great perk: In the winter, the inn lends out ski equipment for free.

104 rooms. Complimentary breakfast. Fitness center. Pool. Golf. $251-350

WHICH RESTAURANTS HAVE THE BEST VIEW?

Salish Lodge & Spa Dining Room:
You might forget you are here for the regional cuisine when you get a glimpse of the gorgeous Snoqualmie Falls and river beyond the window panes.

The Dining Room:
Although the American dishes are like works of art on a plate, your gaze will be fixed on the picturesque snow-capped mountains outside of the big-picture windows.

RUN OF THE RIVER BED & BREAKFAST

9308 E. Leavenworth Road, Leavenworth, 509-548-7171, 800-288-6491; www.runoftheriver.com

This small, quiet inn on the Icicle River is tucked among the towering Cascade Mountains. Activities include hiking, walking or mountain biking through forest trails. Rooms are cozy and individually decorated with rustic furnishings.

6 rooms. Complimentary breakfast. No children allowed. $151-250

SLEEPING LADY MOUNTAIN RESORT

7375 Icicle Road, Leavenworth, 509-548-6344, 800-574-2123; www.sleepinglady.com

Tucked away in the Cascade Mountains, this resort brings its setting into its rooms. The beds and desks are handmade from logs and the airy wood-filled rooms are decorated in pale blue, orange and brown with wildflower-patterned bolsters. And while your room won't come with a TV, it will have complimentary Wi-Fi. There's tons to do at the resort: swim in the rock-lined outdoor pool; sweat it out in the dry sauna; use the free volleyball, horseshoe and badminton rentals; go on an art walk on the property; or visit the spa.

10 rooms. Restaurant, bar. Pool. Spa. Pets accepted. $151-250

WHERE TO EAT

NORTH BEND

★★★SALISH LODGE & SPA DINING ROOM

6501 Railroad Ave., Snoqualmie, 425-888-2556, 800-272-5474; www.salishlodge.com

With views overlooking the Snoqualmie Falls, this rustic restaurant is a prime spot for sampling dishes sourced from the bounty of the area. The menu features entrées such as wild king salmon with Thai basil and English pea coulis, and buttermilk and sage poached pheasant.

American. Breakfast, lunch, dinner, brunch. Closed Monday. Bar. $36-85

WINTHROP

★★★THE DINING ROOM

604 Patterson Lake Road, Winthrop, 509-996-2211, 800-572-0493; www.sunmountainlodge.com

A casual, rustic setting overlooking snow-capped mountains is the backdrop for the fresh regional cuisine served at this restaurant at the Sun Mountain Lodge. The kitchen skillfully combines fish, seafood and meat with a local blend of herbs and vegetables. The dishes are artfully presented; try the antelope tartare or the lobster paella cake. The wine list is extensive and features bottles from around the globe.

American. Breakfast, lunch, dinner, brunch. Children's menu. Bar. $36-85

RECOMMENDED

LEAVENWORTH

CAFÉ MOZART

829 Front St., Leavenworth, 509-548-0600; www.cafemozartrestaurant.com

At this white-tablecloth restaurant, German food is what shines. Choose from "Mozart's Symphony of Schnitzels"—veal, pork or chicken breast—and your preferred preparation as well as sides like housemade spaetzle. If you are dining with a companion, opt for the belly-busting meat feast otherwise known as the

Wolfgang Amadeus Platter, which includes apple-pork bratwurst, red wine and cranberry pork bratwurst, pork shanks, grilled ham, pork schnitzel, Lyonnaise potatoes, spaetzle with wild mushroom sauce, red cabbage and weinkraut. Don't miss the excellent wine list.

German. Lunch, dinner. $16-35

WELCOME TO BRITISH COLUMBIA

BRITISH COLUMBIANS LIVE IN A CORNER OF Canada that sees an explosion of daffodils and cherry blossoms while the rest of the country is still shoveling snow. In this western-most province, life is enormous—from 1,000-year-old trees and everyday mountain vistas to towering city sunflowers.

Six diverse regions make up the whole of the province, each pulling tourists a hundred different ways each day: Vancouver Island, the Vancouver Coast and Mountains, Thompson Okanagan, the Kootenay Rockies, the Cariboo Chilcotin Coast and the vast Northern region.

Vancouver Island has one of the world's most diverse ecosystems: Rainforests, marshes, meadows, beaches, mountains, oceans, rivers and lakes create habitats for multitudes of wildlife species. It all adds up to one of the world's premier locations for golf, whale watching, birding and salmon and trout fishing. The island is blanketed in rare, old-growth rainforest and dramatic mountain ranges, picturesque cities and towns, and smaller island groups that invite ferry-bound adventures at an island pace.

Vancouver Coast and Mountains, which hosted the 2010 Olympic Games, is a phenomenal mountainous city—a mecca of peaks, ocean, lakes, rivers and beaches encircling a cosmopolitan gem that rivals the most spectacular cities in the world. Revel in the four-season resort town of Whistler that is famed worldwide for skiing, great shopping and fine restaurants. Visitors and residents cycle, hike, camp, kayak, golf, ski and snowboard year-round—in fact, the mild climate is such that a "West Coast Special" is an everyday option: Ski in the morning, then golf or sail in the afternoon.

The Thompson Okanagan region is as famous for its pastoral orchards and vineyards as it is for its wildly varied landscape—the highest mountain in the Canadian Rockies is here, as well as a waterfall twice the height of Niagara Falls and Canada's only true desert. The heart of British Columbia's wine-growing region is just a four-hour drive east of Vancouver, where more than 40 wineries are within a 150-mile range.

The Kootenay Rockies region is a vast wilderness of rivers, lakes, waterfalls, beaches, mineral hot springs, alpine meadows and snow-capped mountains. Adventure connoisseurs tackle some of the world's most intense mountain biking, fishing, windsurfing, whitewater rafting and kayaking. Golfers come here for world-class courses with unbeatable scenery, and city slickers turn cowboy at dude and guest ranches that offer authentic cattle rides. You can visit

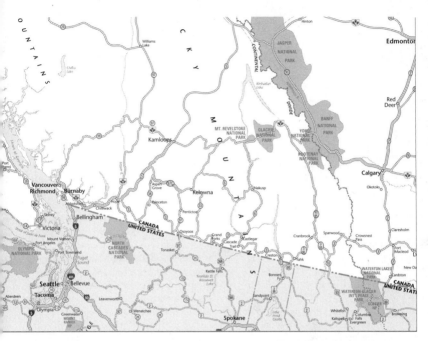

restored heritage towns, thriving art communities and gold rush boomtowns, and in the winter, take in the continent's finest powder skiing and snowboarding.

Thousands of lakes and rivers, plus a magnificent stretch of Pacific Ocean coastline, make the Cariboo Chilcotin Coast, which harkens back to the adrenaline-pumping gold rush era, a top destination for fishing, boating, camping, swimming and kayaking. This is a region whose rich, fascinating history is perhaps only rivaled by its captivating present day—complete with cowboys riding off into the sunset. Roam endless gentle trails or hike, ride and canter strenuous backcountry routes. Tramp through the volcanic mountains of Tweedsmuir Provincial Park, stand at the ancient hoodoos and shifting sand dune of Farwell Canyon, and drive the original Cariboo Wagon Road on the historic Gold Rush Trail, taking in famed local rodeos and stampedes.

Northern British Columbia's vast wilderness comprises more than half the province, a land of jagged mountain peaks, roaring rivers, serene lakes, green valleys, rugged coastlines and ancient island archipelagos. The region is known for its magnificent freshwater and saltwater fishing, canoeing, kayaking, whitewater rafting, and in the winter, powder skiing. A wondrous system of national and provincial parks provides habitats and sanctuary for wildlife. The Queen Charlotte Islands are a living mystery within this region: An untamed, old-growth land rich in Haida culture and with distinct island flora and fauna that have evolved over thousands of years.

VANCOUVER ISLAND

The largest of the Canadian Pacific Coast Islands, Vancouver Island stretches almost 300 miles along the shores of Western British Columbia. It is easily accessible by ferry from the city of Vancouver as well as from other parts of the province and the state of Washington. With most of its population located in the larger cities on the eastern coast, much of the island remains a wilderness and is very popular with outdoor enthusiasts.

Nanaimo is a dominant town, an area known for excellent sandy beaches and beautiful parks. In the center of the island is the Alberni Valley, which includes several parks with excellent swimming and fishing and one of the tallest waterfalls in North America (Della Falls). Because of its location, Nanaimo serves as a fine starting point to visit other attractions on the island, as well as being a vacation highlight in itself. A thriving art, culture and sports scene kicks off your island adventure, a perfect mix of big-city amenities with small-town charm.

Of course the standout city on Vancouver Island is British Columbia's capital, Victoria. One of Canada's most temperate and eminently walkable cities, Victoria has a distinctly British flavor, yet is a heartland of Pacific Northwest indigenous culture. This city of lush parks and gardens bursts with beauty in early spring, when even the five-globed Victorian lampposts are decorated with baskets of flowers. Take a horse-drawn carriage or double-decker bus tour through many historic and scenic landmarks and wander through the bistros, boutiques and colorful alleys of a delightfully compact downtown and Chinatown district that sparkles with history.

WHAT TO SEE

NANAIMO
BASTION
Front and Bastion streets, Nanaimo; www.nanaimomuseum.ca

Built in 1853 as a Hudson's Bay Company fort, this tower has been restored as a museum and features a cannon firing ceremony (summer months at noon). You get a view of Protection and Newcastle Islands from the tower's top.

Admission: adults $2, seniors and students $1.75, children 5-12 $.75. Labor Day-March, Tuesday-Saturday 10 a.m.-5 p.m.; April-June, Monday 11 a.m.-3 p.m., Tuesday-Saturday 10 a.m.-5 p.m.; Memorial Day-Labor Day, daily 10 a.m.-5 p.m.

BC FOREST DISCOVERY CENTRE
North of Victoria, Highway 1, near Duncan, 250-715-1113; www.bcforestmuseum.com

This center features a logging museum with old logging machines and tools as well as hands-on exhibits, a logging camp, a one-mile steam railway ride, sawmill, films, and a nature walk.

Admission: adults $14, seniors and students $12, children $9. Hours vary by season.

BEST ATTRACTIONS

WHAT ARE THE TOP THINGS TO DO ON VANCOUVER ISLAND?

PERUSE THE ART GALLERY OF GREATER VICTORIA

Come to here to see the best collection of Japanese art in Canada. Plus, it has the only Shinto shrine outside of Japan. There are also Canadian and European art exhibits.

TAKE IN BUTCHART GARDENS

Walk along the lovely 55 acres to see rose, Japanese and Italian gardens. Try to visit on a summer night, when the gardens are lit up and perfect for a romantic stroll.

MAKE A TRIP TO CHINATOWN

You'll find authentic Chinese restaurants in this bustling neighborhood, but you'll also see great architecture and the narrowest road in Canada.

GO WHALE WATCHING IN VICTORIA

One of the most popular things to do in Victoria is to hit the ocean in search of whales. Boats line up along Wharf Street to take you on your high-seas whaling adventure.

NANAIMO ART GALLERY
900 Fifth St. and 150 Commercial St., Nanaimo, 250-754-1750; www.nanaimoartgallery.com
This gallery has changing exhibits of art, science and history pieces.

NANAIMO DISTRICT MUSEUM
100 Museum Way, Nanaimo, 250-753-1821; www.nanaimomuseum.ca
This museum features a walk-in replica of a coal mine, turn-of-the-century shops, a restored miner's cottage, dioramas, a Chinatown display and other changing exhibits.
Admission: adults $2, seniors and students $1.75, children 5-12 $0.75. Daily 10 a.m.-5 p.m. Closed Sunday-Monday, December-March.

HIGHLIGHT

WHALE WATCHING

Vancouver Island is known as one of the best places to view migrating and resident whales. Whale-watching tours leave from Victoria and other large city centers on the island. In Victoria, whale-watching boats line both the Wharf Street waterfront and Inner Harbor. Half-day tours display marine life, including orcas, sea lions, seals and porpoises. Victoria Marine Adventures and Prince of Whales operate tours there.

View migrating gray whales during March and April, while orca (killer) whales are best observed between May and October, with July and August as the key months for sightings. Three orca pods totaling more than 80 whales make their home in the waters off of Victoria. North of Vancouver Island, a resident community of 217 whales patrol the Johnstone Strait in 16 pods. Other whales and marine mammals that can be seen off of Vancouver Island include humpback whales, minke whales, otters, seals, sea lions and dolphins.

VICTORIA

ART GALLERY OF GREATER VICTORIA

1040 Moss St., Victoria, 250-384-4101; www.aggv.bc.ca

This gallery is said to have the finest collection of Japanese art in Canada and it includes major holdings of Asian ceramics and paintings. Also housed here are collections of Canadian and European art, with a focus on prints, drawings and decorative arts. The gallery is home to the only Shinto shrine outside of Japan and is the site of many lectures, film screenings and concerts.

Admission: adults $12, seniors and students $10, children 6-17 $2. Monday-Saturday 10 a.m.-5 p.m., Thursday 10 a.m.-9 p.m., Sunday noon-5 p.m. Closed Monday, September-mid-May.

BUTCHART GARDENS

800 Benvenuto Ave., Victoria, 250-652-5256, 866-652-4422; www.butchartgardens.com

At approximately 55 acres, the Sunken Garden was created in the early 1900s by the Butcharts on the site of their depleted limestone quarry with topsoil brought in by horse-drawn cart. Already a tourist attraction by the 1920s, Butchart now includes rose, Japanese and Italian gardens as well as the Star Pond, Concert Lawn, Fireworks Basin, Ross Fountain and Show Greenhouse. The gardens are subtly illuminated at night (mid-June-mid-September), and on Saturday evenings in July and August, firework displays light up the sky.

Daily; hours vary.

EMILY CARR HOUSE

207 Government St., Victoria, 250-383-5843; www.emilycarr.com

Built in 1863, this is the birthplace of famous Canadian painter and author Emily Carr. The ground floor was restored to represent that time period.

May-September, Tuesday-Saturday 11 a.m.- 4 p.m.; rest of year, by appointment.

CHINATOWN

Fisgard and Government streets, Victoria

Chinese immigrants, employed for railroad labor, established Canada's oldest Chinatown in Victoria in 1858. Two key attractions are Fan Tan Alley, the narrowest street in Canada that measures just 3 feet wide at its smallest point, and the Gate of Harmonious Interest, the ornate 38-foot entrance to Chinatown that's guarded by hand-carved stone lions from Suzhou, China. Visit shops with exotic merchandise and great restaurants.

CRAIGDARROCH CASTLE

1050 Joan Crescent, Victoria, 250-592-5323; www.craigdarrochcastle.com

This historic house museum was constructed in 1890 with beautifully crafted wood and stained glass. Inside are period furniture and artifacts.

Admission: adults $12, seniors $11, students $8, children 6-18 $4. Mid-June-mid-September 9 a.m.-7 p.m., mid-September-mid-June 10 a.m.-4 p.m.

CRAIGFLOWER FARMHOUSE & SCHOOLHOUSE HISTORIC SITE

Admirals and Craigflower roads, Victoria, 250-383-4627, 877-485-2422; www.conservancy.bc.ca

This farmhouse was built in 1856 in simple Georgian style and contains some original furnishings. The adjoining 1854 schoolhouse is the oldest in Western Canada. You can see what life was like for schoolchildren and practice your penmanship on old-time slates.

Admission: adults $6, students and seniors $4. May-September 11 a.m.-5 p.m.; rest of year, by appointment.

DOMINION ASTROPHYSICAL OBSERVATORY

5071 W. Saanich Road, Victoria, 250-363-0001; www.hia-iha.nrc-cnrc.gc.ca

The observatory contains three telescopes, two of which are used for research by professional astronomers. The 72-inch Plaskett Telescope is used for public viewings during "Star Parties" (late July-September). Interactive exhibits, film presentations and other special programs are designed to entertain visitors while schooling them about the universe.

Admission: adults $9, students and seniors $8, children 4-12 $5. May-early September, hours vary; rest of year, by appointment.

FORT RODD HILL & FISGARD LIGHTHOUSE NATIONAL HISTORIC SITE

603 Fort Rodd Hill Road, Victoria, 250-478-5849; www.fortroddhill.com

A coastal artillery fort from 1895 to 1956 has casemated barracks as well as gun and searchlight positions. A historic lighthouse is adjacent.

Admission: adults $3.90, seniors $3.40, children 6-16 $1.90. Mid-February-October, daily 10 a.m.-5:30 p.m.; November-mid-February, daily 9 a.m.-4:30 p.m.

HATLEY CASTLE

2005 Sooke Road, Colwood, 250-391-2666, 866-241-0674; www.hatleycastle.com

This turreted castle was once the private estate of James Dunsmuir, the former lieutenant governor of British Columbia. It's now the administrative center of Royal Roads University, but you can find exhibits inside that illustrate the castle's history, starting with its time as an Indian burial site. Buildings are noted for their beauty, as are the grounds, which include Japanese, Italian and rose gardens.

Admission: free. Daily 10:15-3 p.m.

HELMCKEN HOUSE

Elliot Street Square, Victoria, 250-356-7226, 888-447-7977; www.royalbcmuseum.bc.ca

The second-oldest house in British Columbia, it was built in 1852. Most furnishings are original and there is an extensive 19th-century medical collection.

Admission: included with Royal B.C. Museum admission or by donation. June-early September noon-4 p.m.

MARITIME MUSEUM OF BRITISH COLUMBIA

28 Bastion Square, Victoria, 250-385-4222; www.mmbc.bc.ca

This museum depicts the rich maritime heritage of the Pacific Northwest from early explorers through the age of sail and steam as well as Canadian naval wartime history and a large collection of ship models used throughout the history of British Columbia. The Tilikum, a converted dugout that sailed from Victoria to England from 1901 to 1904, is here also.

Admission: adults $12, seniors and students $10, children 6-11 $5, children 5 and under free. Daily 10 a.m.-5 p.m.

PACIFIC UNDERSEA GARDENS

490 Belleville St., Victoria, 250-382-5717; www.pacificunderseagardens.com

Hop aboard a vessel that will descend 15 feet to Inner Harbor for a below-the-surface show. Underwater windows in a floating vessel allow you to get a glimpse of more than 5,000 marine specimens—including crabs, sea stars, anemones, rockfish, salmon, perch and wolf eels—as well as scuba diver shows at this undersea garden.

Admission: adults $10.75, seniors $9.50, children 5-11 $5.50, children 12-17 $7.75, children 4 and under free. September-April, daily 10 a.m.-5 p.m.; April-June, daily 10 a.m.-6 p.m.; June-September, daily 9 a.m.-8 p.m.

POINT ELLICE HOUSE MUSEUM

2616 Pleasant St., Victoria, 250-380-6506; www.pointellicehouse.ca

Step back into Victorian times at this museum, which contains a vast collection of period artifacts, from clothing to teapots. In keeping with the Victorian theme, a proper afternoon tea is served in the lovely restored garden (11 a.m.-3 p.m., reservations recommended).

Admission: adults $6, students $4, children 12 and under $3. May-June, Thursday-Monday 11 a.m.-4 p.m.; July-Labor Day, daily 11 a.m.-5 p.m.; Labor Day-mid-September, Friday-Sunday noon-4 p.m.; mid-November-mid-December, Friday-Saturday 11 a.m.-3 p.m.

ROYAL BRITISH COLUMBIA MUSEUM

675 Belleville St., Victoria, 250-356-7226, 888-447-7977; www.royalbcmuseum.bc.ca

This museum traces the natural and human history of British Columbia through 3-D exhibits. Learn about the province's indigenous people and their culture. There is also a re-creation of a turn-of-the-century town with everything from an herbalist shop in Chinatown to a clothing shop in the Dominion Drapers Building. In the natural history gallery, the exhibits depict British Columbia from the Ice Age to the present.

Admission: adults $27.50, seniors and children 6-18 $18.50. Daily 10 a.m.-5 p.m.

THUNDERBIRD PARK
Belleville and Douglas streets, Victoria

You'll find a collection of authentic totem poles and indigenous carvings, representing the works of the main Pacific Coastal tribes, at this park. Indigenous carvers may be seen at work in the Carving Shed.

May-September.

WHERE TO STAY

MALAHAT
★★★MALAHAT MOUNTAIN INN
265 Trans-Canada Highway, Malahat, 250-478-1979, 800-913-1944;
www.malahatmountaininn.com

Just a short drive from Victoria brings guests to this inn's ocean-view rooms and lofts. If you really want to get up close to the dramatic ocean landscapes and the Saanich Inlet, dine at the onsite restaurant's the outdoor patio. You'll stay cozy in the neutral-colored rooms, which have gas fireplaces, large soaking tubs and bright modern art. But if you do feel the lure of the ocean, just step outside to your balcony to appreciate the beautiful backdrop.

10 rooms. Restaurant, bar. $151-250

NANAIMO
★★★COAST BASTION INN
11 Bastion St., Nanaimo, 250-753-6601, 800-716-6199; www.coasthotels.com

This downtown high-rise hotel offers views of Nanaimo Harbor and nearby islands from every guest room, which are done up in slate, black and pops of yellow. You can gaze at the harbor from your Juliet balcony. Its location is convenient to harbor-front shops, galleries, restaurants and the B.C. Ferry terminal. After a busy day, Minnoz Restaurant is a great place for a delicious traditional West Coast meal. The bar also offers a light tapas menu.

179 rooms. Restaurant, bar. Business center. Fitness center. Spa. Pets accepted. $151-250

★★★CROWN ISLE RESORT
399 Clubhouse Drive, Courtenay, 250-703-5050, 888-338-8439; www.crownisle.com

The Crown Isle course meets the needs and playing levels of both novice and seasoned golfers. Accommodations include fairway rooms, one- and two-bedroom villas and loft villas. Villas come with kitchens, and some have Jacuzzis to soak your weary self after a round of golf and fireplaces. The resort is close to the nearby Aquatics Centre and Fifth Street shopping district as well as beaches and hiking.

56 rooms. Restaurant, bar. Fitness center. Golf. $151-250

★★★KINGFISHER OCEANSIDE RESORT & SPA
4330 S. Island Highway, Courtenay, 250-338-1323, 800-663-7929; www.kingfisherspa.com

Located on wooded grounds in Comox Valley, the Kingfisher is great for people who like to get active outdoors; it has a heated outdoor pool, a sauna, canoe and kayak rentals, and nearby golf. The spa offers many services that use sea-based ingredients, but the highlight is the Pacific Mist Hydropath, where you follow an hour-long trail with stop-offs at a mineral massage pool, waterfalls, a steam cave and more as a form of hydrotherapy and relaxation.

For a quiet dinner, head to the resort's dining room, the Kingfisher Restaurant, where Pacific Northwest cuisine is served and accented by views of Hartley Bay. *64 rooms. Restaurant, bar. Business center. Fitness center. Pool. Spa. Pets accepted. $61-150*

TOFINO

★★★★WICKANINNISH INN

500 Osprey Lane, Tofino, 250-725-3100, 800-333-4604; www.wickinn.com

Famous for its storm-watching events (the luxurious resort is perched on the edge of a particularly volatile stretch of Pacific Ocean), this three-story cedar inn is a rustic retreat on a remote stretch of Vancouver Island. Floor-to-ceiling windows frame dazzling views of the crashing surf. Furnishings crafted from recycled fir, cedar and driftwood add a unique touch in the comfortable accommodations, as do fireplaces, oversized tubs and private balconies. Beachcomb with your pet in tow on Chesterman Beach, and then stop by the pet shower station to freshen up. The superb onsite spa takes its cues from botanicals in the nearby ancient rainforest. The sea is the focus at the Pointe Restaurant, where the ocean's bounty is highlighted.

75 rooms. Restaurant, bar. Business center. Fitness center. Spa. Pets accepted. $351 and up

VICTORIA

★★★ABIGAIL'S HOTEL

906 McClure St., Victoria, 250-388-5363, 800-561-6565; www.abigailshotel.com

This colorfully painted boutique hotel consists of a historic Tudor mansion and converted carriage house. Rooms are individually decorated, but they all have fresh-cut flowers, Italian marble bathrooms and Wi-Fi, and most come with wood-burning fireplaces. The quiet setting belies the inn's location just three blocks from Victoria's Inner Harbor and main tourist attractions. Guests won't go hungry here: You'll be greeted with freshly baked cookies at check-in, a three-course gourmet breakfast is served overlooking the patio and English-style gardens and evening hors d'oeuvres will tide you over till dinner.

23 rooms. Complimentary breakfast. Spa. Pets accepted. $251-350

★★★BEACON INN AT SIDNEY
9724 Third St., Sidney, 250-655-3288, 877-420-5499; www.beaconinns.com

Located in the center of Book Town, this elegant Edwardian-inspired property is the perfect romantic getaway. The rooms are decked out in navy velvet and brocade and rich wood furniture, and all but one has a gas fireplace. A complimentary gourmet meal in the breakfast room (or on the front patio) starts each day. For guests who want pure relaxation, the Ocean Palm Spa is just a few minutes from the inn.

9 rooms. Complimentary breakfast. $151-250

★★★BEACONSFIELD INN
998 Humboldt St., Victoria, 250-384-4044, 888-884-4044; www.beaconsfieldinn.com

This three-story Edwardian mansion on Victoria's south side is a Registered Heritage Property. The gardens are kept in the English style, and high tea and sherry are served each afternoon. Each guest room boasts unique features, such as canopied beds, beamed ceilings, stained-glass windows and fireplaces.

9 rooms. Complimentary breakfast. $251-350

★★★COAST HARBORSIDE HOTEL & MARINA
146 Kingston St., Victoria, 250-360-1211, 800-716-6199; www.coasthotels.com

This location can't be beat. The hotel has an inner harbor spot with a 42-slip private marina and it's close to Victoria International Airport. Though if you want to go for a dip, you can opt for the hotel's two pools or hot tub. All rooms have balconies or terraces, some with marina-side views, and complimentary high-speed Internet access. Visit Blue Crab Bar & Grill for a seafood dinner or a glass of wine—its cellar is stocked with bottles from British Columbia and the rest of the Pacific Northwest.

132 rooms. Restaurant, bar. Business center. Fitness center. Pool. Pets accepted. $151-250

★★★DELTA VICTORIA OCEAN POINTE RESORT AND SPA
45 Songhees Road, Victoria, 250-360-2999, 800-667-4677; www.deltahotels.com

Located on a point between Victoria's Inner and Upper harbors, this elegant, modern hotel offers wonderful views of the waterfront, Parliament Buildings and the Royal British Columbia Museum. Take advantage of the resort experience by participating in fitness classes, booking a tee time on a nearby golf course and playing tennis on one of the hotel's two lighted courts.

239 rooms. Restaurant, bar. Business center. Fitness center. Pool. Spa. Pets accepted. Tennis. $151-250

★★★ENGLISH INN & RESORT
429 Lampson St., Victoria, 250-388-4353, 866-388-4353; www.englishinnresort.com

This unique resort was built to echo an English country village, and its buildings are set amid 5 acres of beautifully landscaped English-style gardens. While the décor varies in each room, they all are spacious and streamlined, with contemporary furnishings. Some come with fireplaces or spa tubs. If you want really roomy digs, book one of the Crown Rooms, the largest on the lot. On the other end of the spectrum, the Garden Rooms are the most compact and good for solo travelers.

30 rooms. Restaurant, bar. Spa. $251-350

★★★THE FAIRMONT EMPRESS

721 Government St., Victoria, 250-384-8111, 866-540-4429; www.fairmont.com

The Fairmont Empress is one of Victoria's most cherished landmarks. Nearly a century old, this storybook castle resting on the banks of Victoria's Inner Harbor enjoys a legendary past, sparkling with royals, celebrities and a bygone era. Rita Hayworth, Katharine Hepburn, Bob Hope, Bing Crosby, Shirley Temple and Roger Moore are just a few of the famous faces who have stayed here. A tradition since the hotel opened in 1908, afternoon tea at The Fairmont Empress is a must for all visitors to Victoria.

477 rooms. Restaurant, bar. Business center. Fitness center. Pool. Spa. Pets accepted. $251-350

★★★★HASTINGS HOUSE COUNTRY HOUSE HOTEL

160 Upper Ganges Road, Salt Spring Island, 250-537-2362, 800-661-9255;
www.hastingshouse.com

Snuggled on Salt Spring Island, the Tudor-style Hastings House captures the essence of the English countryside. Scattered throughout the lovely grounds, the rooms and suites are housed within ivy-covered garden cottages and the timber-framed barn. High tea and pre-dinner cocktails are served daily in the lounge. Be sure to stay for diner; Hastings House boasts one of the most accomplished kitchens in British Columbia. Longtime executive chef Marcel Kauer and his brigade have the great fortune to draw on the area's Pacific Northwest bounty. The wine list, although international in scope, features a slate of reds and whites from B.C.'s Okanagan Valley.

18 rooms. Restaurant. Spa. Closed November-March. $351 and up

★★★HOTEL GRAND PACIFIC

463 Belleville St., Victoria, 250-386-0450, 800-663-7550; www.hotelgrandpacific.com

Located at the southern tip of Vancouver Island, this hotel offers serene water views and easy access to historic Old Town and area businesses. The rooms and suites are light and airy. Fine dining is one of Victoria's hallmarks, and this hotel is no exception. The Pacific Northwest cuisine at the Pacific Restaurant is a standout, while The Mark's regionally influenced dishes are equally delicious.

304 rooms. Restaurant, bar. Business center. Fitness center. Pool. Spa. Pets accepted. $151-250

★★★LAUREL POINT INN

680 Montreal St., Victoria, 250-386-8721, 800-663-7667; www.laurelpoint.com

Every room of this hotel has a balcony and a fabulous view of either the Inner or Upper Harbor. The studio rooms, which are dressed in neutrals with Canadian art on the walls, spoil you with triple sheeting, Molton Brown toiletries and deep-soaking tubs in the marble bathrooms. The grounds include a Japanese-style garden, and the Asian influence is felt in the décor. Relax in the cozy piano lounge, fragrant garden or outdoor patio.

200 rooms. Restaurant, bar. Business center. Pool. Spa. Pets accepted. $251-350

★★★MAGNOLIA HOTEL AND SPA

623 Courtney St., Victoria, 250-381-0999, 877-624-6654; www.magnoliahotel.com

This luxury boutique hotel one block from the Inner Harbor provides comfort and pampering throughout. It starts in the classic, elegant rooms, with crown molding, two-poster beds and marble bathrooms. But you'll get maximum pampering at the spa, which offers a full range of beauty and relaxation regimens and prides itself on using natural products from renewable resources. The signature Spa Magnolia body treatment will leave you utterly relaxed with an invigorating body scrub followed by a hydrotherapy session, a deep-cleansing facial and a massage.

64 rooms. Restaurant, bar. Complimentary breakfast. Fitness center. Spa. Pets accepted. $251-350

★★★MIRALOMA ON THE COVE

2306 Harbour Road, Sidney, 250-656-6622, 877-956-6622

This luxurious seaside property is just 20 minutes from downtown Victoria and five minutes from ferries and the airport. Choose from studios, one-bedroom suites or two-bedroom suites. Each guest room includes pillow-top mattresses, a balcony or patio, spa tubs and heated towel bars. The hotel offers nice touches to make you feel at home, including hot chocolate, cookies, use of mountain bikes and a complimentary breakfast buffet.

22 rooms. Fitness center. Complimentary breakfast. Pets accepted. $151-250

★★★SOOKE HARBOR HOUSE

1528 Whiffen Spit Road, Sooke, 250-642-3421, 800-889-9688; www.sookeharbourhouse.com

Located on Vancouver Island by the sea, this bed and breakfast features beautifully designed guest rooms with light wood and lots of white with fireplaces and spectacular ocean views. The hotel's location is perfect for hiking, whale watching and cross-country skiing.

28 rooms Restaurant, bar. Complimentary breakfast. Spa. Pets accepted. Closed three weeks in January. $251-350

★★★SWANS SUITE HOTEL

506 Pandora Ave., Victoria, 250-361-3310, 800-668-7926; www.swanshotel.com

Built in 1913, this hotel holds two- and two-bedroom suites. Most of the guest rooms have a spacious feel thanks to the loft-style layout with high ceilings and open beams, and some have skylights and private patios. All rooms boast full kitchens, duvets and original artwork. It's a lively place with its own brewery and two popular eating and drinking establishments.

29 rooms. Restaurant, bar. Complimentary breakfast. $151-250

WHERE TO EAT

TOFINO
★★★THE POINTE RESTAURANT

Wickaninnish Inn, 500 Osprey Lane, Tofino, 250-725-3106, 800-333-4604; www.wickinn.com

Perched above the crashing waves of Vancouver Island's west shore is the Pointe Restaurant at the Wickaninnish Inn. The cedar-beamed, circular dining room features a breathtaking 240-degree view of the Pacific Ocean. The adjoining On the Rocks Bar & Lounge is a perfect spot for a pre- or post-dinner cocktail, with a variety of wines by the glass and an extensive selection of single-malt Scotches.

Seafood. Breakfast, lunch, dinner, Sunday brunch. Reservations recommended. $36-85

VICTORIA

★★★CAFE BRIO

944 Fort St., Victoria, 250-383-0009, 866-270-5461;
www.cafe-brio.com

This award-winning restaurant is in downtown
Victoria and offers West Coast/Continental cuisine
with an Italian bent. You'll find an abundance of fresh
wild fish, like white wine-poached halibut and pan-
seared rockfish. The rest of the daily menu offers local,
seasonal, organic foods like roasted summer squash
and goat cheese agnolotti. Be sure to check out the
menu of housemade salumi to kick-start your meal.

*International. Dinner. Closed first two weeks in January.
Reservations recommended. Outdoor seating. $36-85*

★★★DEEP COVE CHALET

11190 Chalet Road, Sidney, 250-656-3541;
www.deepcovechalet.com

This charming and historic country inn has a great view
overlooking the waters of the inside passage. Built in
1914, it was originally a teahouse for a railroad station.
Now it serves French fare like black cod filet en croûte,
Dover sole meunière and beef Wellington.

*French. Lunch, dinner. Closed Monday-Tuesday. Reservations
recommended. Outdoor seating. $36-85*

★★★EMPRESS ROOM

721 Government St., Victoria, 250-389-2727; www.fairmont.com

Dine on classic cuisine like a cilantro-rubbed albacore
tuna steak or a pine nut and roasted garlic lamb rack in
this richly appointed room of tapestries, intricately carved
ceilings and live harp music. The 100-year-old hotel's
waterfront location is full of European style, a great spot
for a romantic meal. If you really want to do something
sweet, share the lip-smacking gianduja-crusted caramel
and roasted marshmallow chocolate cake for dessert.

*International. Breakfast, dinner. Reservations recommended. $86
and up*

★★★LURE

Delta Ocean Pointe Resort, 45 Songhees Road, Victoria,
250-360-5873; www.lurevictoria.com

This contemporary, sophisticated restaurant is inside
the Delta Ocean Pointe Resort and offers excellent
water and downtown views. But equally deserving of
your attention is fresh seafood such as the proscuitto-
wrapped trout filet and the rare seared ahi tuna in a
pool of spicy miso broth.

*Seafood. Breakfast, lunch, dinner. Reservations recommended.
Outdoor seating. $36-85*

★★★★RESTAURANT MATISSE

512 Yates St., Victoria, 250-480-0883; www.restaurantmatisse.com

Restaurant Matisse is a gem of a dining room that has become a destination for simple, traditional French fare among Victoria's dining elite. They come for dishes like the juicy beef tenderloin topped with foie gras butter, red wine and black truffle sauce or the pepper-crusted venison chop with orange gastrique. Of course, delicious desserts such as Grand Marnier croissant bread pudding doused in a warm cognac butterscotch sauce don't hurt, either. While French wines dominate the list, there is also a great selection of California bottles.

French. Dinner. Closed Monday-Tuesday. Reservations recommended. $36-85

★★★SOOKE HARBOR HOUSE

1528 Whiffen Spit Road, Sooke Harbor, 250-642-3421, 800-889-9688;
www.sookeharbourhouse.com

Considered one of the most unique restaurants in Canada—it was one of the country's pioneers in the local food movement—the bistro serves local organic seafood, meat and produce, with all of the salad greens and edible herbs and flowers coming from the onsite garden. The menu changes daily, but expect items like a sunflower seed and panko-crusted lingcod and quinoa and chickpea tarts.

International. Dinner. Closed Monday-Wednesday, December-February.
Reservations recommended. Outdoor seating. $36-85

SPAS

TOFINO

★★★★ANCIENT CEDARS SPA

Wickaninnish Inn, 500 Osprey Lane, Tofino, 250-725-3100; www.wickinn.com

Resting on a rocky promontory jutting into the Pacific Ocean with an old-growth rainforest in the background, this is truly a one-of-a-kind hideaway. The interiors have been designed to bring the outdoors in, with slate tiles, dark colors and cedar decorating this serene space. The treatment menu focuses on relaxation and renewal. Thai, lomi lomi and hot-stone massage are among the bodywork therapies available, or try the signature sacred sea treatment, which uses the renowned Bouvier hydrotherapy tub.

VANCOUVER AREA

Vancouver, the City of Glass, is lauded for its enviable mix of laid-back West Coast living and striking skyline with the snow-capped Coastal Mountains (also known as the Coast Range) as a picturesque backdrop. Surrounded by the waters of the Fraser River and Burrard Inlet, Vancouver has a mild climate and rain forest vegetation that make it an utterly unique North American city. Located on the Pacific Rim, it is a bustling seaport and major trade and tourist destination known for its ethnically diverse population and cosmopolitan urban core. The modern architecture, with glass high-rises dotting the downtown skyline, and lush scenery are so breathtaking, many studios shoot films here. It is an easy stand-in for international cities, earning Vancouver its other nickname, Hollywood North.

HIGHLIGHTS

WHAT ARE THE TOP THINGS TO DO IN VANCOUVER?

SPEND BIG BUCKS ON ALBERNI STREET
Nicknamed Affluent Alley, Alberni Street is lined with shops carrying the world's most luxe labels, including Hermès, Tiffany's and Agent Provocateur.

CHECK OUT CHINATOWN
North America's third-largest Chinese population makes its home in this Chinatown. Don't miss the beautiful Dr. Sun Yat-Sen Classical Chinese Garden.

HANG OUT ALONG COMMERCIAL DRIVE
The funky boho vibe in the shops, cafés and eateries along Commercial Drive makes it a great spot to visit and mingle with the locals. It's one of Vancouver's best neighborhoods.

SPEND THE DAY IN STANLEY PARK
In the middle of Vancouver is a 1,000-acre green oasis, the largest city park in Canada. There are beaches, hiking trails, gardens and aquarium and more.

EXPLORE OLYMPIC VILLAGE
This housed the 2010 Winter Games' athletes, but it's being transformed into a hub with a scenic waterfront walkway peppered with intriguing public art.

WHAT TO SEE

VANCOUVER

ARTS CLUB THEATRE COMPANY

1585 Johnston St., Vancouver, 604-687-1644; www.artsclub.com

Having helped launch the careers of actors Michael J. Fox and Brent Carver, the Arts Club Theatre steals the Vancouver stage spotlight. In addition to its four annual main stage productions at Stanley Theatre (2750 Granville St.), the company mounts four productions at the Granville Island Stage.

BALLET BRITISH COLUMBIA

677 Davie St., Vancouver, 604-732-5003; www.balletbc.com

With a strong company of 15 dancers, this reigns as Vancouver's top dance troupe. The company's repertoire includes dances by famed choreographers such as William Forsythe and John Cranko and commissioned works by Canadian talents. Ballet BC's home stage is the Queen Elizabeth Theatre. *November-May.*

BC FERRIES

1112 Fort St., Victoria, 250-386-3431, 888-223-3779; www.bcferries.bc.ca

Ferry destinations include the Queen Charlotte Islands, Vancouver Island and various spots along the British Columbia coast. Terminals are at Horseshoe Bay, north of Vancouver via Trans-Canada Highway 1 and Tsawwassen near the U.S. border, and south of Vancouver via Highway 99.

BITES-ON SALMON CHARTERS

Bayshore West Marina, 450 Denman St., Vancouver, 604-688-2483, 877-688-2483; www.bites-on.com

Coho, sockeye and chinook salmon school in the waters around Vancouver, which is convenient for urban-bound fishing fans. Granville Island-based Bites-On offers day trips of five or eight hours, during which you can sink a line into the Strait of Georgia on a yacht up to 40 feet long. The charters serve parties of up to 10 people. Other options include day-long or two-day excursions. Peak fishing months are April to October, although charters operate year-round. Boat trips also allow fishermen to spot sea lion, porpoise and whale populations.

BURNABY ART GALLERY

6344 Deer Lake Ave., Burnaby, 604-297-4422; www.burnabyartgallery.ca

This gallery has monthly exhibitions of local, national and international artists. It has a collection of contemporary Canadian works on paper. It is housed in Ceperley Mansion, overlooking Deer Lake and the surrounding gardens. *Admission: free. Tuesday-Friday 10 a.m.-4:30 p.m., Saturday-Sunday noon-5 p.m.*

BURNABY VILLAGE MUSEUM

6501 Deer Lake Ave., Burnaby, 604-293-6501; www.burnabyvillagemuseum.ca

This living museum of the 1920s has costumed attendants and more than 30 full-scale buildings with displays and demonstrations. *Admission: adults $12, seniors and children 13-18 $9, children 6-12 $6. May-September, Tuesday-Sunday 11 a.m.-4:30 p.m. Half-price admission on Tuesday.*

CAPILANO SUSPENSION BRIDGE

3735 Capilano Road, Vancouver, 604-985-7474; www.capbridge.com

The 136-meter Capilano Suspension Bridge towers precariously 230 feet above the Capilano River gorge. Originally constructed in 1889 and rebuilt in 1956, the wooden bridge is engineered of wire rope cemented at both ends. In addition to the bridge, the surrounding park provides walking trails, gardens and a totem pole collection. Audiences crowd around to see the First Nations carvers at work. Arrive early in high season.

Admission: adults $27.95, seniors $25.95, students $21.75, children 6-12 $8.75, children 13-16 $16.65. Year-round; hours vary by season.

THE CENTRE IN VANCOUVER FOR PERFORMING ARTS

777 Homer St., Vancouver, 604-602-0616; www.centreinvancouver.com

Acclaimed Canadian architect Moshe Safdie designed the dramatic center with an arched glass façade and, punctuating the entry, a spiraling glass cone. The auditorium seats 1,800 and features major Broadway tours.

CHAN CENTRE FOR THE PERFORMING ARTS

University of British Columbia, 6265 Crescent Road, Vancouver, 604-822-9197; www.chancentre.com

Located in the University of British Columbia district, the Chan houses three venues for theater and music, all of which share the same light-flooded lobby. Built in 1997, the distinctive zinc-clad cylindrical building stands out amid the verdant campus. With superior acoustics, this is one of the best spots in town to hear concerts by touring soloists, UBC musicians and the Vancouver Symphony.

CHINATOWN

Bordered by Hastings, Keefer, Gore and Taylor streets, Vancouver

This downtown area is the nucleus of the third-largest Chinese community in North America (behind San Francisco and New York). At the heart lies the Chinese Market, where you can buy 100-year-old duck eggs and herbalists promise cures with roots and powdered bones. The Dr. Sun Yat-Sen Classical Chinese Garden provides a beautiful centerpiece. Chinese shops display a variety of items ranging from cricket cages to cloisonné vases. Offices of three Chinese newspapers and one of the world's narrowest buildings are within the community's borders. The resplendent Asian atmosphere offers fine examples of Chinese architecture, restaurants and nightclubs.

CN IMAX THEATRE

201-999 Canada Place, Vancouver, 604-682-4629; www.imax.com

Under the white sails that distinguish waterfront Canada Place, CN IMAX screens wide-format documentary films on subjects ranging from space travel to wildlife conservation.

Show times vary; see website for information.

COMMERCIAL DRIVE

Bordered by Broadway and Venables streets, Vancouver; www.thedrive.ca

In the past 20 years Vancouver's one-time Little Italy has transformed into "The Drive," one of North America's most eclectic and interesting neighborhoods characterized by a boho vibe and counterculture spirit. Lined with Italian coffee shops (look for men crammed around TVs when European soccer matches are on), ethnic eateries (Portuguese, Indian, Japanese, Thai, Italian, Ethiopian and Cuban, to name a few), patios frequented by leisurely laptop users and caffeine drinkers (rain or shine), delis that offer delectable cheeses and meats, and funky clothing and tchotchke shops, this neighborhood is a true original. End your excursion with a pint at St. Augustine's Craft Brewhouse (2360 Commercial Drive), which boasts 40-plus craft beers on tap, the largest selection in Western Canada.

THE COMMODORE BALLROOM

868 Granville St., Vancouver, 604-739-4550; www.livenation.com

It's been swinging since the big-band era, and the Commodore flaunts its age with brass chandeliers and polished wood stairs. A renovation in 1999 restored its elegance (and kept the spring-loaded dance floor) while modernizing its stage wizardry. U.S.-based Live Nation programs the acts that come through the ballroom, ranging primarily from rock to blues with a smattering of world talent.

CYPRESS MOUNTAIN

Cypress Bowl and Highway 1, Vancouver, 604-419-7669; www.cypressmountain.com

With 52 runs and nine lifts, Cypress Mountain claims the region's highest vertical rise at 2,010 feet. But the ski area's bigger claim to fame is its cross-country skiing facilities, which span 12 miles of groomed trails, nearly five of which are lit for night gliding. The region's most popular Nordic destination also offers private and group lessons as well as rental equipment. Snowshoers can tramp on designated trails solo or take a guided tour.

December-mid-April; hours vary by season and weather conditions.

DR. SUN-YAT-SEN CLASSICAL CHINESE GARDEN

578 Carrall St., Vancouver, 604-662-3207; www.vancouverchinesegarden.com

Unique to the Western Hemisphere, this garden was originally built in China circa 1492 and transplanted to Vancouver for Expo '86. Guided tours are available daily.

Admission: adults $10, seniors $9, students $8. Year-round; hours vary by season.

ECOMARINE OCEAN KAYAK CENTRE

1668 Duranleau St., Vancouver, Granville Island, 604-689-7575, 888-425-2925; www.ecomarine.com

To get the full impact of Vancouver's magnificent setting on the coast, troll the waterways under paddle power with a kayak from Ecomarine. The outfitter rents both single and double kayaks at its Granville Island headquarters and at two other outposts at Jericho Beach and English Bay. Tours are available, and first-timers can take a three-hour lesson before getting started. Navigate from placid False Creek to more rugged inlets up the shore.

FORT LANGLEY NATIONAL HISTORIC SITE

23433 Mavis Ave., Fort Langley, 604-513-4777; www.pc.gc.ca

Originally one of a string of the Hudson's Bay Company trading posts across Canada, the Fraser Valley's Fort Langley became the birthplace of modern-day

British Columbia with the Crown Colony Proclamation, an act of protection by the British against an American gold rush influx, which was read there in 1858. In addition to preserving the restored buildings, Fort Langley is garrisoned by costumed re-enactors who demonstrate pioneer activities such as blacksmithing and open-fire cooking.

Admission: adults $7.80, seniors $6.55, children 6-16 $3.90. September-late June, daily 10 a.m.-5 p.m.; late June-August, daily 9 a.m.-8 p.m.

GASTOWN
Vancouver, 604-683-5650; www.gastown.org

Vancouver's historic nucleus consists of a series of Victorian buildings rehabbed to shelter an array of shops, clubs and eateries. Among the highlights, the Gastown Steam Clock pipes up every 15 minutes and the Vancouver Police Centennial Museum covers the most notorious local crimes. To fully appreciate the neighborhood, show up for a free tour sponsored by the Gastown Business Improvement Society in Maple Tree Square (2 p.m. daily mid-June-August).

GRANVILLE ISLAND
Beneath the south end of the Granville Street Bridge, Vancouver, 604-666-5784; www.granvilleisland.bc.ca

A former industrial isle, Granville Island is an urban renewal case study with markets, shops, homes and entertainment fashioned out of decaying wharf warehouses beginning in the 1970s. Its hub is the Public Market, a prime picnic provisioner teeming with fishmongers, produce-vendors, butchers, cheese shops, bakeries and chef demonstrations. A specialized kids' market and a free outdoor water park (Late May-early September) appeal to children. The Maritime Market on the southwest shore serves as a dock for boat owners as well as those looking to hire a fishing charter, hop on a ferry or rent a kayak. Three Granville Island museums showcase miniature trains, ship models and sport fishing. Dozens of bars and restaurants, many with views back across the water to the downtown skyline, drive the after-dark trade. An art school, artists' studios and several galleries lend bohemian flair to Granville, abetted by several theaters and street musicians.

GRANVILLE ISLAND KIDS' MARKET
1496 Cartwright St., Vancouver, 604-689-8447; www.kidsmarket.ca

Vancouver's open food market turns its third floor into something kids can enjoy. More than 20 children's shops, including eight selling toys and another seven hawking clothes, take aim at junior consumers, many of whom, of course, prefer the Kids' Market's indoor play area. Strolling clowns and face-painters amplify the carnival-like setting.

Daily 10 a.m.-6 p.m.

GREATER VANCOUVER ZOO
5048 264th St., Aldergrove, 604-856-6825; www.gvzoo.com

Explore 120 acres housing more than 700 animals. Take a miniature train ride or bus tour of the North American Wilds exhibit.

Admission: adults $18, seniors and children 4-15 $14. May-September, daily 9 a.m.-7 p.m.; October-April, daily 9 a.m.-4 p.m.

GROUSE MOUNTAIN

6400 Nancy Greene Way, North Vancouver, 604-986-6262; www.grousemountain.com

For skiing in winter, hiking in summer and sightseeing year-round, Grouse Mountain draws legions of visitors to Vancouver's North Shore. The area's first ski mountain is still its most convenient, with ski and snowboard runs that overlook the metropolis, as well as a skating rink and sleigh rides available. Hikers have loads of trails to choose from, but the one to boast about is the Grouse Grind, a 1.8-mile hike straight up the 3,700-foot peak. The Skyride Gondola takes the easy route up in an eight-minute ride. At the top, all-season attractions include Theater in the Sky, a high-definition aerial film, and several panoramic-view restaurants with vistas of the Strait of Georgia and the twinkling lights of Vancouver.

HASTINGS PARK RACECOURSE

Renfrew and McGill streets, Vancouver, 604-254-1631, 800-677-7702; www.hastingsracecourse.com

Thoroughbreds run in Vancouver at Hastings Park on the city's east side. Although the lengthy racing season runs late April to early November, most races are held on Saturday and Sunday, with extra meets scheduled for major holidays like Canada Day and Labor Day. Two-dollar bet minimums are encouraged, while self-service betting terminals patiently acquaint you with the track lingo.

H.R. MACMILLAN SPACE CENTRE

1100 Chestnut St., Vancouver, 604-738-7827; www.hrmacmillanspacecentre.com

One of several museums in Vanier Park tucked between Kitsilano Beach and Granville Island, the MacMillan Space Centre appeals to would-be astronauts with a space flight simulator, planetarium and interactive games. After hours, laser light shows integrate music from the likes of Pink Floyd and Led Zeppelin. *Admission: adults $15, seniors, students, children 5-18 $10.75 children 5 and under free. Hours vary by season.*

INUIT GALLERY OF VANCOUVER

206 Cambie St., Vancouver, 604-688-7323; www.inuit.com

Immerse yourself in the rich artistic tradition of coastal natives with soapstone sculptures, native prints, ceremonial masks and bentwood boxes. One of Vancouver's best sources for First Nations art, Inuit represents tribes up and down the Pacific Northwest. In the Gastown district, Inuit is a short walk from the convention center and cruise ship terminal. *Admission: free. Monday-Saturday 10 a.m.-6 p.m.. Sunday 11 a.m.-5 p.m.*

THE LOOKOUT AT HARBOR CENTRE

555 W. Hastings St., Vancouver, 604-689-0421; www.vancouverlookout.com

Glass elevators take you to a 360-degree viewing deck 430 feet above street level, where you can also catch a multimedia presentation, historical displays and tours. *Admission: adults $13, seniors $11, students and children 13-18 $9, children 6-12 $6. May-mid-October, daily 8:30 a.m.-10:30 p.m.; mid-October-April, daily 9 a.m.-9 p.m.*

MUSEUM OF ANTHROPOLOGY AT THE UNIVERSITY OF BRITISH COLUMBIA

6393 N.W. Marine Drive, Vancouver, 604-822-5087; www.moa.ubc.ca

Built as a homage to a First Nations longhouse, the glass and concrete Museum of Anthropology makes a fitting shrine for the art and artifacts of West Coast natives. The Great Hall surrounds visitors with immense totem poles, canoes and feast dishes of the Nisgaa, Gitksan and Haida people, among others. An outdoor sculpture garden sets tribal houses and totem poles, many carved by the best-known contemporary artists, against a backdrop of sea and mountain views. In its mission to explore all the cultures of the world, the MOA also catalogs 600 ceramics works from 15th- to 19th-century Europe.

Admission: adults $12, seniors and students $10. Mid-May-mid-October, daily 10 a.m.-5 p.m., Tuesday until 9 p.m.; early March-mid-May, Wednesday-Sunday 10 a.m.-5 p.m., Tuesday 10 a.m.-9 p.m.

OLD HASTINGS MILL

1575 Alma Road, Vancouver, 604-734-1212

One of the few buildings remaining after the fire of 1886, the structure now houses indigenous artifacts and memorabilia of Vancouver's first settlers.

Admission: free; donation requested. Mid-June-mid-September, Tuesday-Sunday 11 a.m.- 4 p.m.; mid-September-November, Saturday-Sunday 1-4 p.m.; February-mid-June, Saturday-Sunday 1-4 p.m.

OLYMPIC VILLAGE

Southeast False Creek

Built to house 2,800 athletes for the 2010 Winter Games, the Olympic Village is now being transformed into a False Creek community hub and permanent residential housing. The award-winning development (aiming to be 6 million square feet by 2020) is built with ecological and sustainability principles in mind and boasts a stunning waterfront location, a seaside walkway and bike route, a community garden, a non-motorized boating center and whimsical public art like The Birds by artist Myfanwy MacLeod (in front of the restored 1930s Salt Building). With further development slated, the transformation of this space is a must-see for those with an interest in urban eco-architecture.

ROYAL CITY STAR RIVERBOAT CASINO

788 Quayside Drive, New Westminster, 604-519-3660

The late-model paddle wheeler Queen of New Orleans, once stationed on the Mississippi, is now docked on the Fraser River as the Royal City Star. Games of chance include pai gow poker, mini baccarat, blackjack, roulette and Caribbean stud poker. Several bars, a deli and a restaurant take care of patrons.

SAMSON V MARITIME MUSEUM

Westminster Quay, New Westminster, 604-522-6891; www.samsonmuseum.org

The last steam-powered paddle wheeler to operate on the Fraser River now functions as a floating museum. Displays focus on the various paddle wheelers and paddle wheeler captains that have worked the river and on river-related activities.

May-June, Saturday-Sunday noon-5 p.m.; July-early September, daily noon-5p.m.; early September-mid-October, Saturday-Sunday noon-5 p.m.

SCIENCE WORLD BRITISH COLUMBIA
1455 Quebec St., Vancouver, 604-443-7443; www.scienceworld.bc.ca

The massive, golf ball-shaped Science World attracts both architecture and museum fans. Modeled on the geodesic domes of F. Buckminster Fuller, the aluminum ball was erected for Expo '86 and now houses a science center devoted to interactive exhibits on nature, invention, ecology and optical illusions. A play space with a water table and giant building blocks engages the 3-to-6 set, while the dome-projection OMNIMAX theater entertains the whole brood.

Admission: adults $18.75, seniors, students and children 13-18 $15.25, children 4-12 $12.75. Monday-Friday 10 a.m.-5 p.m., Saturday-Sunday 10 a.m.-6 p.m.

SPOKES BICYCLE RENTALS
1789 W. Georgia St., Vancouver, 604-688-5141; www.vancouverbikerental.com

Just across from the Stanley Park entrance on Georgia Street, this cycle shop rents from a vast fleet that includes cruisers, tandems, mountain bikes and hybrid models. Rentals come with complimentary helmets and locks; there are hourly, half-day, daily and weekly rental rates.

Daily 9 a.m.-8 p.m.

STANLEY PARK
West end of Georgia Street, Vancouver, 604-681-6728; www.vancouver.ca

One thousand acres of unspoiled British Columbia in the heart of the city, Stanley Park—the largest city park in Canada—is a green haven with few peers. Towering forests of cedar, hemlock and fir spill onto sand beaches, immersing visitors and residents alike in the wild just minutes from the civilized. Park-goers recreate along forest hiking trails, on three beaches and along the five-mile 1920s vintage seawall, where in-line skaters, runners and cyclists admire skyline and ocean views. Check out the gardens devoted to roses and rhododendrons, and the vivid stand of First Nations totem poles. Providing an appeal for every interest, Stanley Park also hosts the Vancouver Aquarium, Children's Farmyard, Miniature Railway, Theatre Under the Stars and several restaurants.

UBC BOTANICAL GARDEN
6804 S.W. Marine Drive, Vancouver, 604-822-9666; www.ubcbotanicalgarden.org

The UBC Botanical Garden features seven separate garden areas, including Asian, native, alpine and food gardens. Nitobe Memorial Garden, an authentic Japanese tea garden, is behind the Asian Centre.

Admission: adults $8, seniors, students and children 13-17 $6. Monday-Friday 9 a.m.-5 p.m., Saturday-Sunday 9:30 a.m.-5:30 p.m.

VANCOUVER AQUARIUM MARINE SCIENCE CENTRE
845 Avison Way, Stanley Park, Vancouver, 604-659-3474; www.vanaqua.org

With inviting, hands-on exhibits, Vancouver Aquarium in sylvan Stanley Park explores the undersea world from the Amazon to the Arctic, assembling 300 species of fish. For all its globetrotting interests, the aquarium is a top spot to study the local environment as well. In outdoor pools, graceful beluga whales, frisky sea lions and playful otters prove comfortable with the changeable Pacific

Northwest climate. Progeny of salmon released by the aquarium in 1998 from a park river return each winter, roughly November to February, illustrating B.C.'s rich salmon-spawning waterways. Behind-the-scenes tours with trainers provide you a glimpse of the marine mammal rescue and rehab program for which the aquarium is lauded.

Admission: adults $28, seniors $22, children 13-18 $22, children 4-12 $18, children 3 and under free. Daily 9:30 a.m.-7 p.m.

VANCOUVER ART GALLERY

750 Hornby St., Vancouver, 604-662-4719; www.vanartgallery.bc.ca

Most visitors bound up to the Vancouver Art Gallery's fourth floor for a look at the largest collection of works by British Columbia's best-known painter, Emily Carr. The other galleries in Western Canada's largest art museum, housed in an early-20th-century courthouse, are fantastic—subjects range from Group of Seven landscapes to photo conceptual art.

Admission: adults $20.50, seniors $16, students $15, children 5-12 $7, children 4 and under free. Monday, Wednesday, Friday-Sunday 10 a.m.-5:30 p.m.; Tuesday,
Thursday 10 a.m.-9 p.m.

VANCOUVER CIVIC THEATRES

649 Cambie St., Vancouver, 604-665-3050; www.city.vancouver.bc.ca

A symphony orchestra, an opera company and many theater groups present productions at this group of three theaters: Queen Elizabeth Theatre, Vancouver Playhouse and Orpheum.

VANCOUVER MARITIME MUSEUM

1905 Ogden Ave., Vancouver, 604-257-8300; www.vancouvermaritimemuseum.com

Built around the St. Roch, the first ship to navigate Canada's Inside Passage from west to east, Vanier Park's Maritime Museum lets seafaring fans explore the 1928 supply ship from the wheelhouse to the captain's quarters. In addition to the series of historic model ships housed inside the museum, several historic craft are tethered outside its waterfront Heritage Harbor, including two tugs, a rescue boat and the 1927 seiner once featured on Canada's $5 bill.

Admission: adults $10, seniors and children 6-18 $7.50. Mid-May-early September, Tuesday-Saturday 10 a.m.-5 p.m. Sunday noon-5 p.m.; early September-mid-May, daily 10 a.m.-5 p.m.

VANCOUVER MUSEUM

1100 Chestnut St., Vancouver, 604-736-4431; www.vanmuseum.bc.ca

The keeper of city history and another Vanier Park attraction, Vancouver Museum takes a sweeping view of civilization, collecting everything from Egyptian mummies to local vintage swimming garb. In addition to the urban story told in lifelike re-creations of an Edwardian parlor, a ship's berth and a trading post, the museum also examines First Nations' artifacts, the contributions of Asian Rim cultures and world history.

Admission: adults $11, seniors and students $9, children 5-17 $7. Monday-Wednesday, Friday-Sunday 10a.m.-5 p.m., Thursday 10 a.m.-7 p.m. Closed Monday September-June.

VANCOUVER OPERA
835 Cambie St., Vancouver, 604-683-0222; www.vancouveropera.ca

Vancouver Opera stages four productions annually. Established in 1958, the company has hosted a roster of greats, including guest singers Placido Domingo, Joan Sutherland and Marilyn Horne. Performances take place at the Queen Elizabeth Theatre.

VANCOUVER POLICE MUSEUM
240 E. Cordova St., Vancouver, 604-665-3346; www.vancouverpolicemuseum.ca

For fans of the macabre, the Vancouver Police Centennial Museum not only supplies the gruesome details of the city's most lurid crimes but also dramatizes them, crime-scene style. Run by the city's police department, the museum tells the history of local law-keeping and ushers visitors into an eerie mock-forensics laboratory in the former city morgue.

Admission: adults $7, seniors and students $5. Monday-Saturday 9 a.m.-5 p.m.

VANCOUVER SYMPHONY ORCHESTRA
601 Smithe St., Vancouver, 604-876-3434; www.vancouversymphony.ca

Canada's third-largest orchestra, the Vancouver Symphony presents more than 150 concerts annually, most of them at the ornate Orpheum Theatre. The symphony's featured programs broadly encompass classical, light classical, pops and children's works. Most concerts are on weekends with family-oriented matinees.

September-June.

VANCOUVER TROLLEY COMPANY LTD
875 Terminal Ave., Vancouver, 604-801-5515, 888-451-5581; www.vancouvertrolley.com

Take a narrated trolley tour to top attractions and neighborhoods throughout the city. Get on and off at designated stops throughout the day.

Price varies by tour; see website for information.

VANDUSEN BOTANICAL GARDEN
5251 Oak St., Vancouver, 604-878-9274; www.vandusengarden.org

The botanical garden's 55 acres are filled with flowers and exotic plants and offer mountain views. The grounds feature seasonal displays and a restaurant.

Prices and schedule varies; see website for information.

WINDSURE WINDSURFING SCHOOL
1300 Discovery St., Vancouver, 604-224-0615; www.windsure.com

Head to Jericho Beach to catch the offshore drafts in English Bay aboard a windsurfer. Operating out of the Jericho Sailing Center, this school rents both boards and wetsuits, including rigs suitable for children.

April-October, daily 9 a.m.-8 p.m.

THE YALE HOTEL
1300 Granville St., Vancouver, 604-681-9253; www.theyale.ca

Built in the mid-1880s as a hotel for rough-and-tumble miners, fishermen and loggers, The Yale prizes its working-class roots and makes a fitting home for the city's best blues club. Past headliners include John Lee Hooker, Clarence "Gatemouth" Brown, Jeff Healey and Jim Byrnes.

YALETOWN
Bounded by Georgia Street, Richards Street, False Creek and Cambie Street

A former rail yard, Yaletown once held the world record for the most bars per acre. With time and prosperity the redevelopment grew, and the warehouse district is now one of Vancouver's hippest, drawing urban dwellers with an arty bent. The former loading docks along Hamilton and Mainland teem with cafés with umbrella-shaded tables on concrete terraces. Tucked in between are a slew of shops, galleries and clothiers.

WHISTLER
BLACKCOMB SKI AREA
4545 Blackcomb Way, Whistler, 604-687-1032, 866-218-9690;
www.whistlerblackcomb.com

This ski area features seven high-speed quad chairlifts, three triple chairlifts and seven surface lifts. There are more than 100 runs with the longest run at seven miles, with a vertical drop of 5,280 feet.

WHISTLER MUSEUM AND ARCHIVES
4333 Main St., Whistler, 604-932-2019; www.whistlermuseum.com

Discover the rich history of the thriving Whistler community through artifacts, photographs and stories from local community members.

WHERE TO STAY

VANCOUVER
★★★DELTA VANCOUVER SUITES
550 W. Hastings St., Vancouver, 604-689-8188, 888-890-3222; www.deltavancouversuites.ca

This high-rise, all-suite hotel is in the Heritage District of Vancouver and just minutes from newly revitalized urban areas like Gastown and Chinatown. Ideal for business travelers, suites have movable workstations and ergonomic chairs. All the conveniences of home are provided, like in-suite coffee and complimentary newspaper service. For those traveling with family, kids enjoy special privileges, like a welcome package and discounted meals—and all children under 17 stay for free.

225 rooms. Restaurant, bar. Business center. Fitness center. Spa. Pets accepted. $251-350

★★★THE FAIRMONT HOTEL VANCOUVER
900 W. Georgia St., Vancouver, 604-684-3131, 866-540-4452; www.fairmont.com

The Fairmont Hotel echoes the vibrancy of its home city. Grand and inviting, it has been a local favorite since 1939, when it opened to celebrate the royal visit of King George VI and Queen Elizabeth. Today, its unique seafoam-green rooftop is a skyline landmark. The lobby décor nods to the past with ornate furniture, luxurious textures and patterns, high ceilings and classic colors, and the dining areas have a traditional feel with dark woods and neutral and sophisticated palettes. The building is also home to high-end boutiques fit for a queen, such as Louis Vuitton, Gucci and St. John.

556 rooms. Restaurant, bar. Business center. Fitness center. Pool. Spa. Pets accepted. $151-250

★★★THE FAIRMONT VANCOUVER AIRPORT

3111 Grant McConachie Way, Vancouver, 604-207-5200, 866-540-4441; www.fairmont.com

This stylish hotel is inside the airport and features contemporary rooms and suites appointed with crisp white linens, floor-to-ceiling windows with views of the runways, ocean and mountains. It's got techie perks as well, like touch-screen technology for everything from the bathtub jets to the drapes. Airport dining is elevated to new levels at the Globe@YVR, where you can watch approaching and departing jets while enjoying cosmopolitan cuisine. Whether just arriving or on a layover, unwind at the Absolute Spa, which has soothing packages like Flight Fatigue, a massage, facial and anti-swelling leg massage to combat jet lag.

392 rooms. Restaurant, bar. Business center. Fitness center. Pool. Spa. Pets accepted. $151-250

★★★THE FAIRMONT WATERFRONT

900 Canada Place Way, Vancouver, 604-691-1991, 866-540-4509; www.fairmont.com

With state-of-the-art conference facilities, a comprehensive health club and spa, and fine dining, this hotel offers just about everything a business or leisure traveler would need. Strongly committed to the environment, this hotel has lots of eco cred. It has a third-floor herb garden whose bounty is used in the restaurants' culinary creations; honeybees that produce nectar used in the lunch, dinner and cocktail menus; and sustainable, local and organic food options for guests. The rooms are spacious and refined, with plush earth-tone furniture and floor-to-ceiling windows. Surrounded on three sides by the Pacific Ocean, there is an enclosed walkway to the Vancouver Convention and Exhibition Center and the Cruise Ship Terminal, and it's is within walking distance to Stanley Park and Gastown.

489 rooms. Restaurant, bar. Business center. Fitness center. Pool. Spa. Pets accepted. $251-350

★★★★FOUR SEASONS HOTEL VANCOUVER

791 W. Georgia St., Vancouver, 604-689-9333; www.fourseasons.com

After a major renovation in 2009, the Four Seasons Vancouver got a significant facelift, but luckily it didn't lose any of its classic charm. Adjacent to the epicenter of downtown shopping and services, Pacific Centre, the Four Seasons has a good central location. If you have little ones in your group, be sure to provide the hotel with ages and names prior to check-in so that the kids will have pint-size robes and rice crispy "sushi" rolls waiting for them. The rooms offer city or sweeping panoramic views and are decorated in pale, soothing green, cream and amber hues with custom cherry-finished furnishings. Take a dip in the city's only indoor-to-outdoor pool and sit out on the deck for some sun. The hotel also houses Blo blow dry bar, a wash-and-go hair salon where women can quickly get coiffed for a big night out. Where to go? Yew restaurant + bar is a West Coast design wonder—think wood, wood and more wood. Sidle up to the bar for happy hour and spy plenty of professionals doing business over drinks.

373 rooms. Restaurant, bar. Business center. Pool. Pets accepted. $151-250

★★★HYATT REGENCY VANCOUVER

655 Burrard St., Vancouver, 604-683-1234, 800-233-1234; www.vancouver.hyatt.com

Shopaholics will want to make the Hyatt their base of operations. It's within the Royal Centre shopping complex, which also includes two levels of shops,

WHAT ARE THE BEST BOUTIQUE HOTELS IN VANCOUVER?

Le Soleil Hotel:
This hotel aims for a ritzy Old World ambiance with gilded ceilings and Louis XVI-style furniture in the lobby, and rooms filled with gold and crimson.

Opus Hotel:
For a more modern hotel, Opus offers rooms with sleek and minimalist furniture and walls bursting with color, from scarlet red to deep yellow.

Wedgewood Hotel:
Set in busy Robson Square, Wedgewood provides a respite. Whether you go for high tea, delicious restaurant Bacchus or the traditional-looking rooms.

restaurants and a SkyTrain station. The hotel is also steps away from Affluent Alley, Vancouver's most luxurious shopping block. After checking in, take a dip in the heated outdoor pool, get a bite in the Mosaic Bar & Grille (kids eat free) or have an evening cocktail at the Gallery Lounge. Then, relax in the spacious guest rooms, which all feature pillow-top mattresses and flat-screen televisions.

644 rooms. Restaurant, bar. Business center. Fitness center. Pool. $151-250

★★★LE SOLEIL HOTEL
567 Hornby St., Vancouver, 604-632-3000, 877-632-3030; www.lesoleilhotel.com

In the heart of the city's financial and business districts sits this charming boutique hotel. The lobby boasts 30-foot gilded ceilings and a Louis XVI-style collection of imported Italian furniture. Rooms are appointed with ornate wallpaper and gold and crimson furniture, bathrooms awash in marble and luxe European fabrics and linens. Complimentary bottled water and fruit upon arrival are welcome surprises, and the property's restaurant offers a variety of luxury comfort food.

119 rooms. Restaurant, bar. Business center. Pets accepted. $151-250

★★★METROPOLITAN HOTEL
645 Howe St., Vancouver, 604-687-1122, 800-667-2300; www.metropolitan.com

Located in the heart of Vancouver's downtown, the hotel is near local tourist attractions and shopping. The guest rooms are elegant and spacious, with marble washrooms, glass showers, oak cabinetry, warm furniture and art décor, large work desks, down duvets and Frette linens, and some have Juliet balconies. Enjoy a dinner at Diva at the Met, with its international and Pacific Northwest-influenced cuisine. For a real foodie experience, book the renowned chef's table and dine at the most exclusive spot in the restaurant.

197 rooms. Restaurant, bar. Business center. Fitness center. Pool. $61-150

★★★OPUS HOTEL
322 Davie St., Vancouver, 604-642-6787, 866-642-6787; www.opushotel.com

This hip boutique hotel blends contemporary design with great service. Located in the Yaletown area, it is close to all local attractions and the Canada Line (with direct trains to the airport). Guest rooms feature unique décor, like boldly shaded walls in scarlet red and electric blue and sleek modern furniture that's minimalist without losing warmth and comfort.

96 rooms. Restaurant, bar. Business center. Fitness center. Spa. Pets accepted. $61-150

★★★PAN PACIFIC VANCOUVER

300-999 Canada Place, Vancouver, 604-662-8111, 800-937-1515; www.panpacific.com

Awe-inspiring waterfront views take center stage at Vancouver's Pan Pacific Hotel, located minutes from some of the city's best shopping and tourist destinations. Luxurious guest rooms overlook unobstructed mountains and ocean, and some feature private balconies where you can soak in the view. Luxe linens, posh and comfortable furniture and high-end bath products ensure a comfortable stay. Three distinctive restaurants offer international cuisine.

504 rooms. Restaurant, bar. Business center. Fitness center. Pool. Spa. Pets accepted. $251-350

★★★RENAISSANCE VANCOUVER HARBORSIDE HOTEL

1133 W. Hastings, Vancouver, 604-689-9211, 800-905-8582; www.renaissancevancouver.com

Sitting on the waterfront and close to local attractions, this is a great spot for both leisure and business travelers. Some rooms offer a balcony and all rooms have duvets and feather pillows. The rooms have fanciful bursts of bright hues like red and green and fluffy pillows, along with modern touches like flat-panel LCD TVs. Enjoy a meal and the views at p2b bistro + bar, which offers fresh and simple fare for breakfast, lunch and dinner.

442 rooms. Restaurant, bar. Business center. Fitness center. Pool. Pets accepted. $151-250

★★★★SHANGRI-LA HOTEL, VANCOUVER

1128 W. Georgia St., Vancouver, 604-689-1120; www.shangri-la.com

The Shangri-La Hotel makes its North American debut in a grandiose way by occupying 15 floors of the tallest building in downtown Vancouver. The hotel oozes sleek sophistication. The spacious rooms and suites are decadently decorated with warm beige and golden tones as well as contemporary Asian-influenced furniture. All guestrooms feature a 42-inch flat-screen TV, CD/DVD player with surround sound and Nespresso coffee machine. Most suites have a private balcony in which to absorb stunning views of the city. MARKET by chef Jean-Georges offers an unforgettable fine-dining experience by proving four unique "destinations" for diners to choose a table.

119 rooms. Restaurant, bar. Business center. Fitness center. Spa. $350 and up

★★★★THE SUTTON PLACE HOTEL VANCOUVER

845 Burrard St., Vancouver, 604-682-5511, www.vancouver.suttonplace.com

A well-regarded institution on the Vancouver hotel scene, the Sutton Place brings European charm to a city often awash in minimalism. The warm hotel typifies cozy-chic decor, with huge fresh flower arrangements in the lobby, gold fixtures, high ceilings and opulent furniture and rugs. With two options (guestrooms on one side of the building, the long-term Le Grand Residence on the other), guests have their choice of suites and styles. With its spacious layout and full kitchenettes, Le Grand Residence is ideal for groups, families and those on extended stay. On the hotel end, each guestroom has a plush bed, a flat-screen TV and umbrellas—a must-have in Vancouver. The Vida Spa offers a full range of Ayurvedic-inspired treatments, along with steam rooms in the changing area and a plush lounge stocked with magazines and healthy snacks. After dark, the Gerard Room becomes a nightcap hub for a sophisticated crowd, as well as an undercover watering hole for celebrities.

397 rooms (164 long-term residences). Restaurant, bar. Business center. Pets accepted. $151-250

★★★WEDGEWOOD HOTEL

845 Hornby St., Vancouver, 604-689-7777, 800-663-0666; www.wedgewoodhotel.com

Tradition abounds at this independent boutique hotel, which features rooms decorated with classic furnishings, fresh flowers, antiques and luxurious fabrics. Bacchus, the onsite restaurant, offers a full menu plus sumptuous weekend brunch menus, and traditional high tea is served from 2 to 4 p.m. daily. A discreet gem tucked away in a high-profile area of downtown, the Wedgewood Hotel is a favorite of discerning travelers and locals alike. All rooms boast touches of class, including Gilchrist & Soames bath amenities, Frette towels and bathrobes, and a spacious work area with complimentary wireless Internet access.

83 rooms. Restaurant, bar. Business center. Fitness center. Spa. $251-350

★★★THE WESTIN GRAND

433 Robson St., Vancouver, 604-602-1999, 888-680-9393; www.westingrandvancouver.com

All of Vancouver is within reach of the Westin Grand. Sleek and stylish, this all-suite boutique property introduces visitors to the hip side of this western Canadian city. You never leave behind the sophisticated comforts of home here, where all rooms feature well-stocked kitchenettes. Rooms also come outfitted with the Westin's patented Heavenly Beds, cordless phones and soaker tubs. Endorphin junkies can get their fix in the Westin Workout Deluxe suite, which comes equipped with a treadmill or stationary bike, dumbbells, fitness DVDs, towels and water. An outdoor heated pool and whirlpool are surrounded by a lush Garden Terrace. Guests can dine on Pacific Rim dishes at Hidden, the hotel's restaurant and lounge.

207 rooms. Restaurant, bar. Business center. Fitness center. Pool. Spa. $151-250

WHISTLER

★★★THE FAIRMONT CHATEAU WHISTLER

4599 Chateau Blvd., Whistler, 604-938-8000, 866-540-4424; www.fairmont.com

The Fairmont Chateau Whistler is a skier's nirvana. During summer, its golf course and David Leadbetter Golf Academy lend the same status for golfers. The Vida Wellness Spa soothes the tired muscles of active visitors. When it's time to retire, head up to your room, which is traditionally decorated with two-poster beds and dark wood furniture.

550 rooms. Restaurant, bar. Business center. Fitness center. Pool. Spa. Pets accepted. Golf. Ski in/ski out. Tennis. $251-350

★★★★FOUR SEASONS RESORT WHISTLER

4591 Blackcomb Way, Whistler, 604-935-3400, 888-935-2460; www.fourseasons.com

This resort is nestled at the foot of the Blackcomb and Whistler mountains and offers a year-round getaway that features signature Four Seasons service and style. The resort is a five-minute walk to the ski lifts and a 10-minute stroll to the village center. The guest rooms are spacious and beautifully furnished and decorated. The dining room and lounge, Fifty Two 80 Bistro, delights with flavorful food, an extensive wine list and a slew of specialty cocktails. After a day full of activity, retreat to the spa, where body wraps, hydrotherapy, facials and massages will help you unwind.

273 rooms. Restaurant, bar. Business center. Fitness center. Pool. Spa. Pets accepted. $351 and up

★★★PAN PACIFIC WHISTLER MOUNTAINSIDE

4320 Sundial Crescent, Whistler, 604-905-2999, 888-905-9995; www.panpacific.com

Nestled at the foot of Whistler and Blackcomb mountains and facing Skier's Plaza, this all-suite boutique resort offers kitchens, fireplaces and balconies with beautiful views of the mountains of Whistler Village. After a day of skiing, retreat to the onsite spa for a relaxing hot-stone massage or swim in the heated outdoor pool to help your worn body.

121 rooms. Restaurant, bar. Business center. Fitness center. Pool. Spa. $251-350

★★★THE WESTIN RESORT AND SPA

4090 Whistler Way, Whistler, 604-905-5000, 888-634-5577; www.westinwhistler.com

Enjoy dramatic views from the privacy of airy suites done up in tan, cream and brown. For sustenance, retreat to the comfort of the FireRock Lounge après-ski or the Aubergine Grille for fresh cuisine. The Avello Spa & Health Club entices bliss-seekers with more than 75 treatments.

419 rooms. Restaurant, bar. Business center. Fitness center. Pool. Pets accepted. $251-350

RECOMMENDED

VANCOUVER

LODEN VANCOUVER HOTEL

1177 Melville St., Vancouver, 604-669-5060; www.theloden.com

This hip waterfront hotel in the affluent Coal Harbour area is ideal for the jet-set weekend tourist or upwardly mobile business traveler. Far from cookie-cutter lodging, the impressive lobby is outfitted with marble floors, dramatic lighting and modern art. Taking a cue from the stunning natural surroundings, Loden's décor is an earthy palette of chocolate and caramels with punches of color. Five room types are offered, and all boast 42-inch flat-screen TVs, luxury linens, floor-to-ceiling windows and sleek bathrooms awash in light. Take a complimentary yoga mat outside and practice your poses in an urban oasis, surrounded by skyscrapers, giant trees and the Pacific Ocean, or borrow a bike from the concierge and pedal around Stanley Park's famous seawall. The sultry Voya Restaurant & Lounge, a hot spot for hotel guests and locals, serves up global cuisine with a tinge of European influence and a seasonal wine list.

77 Rooms. Restaurant, bar. Business center. Fitness center. Pets accepted. $151-250

WESTIN BAYSHORE VANCOUVER

1601 Bayshore Drive, Vancouver, 604-682-3377; twww.westinbayshore.com

Perched on the edge of Stanley Park, the Westin Bayshore is a luxury resort-style experience in downtown Vancouver's most picturesque neighborhood. The freshly appointed rooms are spacious, airy and modern with wood furniture, white linens and earth tones; all guestrooms have balconies with sliding glass doors, ideal for experiencing stunning views of the coastline and mountains. Outdoor enthusiasts will love the close proximity to the Stanley Park Seawall (a walk, jog, rollerblade or bike around the wall is a summer must-do), but there's no end to nearby cosmopolitan activities as well, including shopping and fine dining. For those looking for R&R, the onsite Vida Spa has a full treatment menu to help you unwind after a long day, and the indoor and outdoor pools have sleek white loungers and umbrellas for sunny weather. The Westin's plush and cozy signature Heavenly Bed ensures a delightful night's sleep. Don't fret if you have a baby or dog on board; Heavenly Cribs and Dog Beds are available to help them catch z's, too.

511 rooms. Restaurant, bar. Business center. Pets accepted. $151-250

WHERE TO EAT

VANCOUVER
★★★BACCHUS
845 Hornby St., Vancouver, 604-608-5319, 800-663-0666; www.wedgewoodhotel.com

This luxurious restaurant is adorned with richly upholstered furniture, décor from Venice and, of course, a large canvas depicting Bacchus, Greek god of wine and revelry. The menu spotlights local ingredients, including seafood, organic chicken and top-of-the-line Alberta beef. Delicious dishes like pan-seared Qualicum Beach scallops served with cauliflower sour cream and roasted rack of lamb are palate-pleasers. The classic afternoon tea service is a whimsical delight with fresh scones with Devonshire cream, chocolate éclairs and gourmet finger sandwiches presented on classic silver tiers, along with your choice of steaming cuppa.

French. Breakfast, lunch, dinner, late-night, brunch. Reservations recommended. $36-85

★★★BEACH HOUSE
Dundarave Pier, 150 25th St., West Vancouver, 604-922-1414; www.thebeachhouserestaurant.ca

Originally built in 1912, this historic waterfront restaurant affords diners beautiful views of Burrard Inlet. The rustic wood shingled building provides a cozy setting where diners can sample dishes such as seared trout with almondine sauce and pan-roasted sablefish with maple syrup and soy glaze. A favorite of tony locals, oysters on a half shell and a glass or two from the vast yet affordable wine list make for a perfect afternoon on the patio.

Seafood, steak. Lunch, dinner, Sunday brunch. Reservations recommended. Outdoor seating. $36-85

★★★★BISHOP'S
2183 W. Fourth Ave., Vancouver, 604-738-2025; www.bishopsonline.com

Intimate, modern and airy, with a loft-like yet upscale feel, this chic duplex restaurant is known for West Coast continental cuisine and has a menu that emphasizes seasonal, organic produce and locally sourced seafood. Created with the freshest local ingredients, the menu is famous for its constant evolution: Diners will never have the same experience twice. For those who like to sample lots of different wines with dinner, Bishop's offers a nice selection of wines by the glass and an outstanding range of wines by the half-bottle. In addition to being a visionary chef, owner John Bishop is a gracious host.

Seafood. Lunch, dinner. Reservations recommended. Outdoor seating. Bar. $36-85

★★★C RESTAURANT

2-1600 Howe St., Vancouver, 604-681-1164; www.crestaurant.com

Located along the boardwalk running under the Granville Building and overlooking the marina, this contemporary seafood house offers a raw bar, an enclosed patio area and more than 900 wines. The sleek, modern décor is a nice complement to the inventive presentations of the fresh, locally sourced and sustainable cuisine. Sample dishes such as New England clam chowder with double-smoked bacon potatoes, and arctic char prepared with a light butter sauce.

Seafood. Lunch (Monday-Friday), dinner. Reservations recommended. Outdoor seating. $36-85

★★★CINCIN RISTORANTE

1154 Robson St., Vancouver, 604-688-7338; www.cincin.net

Located upstairs in a two-story building on trendy Robson Street, this Italian dining room has a mellow Tuscan atmosphere. A wood-fired brick oven emits a wonderful aroma throughout the restaurant and the extensive wine list offers the perfect complement to any meal. The pizzettes are made old-school style in the aforementioned wood-fired oven; choose the traditional Margherita or the West Coast-influenced salmone topped with salmon, crème fraîche, watercress, salmon caviar and chives. Housemade pastas like the tagliatelle Bolognese can be enjoyed as a primi (first course) plate or entrée.

Italian. Dinner, late-night. Reservations recommended. Outdoor seating. Bar. $36-85

★★★FISH HOUSE IN STANLEY PARK

8901 Stanley Park Drive, Vancouver, 604-681-7275, 877-681-7275; www.fishhousestanleypark.com

This landmark seafood restaurant favored by both locals and tourists is in Vancouver's West End at the south entrance to beautiful Stanley Park. The leafy setting is a relaxing spot to tuck into steamed mussels, maple-glazed salmon or cedar-planked arctic char. In the summer, grab a seat on one of the two sunny patios.

Seafood. Lunch, dinner, Saturday-Sunday brunch. Reservations recommended. Outdoor seating. $36-85

★★★FIVE SAILS

410-999 Canada Place, Vancouver, 604-844-2855, 800-937-1515; www.fivesails.ca

Exceptional views of the harbor and neighboring mountains, a talented kitchen that produces creative Northwest cuisine and good service make this restaurant a favorite destination among locals. The affable staff can make recommendations for local or international wines to pair with the fresh seafood on the menu. Adventurous diners will be intrigued by the Austrian-style Gröstl made with butter-poached Atlantic lobster, whipped potatoes, pan-seared foie gras and veal sweetbreads, but there are plenty of classics, like the warm Dungeness crab cake and grilled rack of lamb.

Seafood, steak. Dinner. Reservations recommended. $86 and up

★★★GOTHAM STEAKHOUSE AND COCKTAIL BAR

615 Seymour St., Vancouver, 604-605-8282; www.gothamsteakhouse.com

It's worth the splurge for truly excellent steaks; smooth, friendly service; and a sleek crowd at this downtown destination. Perfectly aged steaks and hearty sides are served à la carte. The prime rib is roasted to perfection, and the hearty grilled beefsteak tomatoes and creamy lyonnaise potatoes are ideal carnivore companions. The dining room, a converted bank, has a modern and opulent feel with leather and velvet banquettes, high ceilings and dark and intimate mood lighting. It's a classic high-end steakhouse experience.

Steak, seafood. Dinner. Reservations recommended. Outdoor seating. Bar. $36-85

★★★HART HOUSE RESTAURANT

6664 Deer Lake Ave., Burnaby, 604-298-4278; www.harthouserestaurant.com

About 20 minutes from downtown Vancouver, Hart House is reputed to have some of the best steaks in the area and one of the most charming and homey dining atmospheres. The house was built in the early 1900s and over the century served many different purposes, from family home to film set, before transforming into a restaurant in 1988. The imaginative menu takes its inspiration from the flavors native to countries around the globe, like the French-tinged duck confit tortelloni with artichokes, marinated beets and orange gastrique. In pleasant weather, the outdoor patio opens up to let diners enjoy the fresh air and views of idyllic Deer Lake.

Steak, seafood. Lunch (Tuesday-Friday), dinner, Sunday brunch. Closed Monday. Reservations recommended. Outdoor seating. $16-35

★★★★LA BELLE AUBERGE

4856 48th Ave., Ladner, 604-946-7717; www.labelleauberge.com

If you crave the glorious food of France's best kitchens, opt for a 30-minute drive from Vancouver to Ladner and enjoy dinner at La Belle Auberge. Set in a charming 1902 country inn, the restaurant comprises five intimate, antique-filled salon-style dining rooms. The kitchen, led by chef and owner Bruno Marti, a masterful culinary technician, offers spectacular, authentic French cuisine. À la carte options include seared foie gras with seasonal fruits and vegetarian lasagna en cocotte with spinach and Gruyère. For an indulgent feast of seasonal dishes, opt for the sumptuous seven-course prix fixe Table d'Hote menu.

French. Dinner. Closed Sunday-Monday. Reservations recommended. Outdoor seating. $36-85

★★★LA TERRAZZA

1088 Cambie St., Vancouver, 604-899-4449; www.laterrazza.ca

This grand Italian restaurant feels like a romantic villa with burnt-sienna walls, murals, massive windows and vaulted ceilings, as well as an impressive wine cellar. The garden patio, lush lounge and bar area, and eye-catching double-sided fireplace add plenty of character and warmth to the expansive space. The menu features classic Italian dishes, from taglierini with sautéed prawns to osso bucco with risotto.

Italian. Dinner. Reservations recommended. Outdoor seating. $36-85

★★★LE CROCODILE

100-909 Burrard St., Vancouver, 604-669-4298; www.lecrocodilerestaurant.com

A wonderful dress-up place, this downtown French bistro's delicious food will make you come back for more. Classically trained chef Michel Jacob creates quintessential French fare, such as tomato and gin soup served with fresh whipped cream and pan-seared veal sweetbreads with black truffle foie gras cream sauce. And for a truly French experience, try the pan-fried frog legs. The atmosphere is dignified and friendly—no upturned noses or snooty attitudes here, despite the sophisticated foodie menu. The extensive wine list spotlights French bottles that pair perfectly with the menu.

French. Lunch (Monday-Friday), dinner. Closed Sunday. Reservations recommended. Outdoor seating. $36-85

★★★★LUMIÈRE

2551 W. Broadway, Vancouver, 604-739-8185; www.lumiere.ca

Under the umbrella of world-renowned chef-owner Daniel Boulud, Lumière's chef Dale Mackay creates contemporary French dishes that exceed the culinary world's highest standards, both in presentation and creativity. The dining room is intimate and inviting with white linens, warm lighting and luxurious leather seating. Lumière pioneered small-plate dining in Vancouver, and today both prix fixe and tasting menus are available, from the accessible seasonal prix fixe to a decadent seven-course feast (wine pairings are optional for all). Using in-season ingredients, the dishes change according to availability of harvest, but diners adore the duo of prime beef, a perennial favorite, and the Hot and Cold Sundae is a legend among dessert aficionados for the sinful combination of ice cream, lady fingers and mousse (depending on the season, tiramisu, chestnut or Black Forest are added in as well). In traditional French fashion, the tantalizing cheese cart is part of the dessert course, so don't let the expertly displayed fromage distract you from dinner.

Contemporary French. Reservations recommended. Bar. $86 and up

★★★RAINCITY GRILL

1193 Denman St., Vancouver, 604-685-7337; www.raincitygrill.com

Located in Vancouver's West End, this eclectic fine dining restaurant has views across a small park to busy English Bay. The delicious à la carte and chef's tasting menus draw almost exclusively on regional sources. Specializing

HIGHLIGHT

JAPA DOG

Vancouver's street food is on the cusp of becoming the next big thing in the dining scene. Leading the way is Japa Dog. The hot dog purveyor has put a Tokyo twist on the American classic, to wildly popular results, as evidenced by the constant lines waiting to gorge on encased meat. What started off as a humble street meat cart at Burrard and Smithe has grown into a tubed-steak empire, with three carts downtown plus a storefront on Robson Street. Kobe beef sausage, pork sausage and bratwurst are on the menu, but these are no ordinary ballpark dogs. Take the Spicy Cheese Teriymayo, for example, a jalapeño and cheese dog topped with Japanese mayo, teriyaki sauce and seaweed. The selection varies by cart, so bring your appetite, patience (for the aforementioned lines) and sense of adventure (topping options include fried cabbage and edamame). It's all part of the street dining experience, where you can get some fresh air, chat with other patrons and try to decipher the specials board's nonsensical Japanese-English.

Japanese. $15 and under. Burrard and Smithe streets (stand), Burrard and Pender streets (stand), Waterfront Station (stand), 530 Robson St., Vancouver; www.japadog.com.

in farm-to-table dishes, each menu item is carefully chosen as much for taste as it is for environmental impact. Salmon is fished specifically for Raincity Grill, and the menu sources organic meats, vegetables and cheese from nearby communities. The crispy Yarrows Meadow duck is a delight, and diners with a passion for eating local will love the 100-Mile ragu and tagliatelle, a dish whose ingredients have been found less than 100 miles from the restaurant.

Seafood, steak. Lunch (Monday-Friday), dinner, Saturday-Sunday brunch. Reservations recommended. Outdoor seating. $36-85

★★★★WEST

2881 Granville St., Vancouver, 604-738-8931; www.westrestaurant.com

West is one of those sleek, heavenly spots that makes sipping cocktails for hours on end an easy task. Especially since the extensive cocktail list is full of revamped classics—the mint julep, sidecar, hot toddy, to name a few—and all libations are mixed with care and garnished with fresh toppings. Located in Vancouver's chic South Granville neighborhood, West also offers diners the chance to sample the vibrant cuisine of the Pacific Northwest region. Stunning, locally sourced ingredients are on display here thanks to the masterful kitchen. Rabbit with green apple mustard jus and Lois Lake steelhead trout are a few of the tantalizing dishes to experience. It is an ideal choice for gourmets in search of an inventive, eclectic meal, as well as those who crave local flavor and seasonal ingredients.

Seafood, steak. Dinner. Reservations recommended. Bar. $36-85

WHISTLER

★★★ARAXI

4222 Village Square, Whistler, 604-932-4540; www.araxi.com

Tables encircle a giant stone urn, the centerpiece of this warm and friendly dining room. A blend of French and Italian culinary styles and fine, regional ingredients have gained this restaurant continent-wide recognition. Go for dishes like the Paradise Valley pork trio with slow-cooked belly, housemade sausage and pork cheek ravioli; local lingcod smothered in peaches and cream corn sauce; or, if you are really hungry, a 20-ounce "Cowboy Cut" bone-in rib-eye.

International. Dinner. Closed two weeks in early May, late October. Reservations recommended. Outdoor seating. $36-85

★★★BEARFOOT BISTRO

4121 Village Green, Whistler, 604-932-3433; www.bearfootbistro.com

Only a hard day of skiing can justify this decadent feast for the senses. Each of three or five courses is handcrafted from a huge range of rare, high-quality ingredients, including caribou and pheasant. Additionally, this is one of the most beautiful locations in North America, making it a truly standout dining experience.

International. Dinner. Reservations recommended. Bar. $86 and up

★★★VAL D'ISERE

4314 Main St., Whistler, 604-932-4666; www.valdisere-restaurant.com

Impressive for both the food and the charming interior, this fine restaurant is in the north village plaza. The menu covers a wide range of culinary influences and includes dishes such as venison flank steak with chanterelle sauce and wild salmon baked in a potato crust.

French. Lunch (summer), dinner. Reservations recommended. Outdoor seating. $36-85

★★★WILDFLOWER RESTAURANT

Fairmont Chateau Whistler, 4599 Chateau Blvd., Whistler, 604-938-8000, 866-540-4424; www.fairmont.com

Tucked inside the Chateau Whistler, this restaurant features a local, organic-laden menu with weekly table d'hote signature dishes, an ever-popular coastal market buffet and a "Flavors of Asia" buffet on Friday and Saturday nights. Try the cedar-wrapped wild salmon glazed with maple syrup or the Mumbai butter chicken with curry.

International. Breakfast, dinner. Reservations recommended. Outdoor seating. $36-85

RECOMMENDED

VANCOUVER

CHAMBAR

562 Beatty St., Vancouver, 604-879-7119; www.chambar.com

Famous for its moules frites (mussels and fries) served Euro-style with mayo, Chambar is a Crosstown favorite for its heritage-building space, buzzing and beautiful crowd, and sexy candlelit ambiance. As expected of a Belgian menu, the beer list is lengthy, including a specialty Chambar Ale, Trappiste beers (brewed by monks) and refreshing Tripels. The unusual and tasty Blue Fig cocktail, oven-roasted figs steeped in gin and frozen, is served with a side of Danish blue cheese for a tarty tipple. The champagne and sparkling list has a healthy selection of French varietals (with one local bottle thrown in for good measure), and the wine list includes a bold Argentine malbec and Chilean chardonnay. Among the fish entrées is pistachio-crusted halibut, and the carnivorous options include slow-roasted pork tenderloin, rib-eye steak and braised lamb shank. Top off your meal with pot du crème au chocolat, lavender milk chocolate with ganache-filled biscuits and tuiles. And have another glass of bubbly, of course.

Belgian. Dinner. $36-85

SPAS

VANCOUVER

★★★★CHI SPA AT SHANGRI-LA HOTEL

1128 W. Georgia St., Vancouver, 604-689-1120; www.shangri-la.com

Relaxation is key at CHI. A self-proclaimed "spa within a spa," the concept is based on the five Chinese elements: metal, water, wood, fire and earth. There are five individual suites representing each element of tailored treatments. A consultation is performed upon arrival to determine which element best suites your needs. If rejuvenation is what you seek, try the Vitality Ritual, which is a four-hour Himalayan experience that includes a bath therapy, mud wrap, healing stone massage and mountain Tsampa rub. The CHI skin polish is also a must-have treatment. The mineral salt and citrus oil scrub will leave your skin glowing and silky smooth.

WHISTLER

★★★THE AVELLO SPA

Westin Resort & Spa, 4090 Whistler Way, Whistler, 604-935-3444; www.whistlerspa.com

The Avello Spa takes a holistic approach in its well-being treatments. Massage accounts for most of the menu, with signature treatments such as the Avello hot-rock massage, and Thai and Chinese therapies. Asian approaches to balance include reiki, acupuncture, reflexology and shiatsu. A wide variety of hydrotherapy sessions are available, from herbal, milk, mustard and mud to soaks using salts from the Dead Sea.

★★★★THE SPA AT FOUR SEASONS WHISTLER

Four Seasons Resort Whistler, 4591 Blackcomb Way, Whistler, 604-935-3400; www.fourseasons.com

This contemporary spa inside the Four Seasons Resort Whistler offers a full menu of massages and body treatments designed to soothe and restore sore muscles after a day on the slopes. Chilly feet are wrapped in warm towels while muscles are warmed with hot stones during the après-ski massage. The men's fitness facial restores wind- and sun-burned skin while the British Columbia glacial clay wrap is a great way to warm up at the end of the day. Those who can't pry themselves from the comfort of their rooms can order up an in-room massage.

WHERE TO SHOP

VANCOUVER

ALBERNI STREET

Bordered by Burrard and Jervis streets, Vancouver

Dubbed "Affluent Alley," this downtown strip hosts some of the world's most luxurious brands, including Hermès, Tiffany & Co., Betsey Johnson, Agent Provocateur, Calvin Klein and Brooks Brothers. Its stable also features the first Canadian outpost of iconic British brand Burberry, and at more than 3,000 square feet, the store has plenty for shopaholics to indulge in, from classic trench coats to runway-to-rack pieces. There are also a few independent gems, like Montreal's m0851 line of buttery-soft leather jackets and bags, and fashionista favorite Blubird boutique, which stocks designers Marc by Marc Jacobs and Stella McCartney, among others.

Hours vary by store.

BASQUIAT

1189 Hamilton St., Vancouver, 604-688-0828; www.basquiat.com

In the heart of trendy Yaletown, Basquiat's brick exterior gives way to a modern boutique with a cool, high-end look and feel. Lined with mostly American and European men's and women's collections, many exclusive to Basquiat, the shop carries well-edited selections of Pringle, Drykorn, Jenni Kayne, Yigal Azrouel and coveted shoes and boots by French designer Barbara Bui. Each item is selected with care and sartorial consideration; neutral palettes and black rule the racks, but the combination of luxe textures and materials make the simplest pieces the most eye-catching. With an irresistible mix of fashion-forward design and high-quality construction, decision-making could become quite difficult, as most pieces are instant classics that fit into any wardrobe. Whatever you walk away with will be worn for years.

Monday-Saturday 11 a.m.-6 p.m., Sunday noon-5 p.m.

HOLT RENFREW

737 Dunsmuir St., Vancouver, 604-681-3121; www.holtrenfrew.com

This bright and airy designer department store stands alone on Vancouver's sartorial scene as the go-to shopping spot for luxury clothing, cosmetics and accessories. The women's shoe department is a dream, stocking sky-high heels from the likes of Christian Louboutin, Manolo Blahnik and Jimmy Choo, while downstairs the men's department has everything the discerning gentleman needs, from Etro socks to made-to-measure Armani Collezioni suits. Both the men's and women's departments boast extensive contemporary collections, with the women's side carrying fashion-editor favorites like Alexander Wang, 3.1 Philip Lim and Twenty8Twelve and the men's section stocked with Modern Amusement, Paul Smith and 7 For All Mankind. Fur services, a concierge, a salon and spa and personal shoppers round out an indulgent shopping trip.

Monday-Tuesday, Saturday 10 a.m.-7 p.m., Wednesday-Friday 10 a.m.-9 p.m., Sunday 11 a.m.-7 p.m.

ROBSON STREET

Robson Street, between Burrard and Jervis streets, Vancouver; www.robsonstreet.ca

The epicenter of Vancouver's street chic, Robson makes a nice window-shopping stroll. A string of shops and sidewalk cafés runs several blocks in either direction from Robson and Thurlow streets. Retailers range from Tommy Hilfiger and Club Monaco to the playful French Connection on down to the delicious treats at Cupcakes by Heather and Lori. Jewelry stores, chocolatiers and craft galleries round out the offerings.

Hours vary by store.

OKANAGAN VALLEY'S WINE COUNTRY

Oenophiles will have a crush on this region nestled in the heart of British Columbia, four hours from Vancouver. The wineries of Okanagan Valley have well-earned the area's nickname as "The Napa of the North," though many of them lack the attitude of their Northern California peers. The valley, which also has hundreds of orchards, offers some 120 wineries, holds wine festivals year-round and rewards the area's best with a VQA (Vintners Quality Alliance) bottle seal, which requires the approval of an expert tasting panel. B.C.'s largest and oldest wine-growing area—which includes Kelowna, Oliver, Summerland, Osoyoos and Penticton—produces a number of varietals, such as pinot noir, pinot gris, merlot and riesling. Its hot, dry climate and varied geography explain the diverse wine offerings. There are snowy mountains, sandy beaches, lakes and Canada's only desert, the Sonoran. Since it gets more sun than any other part of B.C., the Okanagan Valley is a great place for outdoor activities. Hiking and biking are popular, as are water sports—just watch out for Ogopogo, Lake Okanagan's own Loch Ness monster. Whichever sport you choose, it'll help break up the many winery tours throughout the valley. That's where your own crush on the valley itself will begin.

WHAT TO SEE

KELOWNA
CEDARCREEK ESTATE WINERY

5445 Lakeshore Road, Kelowna, 250-764-8866; www.cedarcreek.bc.ca

In 1986, British Columbian Senator Ross Fitzpatrick acquired a small winery and apple orchard along the hills of Kelowna, but he didn't want to mix apples and grapes. Instead, he converted it all into a vineyard. It was a good hunch, since the family-owned CedarCreek went on to win numerous accolades. Almost half of the vineyard's 50 acres are devoted to CedarCreek's signature wine, pinot noir. Pair it with wine-friendly food at the CedarCreek's Vineyard Terrace Restaurant (open June-September). The alfresco eatery wraps around the wine shop, which is helpful in case you find your glass suddenly empty. Watch the sun set against the picturesque mountains as you tipple, and if you are lucky, you might catch a concert on the terrace, which will provide a nice soundtrack for the evening.

November-April, daily 11 a.m.-5 p.m.; May-October, daily 10 a.m.-6 p.m.

MONASHEE ADVENTURE TOURS

1591 Highland Drive North, Kelowna, 250-762-9253, 888-762-9253;
www.monasheeadventuretours.com

If you prefer traveling via two-wheeler, Monashee leads 10 different winery bike tours to accommodate all levels of riders. The daylong South Okanagan Wine Country Cycle Tour hits Kelowna and Oliver—two Okanagan Valley biggies—and the Sonoran Desert, as well as two wineries. To change things up a bit, try the Peddle and Paddle Tour, where you ride to Okanagan Lake, canoe to shore and then head to a winery for lunch and a tour.

OKANAGAN WINE COUNTRY TOURS

1310 Water St., Kelowna, 250-868-9463, 866-689-9463; www.okwinetours.com

Duffers should sign up for the Chip & Sip, a tour that splits the day between wineries and pre-selected golf courses, with transportation provided to both. The more adventurous will take the Floatplane Wine Tours, which include a 45-minute ride that ends with a landing on Osoyoos Lake. From there, a guide will escort you to a custom-designed luxury vehicle as you shuttle off to five award-winning wineries and end with lunch at Burrowing Owl Estate Winery.

QUAILS' GATE

3303 Boucherie Road, Kelowna, 800-420-9463; www.quailsgate.com

The Stewart family, which settled in the Okanagan Valley in 1908, took its love for red wine to the next level by opening this vineyard in the 1980s. Still family-owned, the winery is known for its award-winning pinot noir, but has expanded into whites, with chardonnay as another one of its trademark vinos. Aside from the wine, visitors come to Quails' Gate to eat at Old Vines Restaurant, which has a seasonal menu tailored for food-and-wine pairings and a patio that offers lovely views of the vineyard. After you've gorged yourself, walk it off around the lush garden. You may catch a whiff of lavender or trumpet vine, but your sniffer likely will be overwhelmed with the more than 500 roses on the grounds. Among the plants and flowers, you'll find the 100-year-old cabin that houses the Wineshop. Stop in for a nightcap.

Daily year-round, hours vary.

SUMMERHILL PYRAMID WINERY

4870 Chute Lake Road, Kelowna, 250-764-8000, 800-667-3538; www.summerhill.bc.ca

Who says wine and new age don't mix? Okay, maybe nobody says that, and that's probably why Summerhill is so successful as Canada's largest certified organic vineyard. Founder and owner Stephen Cipes quit his job in 1987 and moved to the Valley from New York to test whether metaphysical energy would affect an Old World practice. To this day, Summerhill ages wine inside a giant pyramid on the shores of Okanagan Lake. The winery consistently wins awards for its ice wine and bruts, though it'd be downright silly not to try one of the organically grown varietals, which include rieslings, chardonnays, pinot noirs and gewürztraminers. The onsite bistro cooks up delicious dishes using organic veggies grown on the property.

April-December, daily 9 a.m.-9 p.m.; January-March, daily 9 a.m.-5 p.m.

OLIVER
BURROWING OWL ESTATE WINERY
100 Burrowing Owl Place, Oliver, 877-498-0620; www.bovwine.ca

Since Burrowing Owl is in one of Canada's most endangered ecosystems, the locals hold a special concern for the surrounding habitat. The winery's name pays homage to the area's endangered desert and grasslands bird that roosts and nests in already dug burrows. Burrowing Owl uses environmentally safe fertilizers, relocates snakes that happen onto the property and employs nature's own form of pest control in the form of 100 bluebird boxes and two bat nurseries on the vineyards. All of this goes a long way in making the winery's yummy cabernet franc and cabernet sauvignon—which both took silver medals in the 2008 New World International Wine competition—go down even easier. To get the full Burrowing Owl experience, stay in the property's guesthouse, which comes equipped with a pool, a hot tub and airy rooms overlooking the vineyards. For more wine-related fun, order in-room spa treatments, such as the Essential Chardonnay manicure or the merlot-scented Wine Country scrub.
Daily 10 a.m.-5 p.m. Closed January 2-February 14.

INNISKILLIN OKANAGAN VINEYARDS
Road 11, Oliver, 250-498-6663; www.inniskillin.com

Like its sister winery in the Niagara Peninsula, the British Columbia outpost of Inniskillin specializes in ice wine. This dessert wine is made by picking frozen grapes and pressing them before they thaw, a process that yields only a few precious drops of concentrated liquid to use for the wine. Originally a German drink and known as Eiswein, ice wine has become one of Canada's more tasty exports, and Inniskillin's brand is sold in more than 59 countries. The founders of the company are the unlikely godfathers of Canadian wine. Austrian-born chemist Karl Kaiser and Italian-Canadian agriculture graduate Donald Ziraldo started their winery in a converted packing shed. Despite the winery's modest setting, the duo's wine got a lot of attention. The pair no longer runs the company, as Kaiser retired and Ziraldo went on to be the founding chair of the Vintners Quality Alliance. But their legacy lives on at this Okanagan vineyard, which is only about 12 miles north of the Washington State border.
Winter, daily 10 a.m.-4 p.m.; summer, daily 10 a.m.-5 p.m.

OSOYOOS
NK'MIP CELLARS
1400 Rancher Creek Road, Osoyoos, 250-495-2985; www.nkmipcellars.com

Created by Osoyoos Indians, Nk'Mip (pronounced "in-ka-meep") is North America's first aboriginal-owned winery. The lakeside winery, located in Canada's only desert, is just one component of a massive one-stop tourist destination. Stay in a luxurious villa at the Spirit Ridge Vineyard Resort and Spa or rough it at Nk'Mip's Campground and RV Park. Onsite amenities include a nine-hole golf course and a spa featuring an aboriginal-inspired Dreamcatcher aromatherapy massage. You can learn more about the area's native traditions and one of Canada's endangered ecosystems at the Nk'Mip Desert Cultural Centre. Just don't forget to indulge in the best offering of all: Nk'Mip's award-winning chardonnay, pinot blanc, merlot and pinot noir.
Winter, daily 10 a.m.-4 p.m.; summer, daily 9 a.m.-5 p.m.

SUMMERLAND
DIRTY LAUNDRY VINEYARD
7311 Fiske St., Summerland, 250-494-8815; www.dirtylaundry.ca

This cheeky boutique winery rests high on a plateau overlooking the original Summerland township, just 50 minutes from Kelowna. Though one of the newer kids on the block, it's already produced some award-winners, most notably for its Riesling and three gewürztraminer varietals. From the patio—which is shaded by a canopy of vines—you'll be able to see Okanagan Lake, the Trestle Bridge and, if you time it right, the Kettle Valley Steam Train in high season. Check the events portion of the website or call prior to going—during the summer, the vineyard hosts live music concerts.

Daily 10 a.m.-5 p.m. Call for off-season hours.

SUMAC RIDGE ESTATE WINERY
17403 Highway 97N, Summerland, 250-494-0451; www.sumacridge.com

Sumac is pushing 30, and in this young but prolific wine-producing region, that makes it one of the oldest wineries. But this is the right industry in which to be of age, and the winery has several advantages over its younger neighbors: It was one of the region's ice wine pioneers, and it was the first to produce merit age outside of the U.S. Standout wines include gewürztraminer and Riesling, which come from grapes grown on a gently rolling vineyard near Lake Okanagan, and cabernet sauvignon, pinot blanc and merlot (grown in the 115-acre Black Sage Vineyard just south of Okanagan). The winery's onsite restaurant, Cellar Door Bistro, serves regional cuisine that's also locally sourced, which means that as you sit on the patio with a spectacular view of a shimmering Lake Okanagan, you'll feel like you're not just tasting the valley's bounty, but living it.

April-October, daily 9 a.m.-9 p.m.; January-February, daily 9 a.m.-5 p.m.; November-December and March, Tuesday-Saturday 9 a.m.-8:30 p.m., Sunday-Monday 9 a.m.-5 p.m.

WESTBANK
MISSION HILL FAMILY ESTATE
1730 Mission Hill Road, Westbank, 250-768-6448; www.missionhillwinery.com

Perched atop a hill, the Mission Hill Family Estate offers stunning views of Lake Okanagan and its own vineyards of chardonnay and pinot noir grapes. The only thing that rivals the scenery is the winery's architecture. When you enter the estate through the imposing arches and keystone, you'll see a contemporary take on an old-time mission. Mission Hill boasts a 12-story bell tower; the Chagall Room, a reception hall that showcases a rare tapestry from the Russian artist; and a cellar that was formed by underground volcanic rock. But you won't want to spend your time indoors. Head to the open-air Terrace restaurant or the outdoor amphitheatre to catch a concert, dance performance, movie or play. Also be sure to grab a glass of Oculus, Mission Hill's signature Bordeaux-inspired wine, for the outing.

Daily 10 a.m.-6 p.m. Call for off-season hours.

INDEX

T

ALASKA

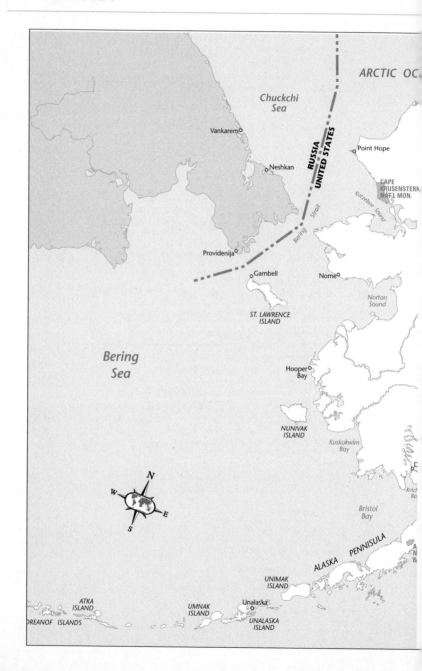

ARCTIC OC.

Chuckchi
Sea

Vankarem

RUSSIA
UNITED STATES

Point Hope

Neshkan

CAPE
KRUSENSTERN
NAT'L MON.

Kotzebue Sound

Bering Strait

Providenija

Gambell

Nome

Norton
Sound

ST. LAWRENCE
ISLAND

Bering
Sea

Hooper
Bay

NUNIVAK
ISLAND

Kuskokwim
Bay

Kvich
Ba

N
W   E
S

Bristol
Bay

ALASKA PENINSULA

UNIMAK
ISLAND

ATKA
ISLAND

UMNAK
ISLAND

Unalaska

DREANOF ISLANDS

UNALASKA
ISLAND

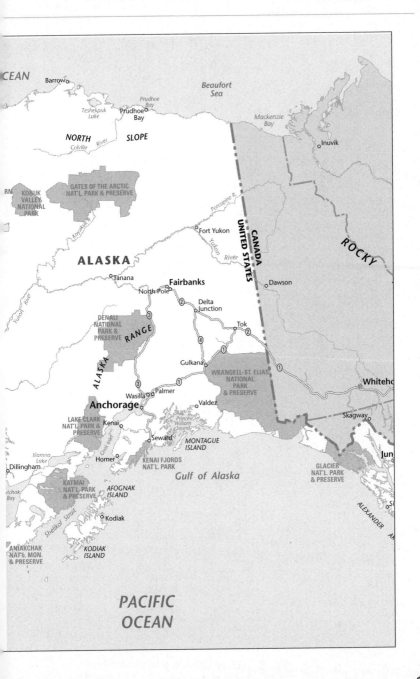

OREGON

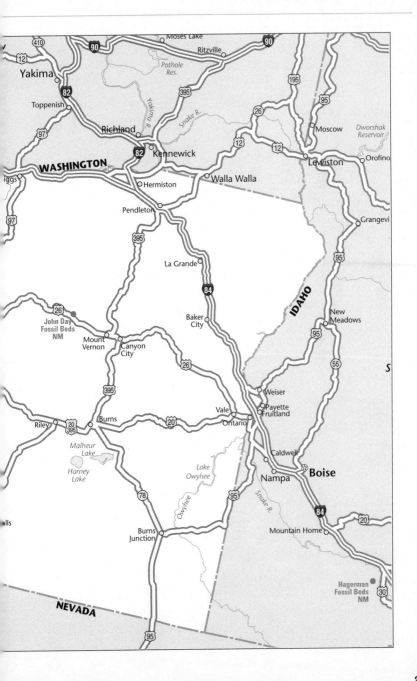

WASHINGTON

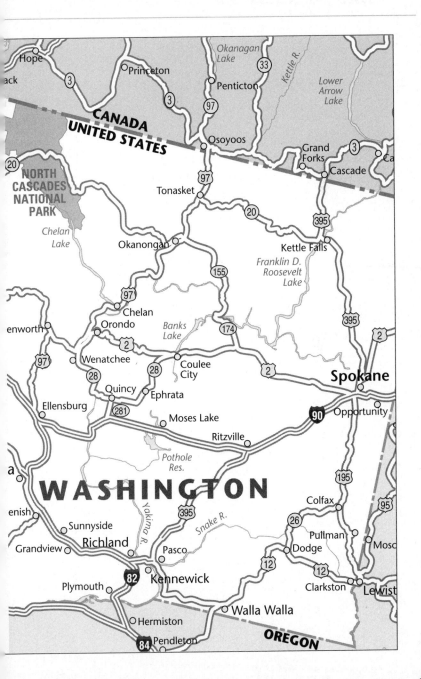

BRITISH COLUMBIA

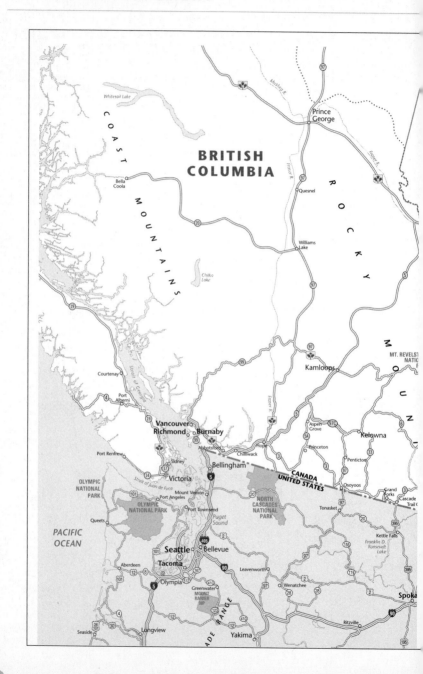

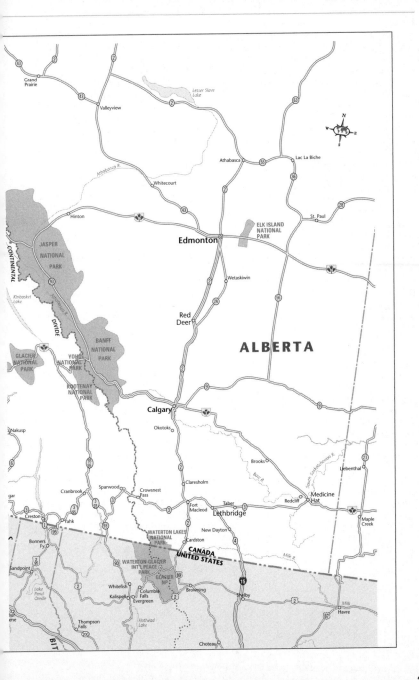

IDAHO

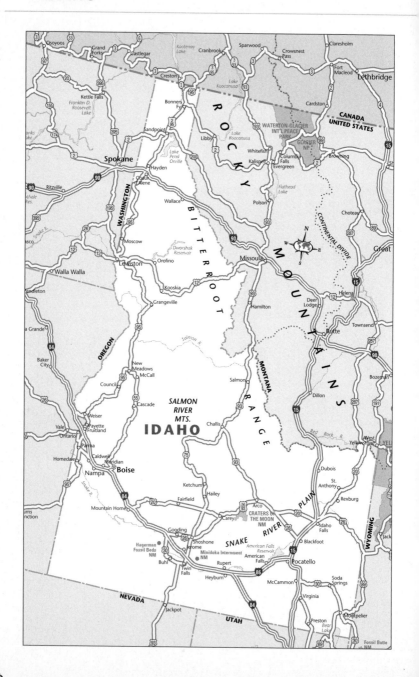